NEW ACCENTS

General Editor: TERENCE HAWKES

Alternative Shakespeares

IN THE SAME SERIES

The Empire Writes Back: Theory and practice in post-colonial
    literatures *Bill Aschcroft, Gareth Griffiths, and Helen Tiffin*
Translation Studies *Susan Bassnett*
Critical Practice *Catherine Belsey*
Formalism and Marxism *Tony Bennett*
Dialogue and Difference: English for the nineties ed. *Peter Brooker and
    Peter Humm*
Telling Stories: A theoretical analysis of narrative fiction *Steven Cohan
    and Linda M. Shires*
The Semiotics of Theatre and Drama *Keir Elam*
Reading Television *John Fiske and John Hartley*
Making a Difference: Feminist literary criticism ed. *Gayle Greene and
    Coppélia Kahn*
Superstructuralism: The philosophy of structuralism and
    post-structuralism *Richard Harland*
Structuralism and Semiotics *Terence Hawkes*
Subculture: The meaning of style *Dick Hebdige*
Dialogism: Bakhtin and his world *Michael Holquist*
The Politics of Postmodernism *Linda Hutcheon*
Fantasy: The literature of subversion *Rosemary Jackson*
Sexual/Textual Politics: Feminist literary theory *Toril Moi*
Deconstruction: Theory and practice *Christopher Norris*
Orality and Literacy *Walter J. Ong*
Narrative Fiction: Contemporary poetics *Shlomith Rimmon-Kenan*
Adult Comics: An introduction *Roger Sabin*
Criticism in Society *Imre Salusinszky*
Metafiction *Patricia Waugh*
Psychoanalytic Criticism: Theory in practice *Elizabeth Wright*
Alternative Shakespeares ed. *John Drakakis*

Alternative Shakespeares

Volume 2

Edited by
TERENCE HAWKES

London and New York

First published 1996
by Routledge
11 New Fetter Lane,
London EC4P 4EE

Simultaneously published in
the USA and Canada
by Routledge
29 West 35th Street,
New York, NY 10001

Routledge is an
International Thomson Publishing
company

© 1996 Terence Hawkes, selection and
editorial matter; the contributors,
individual chapters. Terence Hawkes
asserts his moral right to be identified
as the editor of this work.

Typeset in Baskerville by
Ponting–Green Publishing Services,
Chesham, Buckinghamshire
Printed and bound in Great Britain by
Clays Ltd, St. Ives PLC

British Library Cataloguing in
Publication Data

A catalogue record for this book is
available from the British Library

Library of Congress Cataloguing in
Publication Data

A catalogue record for this book has
been requested

ISBN 0–415–13486–2

Contents

Illustrations

Contributors

Philip Armstrong: Lecturer in English, University of Auckland, New Zealand

Catherine Belsey: Professor of English, University of Wales, Cardiff

Dympna Callaghan: Associate Professor of English, University of Syracuse, New York

Margreta de Grazia: Professor of English, University of Pennsylvania

John Drakakis: Reader in English, University of Stirling

Keir Elam: Professor of English, University of Florence, Italy

Terence Hawkes: Professor of English, University of Wales, Cardiff

Ania Loomba: Associate Professor of English, Jawaharlal Nehru University, New Delhi, India

Steven Mullaney: Associate Professor of English, University of Michigan, Ann Arbor

Alan Sinfield: Professor of English, University of Sussex

Bruce R. Smith: Professor of English, Georgetown University, Washington D.C.

General editor's preface

How can we recognize or deal with the new? Any equipment we bring to the task will have been designed to engage with the old: it will look for and identify extensions and developments of what we already know. To some degree the unprecedented will always be unthinkable.

The *New Accents* series has made its own wary negotiation around that paradox, turning it, over the years, into the central concern of a continuing project. We are obliged, of course, to be bold. Change is our proclaimed business, innovation our announced quarry, the accents of the future the language in which we deal. So we have sought, and still seek, to confront and respond to those developments in literary studies that seem crucial aspects of the tidal waves of transformation that continue to sweep across our culture. Areas such as structuralism, post-structuralism, feminism, Marxism, semiotics, subculture, deconstruction, dialogism, postmodernism, and the new attention to the nature and modes of language, politics and way of life that these bring, have already been the primary concern of a large number of our volumes. Their 'nuts and bolts' exposition of the issues at stake in new ways of writing texts and new ways of reading them has proved an effective statagem against perplexity.

But the questions of what 'texts' are or may be has also

become more and more complex. It is not just the impact of electronic modes of communication, such as computer networks and data banks, that has forced us to revise our sense of the sort of material to which the process called 'reading' may apply. Satellite television and supersonic travel have eroded the traditional capacities of time and space to confirm prejudice, reinforce ignorance, and conceal significant difference. Ways of life and cultural practices of which we had barely heard can now be set compellingly beside – can even confront – our own. The effect is to make us ponder the culture we have inherited; to see it, perhaps for the first time, as an intricate, continuing construction. And that means that we can also begin to see, and to question, those arrangements of foregrounding and backgrounding, of stressing and repressing, of placing at the centre and of restricting to the periphery, that give our own way of life its distinctive character.

Small wonder if, nowadays, we frequently find ourselves at the boundaries of the precedented and at the limit of the thinkable: peering into an abyss out of which there begin to lurch awkwardly-formed monsters with unaccountable – yet unavoidable – demands on our attention. These may involve unnerving styles of narrative, unsettling notions of 'history', unphilosophical ideas about 'philosophy', even unchildish views of 'comics', to say nothing a host of barely respectable activities for which we have no reassuring names.

In this situation, straightforward elucidation, careful unpicking, informative bibliographies, can offer positive help, and each *New Accents* volume will continue to include these. But if the project of closely scrutinizing the new remains nonetheless a disconcerting one, there are still overwhelming reasons for giving it all the consideration we can muster. The unthinkable, after all, is that which covertly shapes our thoughts.

TERENCE HAWKES

Acknowledgements

Collections such as this depend wholly on the energy, goodwill and cooperation of individual contributors. Everyone involved in the present volume gave unstintingly of those resources in addition to the scholarship and critical acumen for which they had been recruited. They deserve my warmest thanks. The enthusiastic help of John Drakakis in the planning and development of the project was crucial as well as characteristic. For the period of study leave which enabled me fully to engage with it, I am extremely grateful to my colleagues at the University of Wales, Cardiff. My greatest debt of gratitude remains, as always, to my wife.

T.H.

NOTE

Shakespearean references are to the Arden edition of individual plays throughout, unless otherwise stated.
References to other works are given in full in a consolidated bibliography at the end of the book.

1
Introduction
TERENCE HAWKES

I In Lieu

Alternative to what? It isn't as if we were short of competing critical accounts of Shakespeare's plays. Their quantity is notorious, their disparity scandalous: this, at least, is the popular belief. And yet, for all their apparent variety, the 'alternatives' on offer too often seem to embody mere surface differences. However noisily they vie for our attention, many turn out to be conceptual stable-mates, thriving on a diet of common presuppositions.

Part of the problem is that in our culture the phenomenon called 'Shakespeare' operates simultaneously on a number of levels. Its 'popular' dimension manages at the same time to be both at odds and at home with the more arcane perceptions of an academic world in which the works also have a striking centrality. Shakespeare appears world-wide on T-shirts, postage stamps and credit cards as well as in the titles of learned monographs and Ph.D. dissertations. His name is as familiar in bars and restaurants as it is in classrooms and lecture-halls.

So deep and complex a penetration of English-speaking culture and beyond suggests that his image speaks to and fosters a number of powerful prejudices, the more potent for being rarely examined. Transmitted through a kind of unlearned, unofficial folk-lore as well as by means of an all-embracing education system which, in Britain at least, makes the study of 'English' enforcible by law; it has become part of the ideological landscape of national life in Europe, North America and beyond.

II Myth

This astonishing development was by no means immediate, but within two hundred years of the Bard's death a remarkable acceleration in it became quite evident. 'Nothing can please many, and please long, but just representations of general nature' announced Dr Johnson in the *Preface* to his famous edition of *The Plays of William Shakespeare* (1765), going on to leave readers in no doubt that the Bard's special gift lay precisely in his command of that capacity for faithful and exact depiction. Its exercise, he says, ensures that Shakespeare stands above all writers as 'the poet that holds up to his readers a faithful mirror of manners and of life' (Johnson 1969: 59). To this day, that remains, in general terms, the grounding claim popularly made on behalf of the Swan of Avon and it has, accordingly, become the foundation stone of the 'Shakespeare' edifice. The Bard, we can depend upon it, tells it like it is. However, Johnson's admiration fell well short of idolatry on other grounds: Shakespeare's lack of discipline, for instance; his tendency to be overwhelmed by the onrush of his own invention. The result was a number of pointed rebukes, amongst them, infamously, an objection to Macbeth's affecting lines '. . . Here lay Duncan, / His silver skin laced with his golden blood,' (*Macbeth* II. iii. 111–12). In Johnson's judgement, these metaphors fail utterly. They offend against common sense and simple observation. He dismisses them as 'forced and unnatural'. After all, skin is not silver, blood is not golden. 'No amendment can be made to this line, of which every word is equally faulty, but by a general blot' he thunders (Johnson 1969: 132).

   Yet few twentieth-century students of the play would agree. Indeed, under the pressure of essays and examinations, they might even rush to admire the use of 'royal' metals in the description of a king's dead body as an instance of Shakespeare's metaphorical skill, to say nothing of its witty manipulation of some of the crucial counters of Jacobean ideology.

Far from judging the words 'forced and unnatural' they might be persuaded to applaud their disturbing intricacy. Few would hesitate to point out that the soft complexities of 'laced' serve paradoxically to confirm the reductive nature of such butchery – Duncan's royal body 'laced up' in dribbled blood like a mere piece of leather. They might even add that the enormous scale of the depredation is suggested by the further implication that its stain darkens even the social conventions of dress, so that the 'lace' ruff apparently worn about the King's neck turns out to be made of blood. The situation is distinctly odd. How is that the most callow of twentieth-century undergraduates can turn out to be wiser in a crucial matter of literary judgement than the great Cham of English letters himself?

Any response to that question is forced to engage with matters of principle. We can historicize Johnson. As a result, we can tell – we think – that he is unable to look at Shakespeare except through the spectacles of his own time. The standards he applies – they seem unchallengeable – are not in fact universally applicable, but have been forged in, by and for a specific time and place, and in response to the pressures of a particular context to which he is as much anaesthetized as we are to our own. For instance, we might question his overall view of drama. Compared to ours, it seems irredeemably literary: 'A dramatic exhibition is a book recited with concomitants that increase or diminish its effect. Familiar comedy is often more powerful on the theatre than in the page; imperial tragedy is always less' (Johnson 1969: 71–2). We might also, not un-reasonably on the basis of our century's studies of history and of comparative anthropology, question the existence of a 'general' human nature. Once we do that, the idea that representations of such an entity constitute the only proper object of art begins to look more like a response to a series of specific historical moments than an eternally valid perception. In the event, Dr Johnson seems to be judging Shakespeare as if he were – indeed he is effectively turning him into – an eighteenth-century poet.

To look at Dr Johnson's great successor as a critic of Shakespeare, Coleridge, is inevitably to notice something sim-ilar. In general terms, Coleridge pushes aside Johnson's ob-jections to Shakespeare's wilder effusions on the grounds that, as a great poet, his commitment is to an 'organic' rather than a 'mechanic' regularity. That is – and Coleridge here draws on one of the central metaphors of the Romantic poets – his plays are like great trees, in which an apparent irregularity in outline and shape is underpinned by a fundamental cohesion, whereby the tiniest outermost leaf on the furthest branch of the tree is connected, via the great trunk, to the sustaining roots in the ground below. In Coleridge's lecture on *The Tempest*, for instance, he justifies the rhetorical flourish of Prospero's injunction to Miranda, 'The fringed curtains of thine eye advance / And say what thou seest yond' (I. ii. 411–12) – a line which a modern reader would find hard to assess as anything other than a rather wordy excrescence – by pointing out how, in its reference to ornate curtains suddenly raised to reveal some surprising new object, Prospero's role as prestidigitator, conjuror, magus, is not only underlined, but, with great subtlety, immediately linked with and woven into the organic unity of the play as a whole (Coleridge 1969: 229–30, 239). In short, Coleridge's insistence upon Shakespeare's commitment to and pursuit of that unity virtually turns the Bard into a Romantic poet.

It might be added that Coleridge is not just involved in an attempt to popularize his views of the Bard, although he was most successful in doing that. Political issues are also in play, and his Shakespearean criticism – despite its own implicit claims about the 'universality' of what is at stake – perhaps represents the beginning of the committed use of Shakespeare as an element in the forging of a nation's ideology. The point could be even more crudely put, in terms of the party politics of the day. There is certainly a case for arguing (as Jonathan Bate has done) that William Hazlitt stands as the 'radical' to Coleridge's 'conservative' in this respect and that their lectures function as salvoes in the battle for possession of the Bard that was a feature of British cultural skirmishing in the first quarter of the nineteenth century.[1]

Any long view of modern Shakespearean criticism must pause at A. C. Bradley's monumental work *Shakespearean Tragedy* (1904).[2] This classic turn-of-the-century analysis contains a host of acutely intelligent observations. Nevertheless, in presenting the plays almost as portrait galleries of notable 'characters' Bradley virtually makes them over into Victorian novels. Interestingly, the influence of this book remains world-wide and astonishingly strong, despite the brilliance of L. C. Knights's devastating attack 'How Many Children had Lady Macbeth?', made in 1933.[3] As a result, Bradley's commitment to the almost palpable existence of single, unitary individuals and the developing relations between them as the core of each play's interest still seems the 'natural' and 'obvious' one to large numbers of people. It does so to an extent that suggests that the concern with individual personality fundamental to such a stance may ultimately reflect deep-lying dimensions of Western ideology, thus making it virtually 'invisible'. As a result, this highly theorized, highly partial study is still presented as open-handed and theory-free; an example of 'pure' Shakespearean criticism 'itself'. Large numbers of people who have never read a word of Bradley espouse his principles as if they embodied the anonymous accents of truth. His 'Shakespeare' is one of our century's most representative myths.

III History

Of course, opposition to it has also flourished. In Britain, the work of both G. Wilson Knight and L. C. Knights long ago put the case that, far from being quasi-novels, portrait galleries of interesting persons with plots that developed in an incremental, linear mode, the plays were effectively long poems. As such, they were not finally susceptible to the sort of analysis which presupposed a sequential and coherent story-line, which probed the extent of their 'truth to life' or the subtlety of their depiction of the quirks of 'character'. Bradley's dogged pursuit of quasi-'real-world' issues, his infamous enquiries into 'Events before the opening of the action in *Hamlet*', the Prince's age, his location at the time of his father's death, or the number of Macbeth's children, began to seem flat-footed. Questions such as 'Did Lady Macbeth really faint?' were manifestly preposterous, fundamentally inappropriate and systematically misleading.[4] In any case, solid material research concerning the way of life of Elizabethan and Jacobean Britain, the structure and social role of its theatres and their relation to the broader community and its institutions, had already established that that society was not the simple precursor of Victorian Britain that Bradley appears to suppose. E. K. Chambers's four-volume *The Elizabethan Stage* (1923) offered a close account of its uniquely structured playhouse and gave specific details of the complex culture from which it grew and to which it spoke. Other studies focused on the emblematic, non-representational dimensions of early modern art, the non-naturalistic style of Elizabethan acting, the highly sophisticated deployment of male actors in female roles, and attempted, in the case of E. M. W. Tillyard's complex contributions, *The Elizabethan World Picture* (1943) and *Shakespeare's History Plays* (1944), to outline an Elizabethan 'world view', with its own integrity, its own sense of the past and of a relationship to it, that was very different from our own. The stable, ordered, hierarchical world of Tillyard's account, with its 'Chain of Being' and its precise gradations of cosmic social and economic status, was presented as the world which Shakespeare's plays seemed designed to address, and the solid ground from which they evidently derived.

Tillyard's books seemed initially to be definitive and became vastly influential: they certainly determined the view of the early modern period taken by a generation. And yet they in their turn could hardly step aside from the process of history. Published in 1943–4, their vision of a golden age of order, stability and established hierarchy, subscribed to by an entire society, was itself the product of a period of spectacular disorder, instability and change. By the 1970s they had come to be perceived as in part a response to the Second World War in Europe; fashioned, almost in a spirit of nostalgia, as the bombs fell upon the remnants of the civilization they were apparently intending to memorialize. Certainly – and once more, political reasons for this are not hard to find – the conclusions of Tillyard and others could afford to take little account of the impulses to disorder that such a society inevitably contained and attempted to hold in balance.

Not inappropriately, opposition to Tillyard's picture of the early modern period took its stand precisely on the use of history. In fact, by the 1980s, how we perceive the past and the role we give to it formed the main concern of the most significant British and American Shakespearean criticism. However, a major methodological readjustment now seemed apt. No longer, in the manner of *The Elizabethan World Picture*, would historical material be treated as a 'background' against which literary texts might be placed. After all, the covert distinction at work here between text and context, foreground and background, clearly operates on behalf of some major presuppositions. One of them, by its promotion of the 'literary' text as a privileged vehicle of communication, ultimately independent of its context, involves a direct projection of the values of our own near-universally literate culture onto a way of life quite differently based, that could at the very least be styled 'pre-literate'. Another reflects an undeclared investment in a particular view of history moulded by a primary commitment to the academic study of literature.

It is well known that the two most significant attempts to forge a new role both for history and the notion of culture in literary criticism have taken place under banners bearing a strange device: either that of New Historicism or that of Cultural Materialism. The terms 'historicism' and 'cultural' reflect these linked concerns. A central focus of both is the renegotiation, in the name of a new use of history, of that distinction between foreground and background mentioned above. Another is the relocation and re-reading of literary texts in quite a different relation to the other material signifying practices of a culture. Both approaches are committed to the abandonment of 'organic unity' as the appropriate model for a way of life's ideal condition, as well as the chief aesthetic value to which the practice of art within it should aspire. Both seek rather to interpet early modern culture as the inherently shifting and always potentially re-forming product of an ensemble of signifying practices. It is for fear of pulling off balance the concrete relationship between those practices that they decline to privilege literature, or to accord writing the 'transcendent' dimension or quality that strikes us late-coming students of 'English' as appropriate. Such a materialism will always see the shape of any culture as volatile and provisional, never complete or 'finished'. By its lights, the committed pursuit of a 'world picture' is quite out of the question.[5]

IV Culture

The aim of such analysis is to locate all of a culture's signifying practices squarely and accurately in the context of the larger material social process. To some extent it involves what the American anthropologist Clifford Geertz calls – borrowing the notion from the British philosopher Gilbert Ryle – 'thick description'. Fundamentally, as Steven Mullaney's essay points out, this focuses on the 'symbolic' dimension of the social actions in which humans engage, placing them in the context of the cultures in which they occur and construing them as events whose raw content (available in 'thin' description) is ultimately overridden by a larger cultural function. Like 'phonation in speech, pigment in painting, line in writing, or sonance in music' human activities are seen to be wholly involved in signification, and what they signify is ultimately directed towards and is for the benefit of participants in the culture that engages in them. The question to ask of such activities – they include the social practice of winking, sheep-stealing in Morocco and, in a highly complex analysis, the 'sport' of cock-fighting in a Balinese village – is not what their ontological status is, or what they 'mean' in themselves. The question to ask, and which 'thick description' tries to answer, is what their larger 'import' may be for those who take part in them. What is it that, by means of their occurrence and through their agency, 'is getting said'?[6] To use phrases that I have employed elsewhere, this proposes that human actions, activities, the 'things of this world', don't in themselves 'mean'. It is *we* who mean, *by* them.[7]

Geertz is right to acknowledge a clear link between 'thick description' and the activity of literary criticism. The 'semiotic concept of culture' he proposes calls emphatically for an interpretative stance from its beholders. In this mode, cultures, or ways of life, present themselves as assemblages of 'texts' – not all of them written – threaded through with elaborate structures of meaning in terms of which whatever people get up to always acquires larger dimensions of signification. What makes a different culture impenetrable to us is always, in Geertz's words, 'lack of familiarity with the imaginative universe within which their acts are signs' (Geetz 1973: 448–9). We need – bearing in mind Mullaney's reservations – to learn how to 'read' those signs. The achievement of precisely that degree of familiarity is central to the project of both New Historicism and Cultural Materialism.

V Meanings

But our opening question is insistent. Alternative to what? What views of Shakespeare do the essays collected here neces-

sarily oppose? In general terms we can begin with the hint
offered by Geertz. Thus, in place of a quest for what Shakespeare's plays 'mean' for all time and for all people, they are
committed first to the principle that any and all 'meaning' will
be historically determined, and second – but simultaneously –
to the notion that what is important is not such meaning in itself
(it has no existence 'in itself'), but how it operates as part of the
ensemble of meaning-making discourses by which that culture
makes sense of the world it creates and inhabits. They thus
oppose themselves, and offer alternatives to, a set of general
beliefs whose roots in Dr Johnson, Coleridge, Bradley and   to
a degree – Tillyard may now, to some extent, be clear, despite
their claim to the status of transparent self-evident truth, even
'common sense'. These might roughly, but not unjustly, be
schematized as follows:

1 That Shakespeare is an all-wise, all-knowing genius, possessed of astounding capacities of insight into the human
   psyche.
2 That his plays present portrait galleries of individual human
   figures, exemplifying characteristic faults or virtues, which
   the Bard's insight permits him to probe and exhibit.
3 That his work is universally valid and speaks to human
   beings across the ages, as clearly now, had we the wit to see
   it, as it did then.
4 That to encounter his plays is thus finally to come across
   ourselves, to receive a trenchant and accurate diagnosis of
   our failings and possibilities and, by implication, to develop
   the capacity to engage at last with the contours of our own
   nature. In the portentous words of Harold Bloom, the true
   'use' of Shakespeare (along with other great writers) is 'to
   augment one's own growing inner self', a process that will
   bring 'the proper use of one's own solitude, that solitude
   whose final form is one's confrontation with one's own
   mortality'. Shakespeare 'may teach us how to overhear
   ourselves when we talk to ourselves', and finally help us to
   prepare for, even to accept, the solitary end that is the
   inescapable human fate (Bloom 1994: 30–31).
5 That, in short, Shakespeare's plays present us with nothing
   less than the truth, the whole truth and nothing but the truth
   about the most fundamental matters of human existence:
   birth, death and the life that comes between.

6 That, in addition, he is entertaining. He makes us laugh and cry like billy-oh, and can command our rapt attention like no other writer.

These claims, it could be argued, rest on the following, perhaps even more dubious and certainly deeply occluded principles:

1 That human nature is permanent, one and indivisible, regardless of place, race, creed and culture. In the end, under the skin, we are all the same and it is to this sameness that Shakespeare speaks.
2 That the passage of time, history, makes no difference to this.
3 That, construed aright, and analysed with sufficient ingenuity, application, vigour and flexibility, Shakespeare's plays are able to address all people at all times, and everywhere.
4 That to deny any of the above is to reveal serious deficiencies in one's humanity, such as characterize the ravings of the deranged, the perverse, the envious and the politically and socially deviant.

To the extent that these, or something not unlike them, still represent the common coin of responses to Shakespeare, both within and without the academic community, the present volume of essays can certainly be said to offer a series of alternatives.

VI Options

What will they look like? Clearly, on the basis of what has already been said, ideas about history and culture must be well to the fore. A sense of the concrete differences between past and present and their respective ways of life will always be the first casualty of a process that invests in a timeless Bard of universal appeal. To prise any creation out of the material historical context from which it derives and with which it traffics will inevitably distort some of its dimensions, usually by masking others. As Steven Mullaney comments, in his incisive account of New Historicism and the developments subsequent to it, the 'aesthetic analysis of literary texts' can no longer constitute an appropriate project for literary criticism, particularly of Shakespeare. Its expansion to embrace 'the ideological analysis of discursive cultural practices, including but not restricted to the literary, and non-discursive practices as well' stands as one of the first requirements of an alternative approach. Catherine Belsey's essay is a good example of exactly that sort of criticism in action. By means of a close reading of the text of *Antony and Cleopatra*, vividly relocated amidst the discourses of which it once formed a part, she is able to trace a dimension of sexuality submerged since the early modern period. Margreta de Grazia's account of how metaphors derived from the technology of printing worked their way into a large number of early modern discourses follows a similarly rewarding path. Pursuing it, her analysis of some crucial Shakespearean images offers a powerful purchase on the ways in which cultures can covertly – and almost casually – reinforce and disseminate particular notions of the relation between male and female.

Sexuality, sexual behaviour and the presuppositions of a society committed to a heterosexual and firmly gendered viewpoint also provide the focus for the contributions of Bruce R. Smith and Alan Sinfield. Both offer readings of Shakespearean texts whose 'alternative' dimension lies in a refusal to neglect the implications, and indeed the history, of precisely that viewpoint. In Smith's case, this derives from a conviction, based upon historical research, that our category of 'homosexual' is a modern invention, the product of economic, social and political changes specific to a particular period of history. His account of a new model of sexual behaviour appropriate to the early modern period thus begins, as it must, with a sceptical look at notions of 'sex' and 'sexuality' as objects of enquiry. Sinfield's essay takes up the 'positive' assessment of homosexuality such a view would support, and asks how subcultures or 'minority out-groups' may relate to the powerful – and heterosexual – cultural icon that Shakespeare has become. Must gay men, for instance, inevitably be excluded from engagement with a play like *The Merchant of Venice*? It is an odd prospect, considering, as he points out, that the play apparently treats, *inter alia*, two men's love for each other.

Probably one of the major limitations of traditional Shakespearean criticism lay in its commitment to the 'literary'; to the plays as instances, not merely of language, but of that particular form of it called writing. As a major component of the monolith 'English Literature', Shakespeare's works helped to reinforce a particularly restrictive notion of the culture of Britain and elsewhere, one of whose central aspects was its denial of the body. And yet the plays are designed as vehicles for the body, as well as for the voice. As Keir Elam points out in his essay, one of the more striking events in recent critical developments has been the shift from a primary concern with disembodied 'language', to a focus on the entity of flesh and blood which guarantees as well as houses it. This involves grasping the full extent to which, in a still-oral society, the embodied physical utterance dominated human life and art. It also requires an analytic tool – a semiotics – capable of matching the complexity newly at stake. The actor's body, from which drama is ultimately made, becomes a primary focus of such analysis. On the basis of an acute probing of the signifying power of bodies in *Twelfth Night*, *Timon of Athens* and other plays, Elam proposes a vital poetics of signification which can act as the basis of a newly historicized and materialized semiotics.

Like the questions of sexual difference, and of its physical embodiment, the issue of racial distinction and integrity will necessarily be neglected by a project concerned to foster the notion of a universal and unchanging human identity, and a common, reachable 'human nature', palpable beneath the cultural veil. Not surprisingly, in a world frequently and horrifically torn by interracial dispute, this issue bulks large in the present collection. Ania Loomba's account of the racial structures at work in early modern Britain and their eruption through the surface of the plays, offers a timely example of how the introduction of a topic as crucial as this can disturb and disrupt the smoothing gestures of a universalizing criticism. In similar vein, Dympna Callaghan's focus on the use of black and white make-up on stage and in 'real life' becomes a penetrative means of exploring the relation of racial to gender difference in the matter of representation, particularly in *Othello*, where the notion of miscegenation plays so crucial a role.

All of this, so much Shakespearean criticism fails to notice, involves the most vital ingredient of any play: an audience. We know that early modern audiences engaged in a cultural transaction of a very specific kind in the building they called the 'playhouse'; one quite different from that which takes place in the building we now call the 'theatre'. Nowadays, a highly literate body of people settles down in relatively comfortable,

individually rented seats, in a temperature-controlled environ-
ment, and in a darkness which reinforces a sense of separate
and individual involvement with the lighted cynosure of a stage
(a procedure which perhaps repeats and confirms a dominant
mode of individual engagement with the printed page). There
it steels itself for a complex encounter with that benign (not to
say state-subsidized) scourge of middle-class pretensions called
Art. The hushed occasion, the absence of the elements, and the
darkness, exalt the experience to the extent that the building
virtually becomes a temple to that abstract sense of individual,
private and personal being, worth and involvement which – for
the last one hundred and fifty years at least – we have taken
almost as a birthright.

In the early modern playhouse, on the other hand, there is
noise and daylight, wind and weather, small sense of a private
individuality (perhaps that has yet to be invented) and in any
case little opportunity to indulge it. Members of the audience
see and respond to each other in precisely that collective role,
clearly and directly, as in a modern football stadium. There is
also little enough sense that we are in the presence of anything
as forbidding as Art. Shakespeare's theatre operated, the point
has already been made, as part of an ensemble of spectacular
'entertainment' available in London: one which included bear-
baiting, brothels, the stocks, the pillory, the exhibition of the
mentally disturbed, public beheading and evisceration, and
royal processions. These competed – on equal terms – with the
theatre for an audience; one which, given the state of its own
literacy, was much drawn to public, eye-catching displays. The
'gaze' of this crowd was perhaps its most formidable and, for
the businessmen who ran the theatres, its most desirable and
exploitable characteristic. Philip Armstrong's essay responds to
an awakening interest in these matters, which has joined a
renewed concern with the insights of post-Freudian concepts of
the modes of human interaction. His use of models developed
by Jacques Lacan and others brings a wholly new dimension to
our sense of the sort of communication that was at issue
between the Shakespearean stage and those onlookers on
whose response everything depended.

The kind of access to the plays which is sought here
ultimately depends upon the abandonment of any sense of a
'final' meaning that must necessarily be dug out of them. To

accept that they have no once-and-for-all essential or stable identity is precisely what permits a probing of the plays' unique legacy: it may even help to create it. That they seem to foster these siftings differently from generation to generation as well as from performance to performance is an inescapable – and happy – conclusion. Those who believe that Shakespeare can still engage modern audiences will find their case fully supported by such stratagems, without needing to locate a phantom quality of 'transcendency' in the plays, or to construct ghostly entities vaguely promoted as the plays 'themselves'.

On this basis, the present collection retains, and insists on, the plural 'Shakespeares' of its title. There is an additional advantage in such a styling. It immediately avoids the tedium of conjuring up yet once more that elusive yet coherent 'personality' of genius supposed to lurk 'behind' or even 'in' the plays; a shadowy, blank-faced British agent, bald, bearded, but dashing, licensed to elaborate plot and develop character whilst magically able to 'pass' undetected from one culture or historical period into any other in order to propagate his everlasting truths. The persistence of this English fantasy of empire and espionage is legendary. It runs from the Scarlet Pimpernel to James Bond and the novels of John Le Carré, via Rudyard Kipling's peculiarly resonant and resolutely English novel *Kim*. (In fact, its echoes extend as far as the personality of one of the most subversive 'Englishmen' of his generation, the spy Kim Philby, whose deliberate and mocking acquisition of that very name predictably failed to ring any bells with his superiors.) Its dangers are evident. Effectively, such a chimera's commitment to values and responses that supposedly cross all barriers and exist for 'all time' reinforces the fiction of a free-floating, permanent 'human nature'. And insofar as that distracts us from the important differences between people and cultures, present and past, it eventually drains away our own experience and our own history.

It follows that a contemporary Shakespearean criticism is bound to cultivate a general awareness of something that any serious concern with the operation of history and the structures of culture cannot neglect: the pressures of our own time, our own involvement in history and the material concerns of our own way of life. Nobody witnessing, or undergoing, the triumph of the English language as a political and economic force in the twentieth century, can fail to be aware of the use of Shakespeare as an instrument of cultural meaning, and in particular of the role played in the process by academic literary criticism. The current undertaking thus necessarily involves an attempt to historicize salient features of recent Shakespearean criticism – it is partly the project of this Introduction – and to draw attention to a more substantial quarry, which perhaps remains to be pursued on other occasions: the complex operation of those institutions and cultural forms which that criticism both generates and is generated by.

VII Getting it wrong

Serious conundrums remain. If we abandon the notion either of an absolute 'truth' about Shakespeare the dramatist, or of a 'truth' that his plays embody or entail, what can we make of the concept of an 'alternative' to the truth? At the very least we might try to enrich that notion by ceasing to think of truth's alternative as merely 'error', something 'wrong' as opposed to truth's 'right'.[8] Modern anthropology teaches us that much of what we respond to as 'error', or as 'wrong' in another way of life, may be more profitably classified as the lineaments of 'culture'.[9] The very idea of 'culture' as a committed and wholesale 'wrongness' which may in different circumstances be perceived as a self-evident 'rightness', brings into question the notion of objective truth. History and the study of other social formations demonstrate time and again that ideas or behaviour we confidently condemn as 'silly' or 'stupid', 'wrong' or 'mistaken', often merely announce the presence of unfamiliar structures of thought. To a considerable degree, the imperative to continuing readjustment urged by that situation propels this collection of essays. Getting Shakespeare and early modern culture 'right' is not its aim. Getting to grips with what our inherited notions of 'right' conceal from us is.

These are issues that were confronted in the initial New Accents collection *Alternative Shakespeares*. They remain, and are also confronted here. Published in 1985, that earlier volume seemed to make an impression on Shakespeare studies. For that reason, the format of the present volume remains essentially the same as that of the first, and the contributors have been no less carefully selected. About half of them appeared in the initial collection and their points of view will be seen variously to have developed or changed. The new contributors represent positions that by and large have more recently emerged.

The problems raised in the first volume were confronted with no expectation that they would be solved. At the best it was hoped to make some impact and to generate some reaction. Both impact and reaction – often in terms of sound and fury – far exceeded the expectations of those involved, indicating a degree of interest to which the present collection is a response. To preserve a kind of continuity with the original enterprise, John Drakakis, the editor of *Alternative Shakespeares*, has agreed to contribute an 'afterword' to *Alternative Shakespeares 2* in which his aim is to single out and address the concerns that link the second volume to the first.

The debate, for that is what the present collection of essays regards itself as part of, will continue. Its topic is not a vanished past, but those texts and activities which, located there, are nonetheless only ever available to us in our readings of them, here and now. An 'alternative' Shakespeare can thus never be a 'finished' – and so diminished – Bard. With our contributors jostling impatiently in the wings, it seems far more likely (to invoke the most radical sort of alternation) that the reverse will continue to be the case.

2
After the new historicism
STEVEN MULLANEY

In his 1986 Presidential Address to the Modern Language Association, J. Hillis Miller noted with some alarm a recent and pervasive transformation of literary studies:

> As everyone knows, literary study in the past few years has undergone a sudden, almost universal turn away from theory in the sense of an orientation toward language as such and has made a corresponding turn toward history, culture, society, politics, institutions, class and gender conditions, the social context, the material base ... conditions of production, technology, distribution, and consumption.
>
> (Miller 1987: 283)[1]

Miller's list of unhappy developments was (and is) generous enough to encompass a great many recent trends in the field, among them new historicism, cultural materialism, feminism, various forms of revisionary Marxism, and cultural studies. Not everyone 'knows' this reorientation, however, in terms of the trajectory Miller describes – as a universal turn away from theory.

A great many others, including most of those involved in critical projects of the kind Miller questions, would be more likely to characterize the turn toward history, culture, society, *et al.* as a recent development *within* (and not away from) post-

structuralist theory, although the direction this reorientation
has taken is clearly not a road J. Hillis Miller regards as well
chosen or even on the map. In describing 'theory' as 'an
orientation toward language as such', Miller in fact stakes out
a markedly parochial domain, one identified with certain
reduced and strictly American versions of deconstruction –
what amount, in fact, to rather faulty translations of Derrida
as he was incorporated into formalist modes of literary analysis
in the United States. Derrida's emphasis on the overdetermined
structures of certain hierarchized binary oppositions in Western
culture is highly fraught in its implications for the study of
social, political and ideological formations, and has provided a
useful tool for cultural analysis, not only for literary critics but
also for some historians.[2] In the strand of American literary
deconstruction Miller himself has promoted, however, Derrid-
ean *overdetermination* becomes a linguistic and rhetorical *indeterminacy* of meaning; Derrida's famous and much misunderstood
statement that 'there is nothing outside of the text' (*il n'y a pas
de hors-texte*) becomes instead an assertion, endlessly reiterated
in close readings of canonical literary works, that there is no
way of *getting* outside the (literary) text, due to its tropological
*aporia*s of meaning. Miller's 'theory' can stand in opposition to
'history, culture, politics, institutions, class and gender conditions' only because, as Louis Montrose has suggested, Miller
radically polarizes the discursive and the social. 'The prevailing
tendency across cultural studies', Montrose notes, 'has been to
emphasize their reciprocity and mutual constitution: on the
one hand, the social is understood to be discursively constructed; and on the other, language-use is understood to be
always and necessarily dialogical, to be socially and materially
determined and constrained' (Montrose 1989: 15).

Not a turning away from theory in general, then, but a
turning toward a great deal else: reformulated in such terms,
Miller's generous list is indeed both useful and clarifying, for it
highlights some of the common ground shared by the various
modes of socio-political and historical criticism that have
emerged in recent years (for similar developments in other
disciplines, see Ortner 1984). Although diverse in their theoretical origins and assumptions and sometimes at apparent if not
fundamental odds in their ideological agendas, these movements have generally shared in an effort to redraw the bound-

aries of literary studies, to reconceive, in terms of a mutually constitutive and open-ended dialectic, the relationship between literary and other cultural discourses, the discursive and the social. Although neither as sudden nor as universal as Miller hyperbolically suggests, such a reorientation does challenge and has begun to alter some traditional paradigms and practices of literary criticism: the aesthetic analysis of literary texts, regarded as relatively self-contained linguistic artifacts, is being displaced by the ideological analysis of discursive cultural practices, including but not restricted to the literary, and non-discursive practices as well; the interpretation of literature within a strictly *literary* history, a diachronic sequence of canonical texts in dialogue with one another but otherwise relatively autistic, is being opened up to a less teleological but decidedly more heteroglossic interpretation of the social, political and historical conditions of possibility for literary production, and of the recursive effects of literary production and dissemination upon those conditions. The literary is thus conceived neither as a separate and separable aesthetic realm nor as a mere product of culture – a reflection of ideas and ideologies produced elsewhere – but as one realm among many for the negotiation and production of social meaning, of historical subjects and of the systems of power that at once enable and constrain those subjects.

This emphasis on the literary as both a form of and a forum for cultural practice, on literary analysis as a vehicle rather than an end in itself – a means of gaining access to other cultural forums and to the complex and heterogeneous processes through which social meaning and subjects are produced – was a distinguishing characteristic of what eventually became known as 'the new historicism'. Stephen Greenblatt first coined the phrase in 1982, seeking to describe a body of work that had been published, primarily by North American Renaissance scholars,[3] since the late seventies – work that was highly interdisciplinary and distinct from then current critical practices, that shared certain methodological and theoretical assumptions but was also heterogeneous enough in its concerns and assumptions that few of those associated with the work felt at all comfortable with the singularity attributed by Green-blatt's discussion of 'the' new historicism, suggestive of a unified theoretical movement or school despite disclaimers on this front (Greenblatt 1982: 5). Adding to this discomfort were the various ghosts raised by the invocation of 'historicism' (Greenblatt has since professed not to have considered the reverberations with nineteenth-century historicism) and the undue emphasis that the name places on the use (or abuse) of history in such criticism, as though there had never been an historically oriented literary criticism in the past.[4] Despite such problems and qualms, the label definitely caught on, and new historicism has consequently received a great deal of debate and discussion in recent years, in both academic journals and the popular press. It has been characterized by Edward Pechter as a Marxist 'specter . . . haunting criticism', although Pechter's sense of what unites and defines various Marxisms is, it must be said, decidedly curious ('they all view history and contemporary political life as determined, wholly or in essence, by struggle, contestation, power relations, *libido dominandi*' [Pechter 1987: 292]). Conversely, it has been viewed as a politically evasive, essentially liberal movement complicit in the structures of power and domination it purports to analyse, although in terms that come close to equating any critical analysis of a dominant power structure *with* such complicity (see Porter 1988). Some see it as part of a pernicious conspiracy, allied with feminism and ethnic studies, bent on perverting immortal literature and timeless, universal values (see Montrose 1989: 29). Certain feminists, however, would deny the alliance, viewing new historicism as a largely male appropriation, displacement and/or erasure of feminist concerns and critical practices (Newton 1989; Boose 1987b; Neely 1988).[5] It has been characterized as a break from and critique of the various, pre- and post-structuralist formalisms that have dominated literary studies (Greenblatt 1982, 1989), and as the latest manifestation of such formalism (Liu 1989; Montrose 1989). Adding to the confusion have been recent volumes that purport to define and exemplify new historicism but betray a considerable disregard for critical accuracy or rigour.[6] On the right and the left and various ideological and critical positions in between, people have been 'after' new historicism for some time.

Given the lack of consensus within literary studies about new historicism – what it is (or was), what it isn't, and what any right- (or left-) thinking person is to think about it – a general caution is in order: no survey, the present one included, is to be entirely trusted. This essay is a partisan account of new historicism, then, written from within the movement but not, I hope, uncritically so. It is also necessarily partial, in the sense that it does not profess to give a complete or synoptic view of the current state of literary studies in general, or of work that has been either celebrated or attacked as new historicism beyond the field of Renaissance literary studies. In the discussion that follows, I have tried to focus on those aspects of Renaissance new historicism which are at once most fundamental to it, most controversial and (partly as a consequence) most often misrepresented. From its early focus on the relationship between cultural forms and structures of state and institutional authority, new historicism has been an enquiry, or rather a series of not always harmonious enquiries, into the power such forms and structures have to determine ideas and ideologies, historical subjects and their actions, cultural practices and their potential for either reinforcing or contesting that power and those structures.

I

Unlike other disciplines, literary studies have traditionally been oriented toward the examination of a specific canon of texts, oftentimes conceived as relatively autonomous cultural artifacts. Even when such study has been in some sense historical, the relationship between literature and history has customarily been constrained by the reflectionist model implicit in the binary opposition of literary text and historical context. Early definitions of new historicism emphasize its departure from such approaches. Thus Greenblatt speaks of literary works as 'fields of force, places of dissension and shifting interests' rather than 'as a fixed set of texts that are set apart from all other forms of expression . . . or as a stable set of reflections of historical facts that lie beyond them'. Such an approach 'challenges the assumptions that guarantee a secure distinction between . . . artistic production and other kinds of social production' and shifts analysis from the literary in itself to the role that literary production plays in the larger social formation:

These collective social constructions on the one hand define the range of aesthetic possibilities within a given representational mode and, on the other, link that mode to the complex network of institutions, practices, and beliefs that constitute the culture as a whole.

(Greenblatt 1982: 6)

Such a shift shares certain assumptions with recent developments in British Marxist literary studies, characterized by its practitioners as a form of cultural materialism. Although not avowedly Marxist in terms of its politics, new historicism is also strongly indebted in its theoretical orientation to the work of Raymond Williams (from whom the phrase 'cultural materialism' derives), especially to his articulation of the nature and functioning of hegemonic culture.[7] In Williams's development of Antonio Gramsci's concept, hegemonic culture is neither singular nor static, nor is hegemony synonymous with cultural domination; on the contrary, the culture of any given historical period is conceived as a heterogeneous and irreducibly plural social formation, and as a dynamic process of representation and interpretation rather than as a fixed ensemble of meanings and beliefs. In such a view, culture is an ongoing production, negotiation and delimitation of social meanings and social selves, composed through both discursive and non-discursive means and in various and competing forums. Moreover, as Williams reminds us, the dominant culture of any given period is never either total or exclusive, never an accomplished fact but rather an ongoing process that 'has continually to be renewed, recreated, defended, and modified' because it is being 'continually resisted, limited, altered, challenged by pressures not at all its own' – by marginal, residual and alternative cultures that, together with the dominant, comprise the hegemonic (Williams 1978: 112).

In calling for a cultural as opposed to a historical materialism, Williams did not of course intend to suppress history but rather to move away from overly teleological models of history associated with classical Marxism, and to displace the economic as the final ground of materialism by focusing historical analysis instead upon what might be called the symbolic economy of any given period.[8] This entails, to my mind, a methodological shift toward a form of cultural or anthropological criticism capable of addressing a level of historical and cultural specificity that exceeds the grasp of ideological criticism *per se*, especially insofar as such specificity relates to the diverse, heterogeneous and often non-discursive cultural practices and processes of the social formation – what Williams called the 'internal dynamic relations' of hegemonic cultures, and whose dynamics he seemed principally concerned to open up to a more broadly conceived ideological/cultural analysis.

New historicism has a great deal of cultural or anthropological torque to it, supplied in part by cultural historians such as Natalie Davis, Robert Darnton and Carlo Ginzburg, and symbolic and Marxist anthropologists and sociologists such as Marshall Sahlins, Mary Douglas and Pierre Bourdieu. The most prominent signatures on the movement, however, are those of Clifford Geertz and Michel Foucault. In his anti-Burckhardtian study of the social construction of and constraints upon Renaissance selves, Stephen Greenblatt aligns his own project, which he calls a 'poetics of culture' (Greenblatt 1980: 5), with Geertz's loosely semiotic model of cultural systems of meaning (Geertz 1973: 44). Others have emphasized Geertz's approach to cultural practices as interpretive forms or 'cultural performances' (Mullaney 1988) or his focus upon the symbolic dimensions and construction of the real (Goldberg 1983).

But as Geertz himself has acknowledged, his semiotic model of culture is hardly original to him or, in its general outlines, unique to his own brand of symbolic anthropology. As Louis Montrose suggests, the more telling Geertzian influence on new historicism is a methodological one, an adoption and adaptation of the ethnographic practice Geertz described (Geertz 1973: 3–30) as 'thick description':

> Geertz's work offered to literary critics and cultural historians not so much a powerful *theory* of culture as an exemplary and eminently literary *method* for narrating culture in action, culture as lived in the performances and narratives of individual and collective human actors. . . . 'Thick description' might be more accurately described as 'interpretive narration': it seizes upon an event, performance, or other practice and, through the interrogation of its minute particulars, seeks to reveal the collective ethos of an alien culture.
>
> (Montrose 1992: 399)

Geertzian 'thick description' is indeed easy to align with the literary practice of providing an intensive 'reading' of a text or set of texts, and is 'eminently literary' in this relatively neutral or at least strictly methodological sense. Geertz's work is also, however, clearly invested in a particular ideology of form that is itself strongly associated with certain approaches to art and literature. His analyses tend to aestheticize the political and ideological domain,[9] explicating and even celebrating the cohesion of cultural meanings rather than analysing their fragmentary and contested production, treating texts, events and practices as collective *expressions* of a cultural essence or ethos rather than as ideological *constructions* of the collective or the essential. Describing man as 'an animal suspended in webs of significance he himself has spun' (1973: 5), Geertz traces the semantic intricacy of the web with extraordinary skill and verve, but pays scant attention to the social, political or ideological intricacies – and inequities – that allow the web to be spun. 'Cultures are webs of mystification as well as significa-tion,' as Roger Keesing comments. 'We need to ask who *creates* and who *defines* cultural meanings, and to what end' (Keesing 1987: 161–2). When Geertz describes ethnographic events as 'texts', he invokes not only a semiotic but also an aesthetic model, and the aesthetics informing much of his work seem close to the formalism of literary New Criticism, which was still dominant in literary studies in the late 1960s and early 1970s (when the essays collected in *The Interpretation of Cultures* were written). The Balinese cockfight is an 'art form' (Geertz 1973: 443), and at times in Geertz's explication and appreciation of its nuances it resembles nothing so much as a literary work in the hands of a New Critic: a complex, ambiguous but ultim-ately unified and coherent expression of cultural (or literary) sensibility. In this regard, Keesing's critique of Geertz echoes new historicist concerns with such formalism, New Critical and post-structuralist, in literary studies; both are

> silent on the way cultural meanings sustain power and privil-ege. . . . blind to the political consequences of cultures as ideologies, their situatedness as justifications and mystifica-tions of a local historically cumulated status quo. Where femin-ists and Marxists find oppression, symbolists find meaning.
>
> (Keesing 1987: 166)

Like a great many anthropologists indebted to Geertz but critical of such tendencies, new historicists – many, like myself, equally indebted – attempt to 'synthesize cultural and Marxist (or at least politically informed) analyses' (Biersack 1989: 84), to combine, however successfully, a poetics with a politics of culture.[10]

As Marxist critics especially have noted, however, new historicist analyses of the processes through which cultural meanings are produced, systems of power and privilege sustained, negotiated or contested, operate primarily within a synchronic field or cultural system rather than on a diachronic axis. Thus, while registering its similarities with Marxism, Walter Cohen also stresses, as a fundamental difference, that 'new historicism describes historical difference, but it does not explain historical change' (1987: 33). The focus upon historical difference is not a superficial trait, although it is reflected in new historicism's characteristic penchant for the unusual, uncanny and even bizarre historical detail – sometimes narrated as a paradoxically illustrative anecdote, oftentimes subjected to full analysis as part of a broader cultural pattern or logic. Nor is the delineation of historical difference absolute. As in Foucault's later work, new historicist practices of defamiliarization are oftentimes strategic efforts to displace traditional accounts of the past in order to clarify both similarities and differences with the present – to open up perspectives, however partial and incomplete, upon the production of historical subjects in the present and 'to experience facets of our own subjection at shifting internal distances – to read, as in a refracted light, one fragment of our ideological inscription by means of another' (Montrose 1992: 414; see also Mullaney 1988: xii).

Although primarily focused on discrete historical moments and silent about processes of historical change, a great deal of early new historicism was also (contrary to many descriptions of it) focused on the internal distances that open up within those historical moments, on the fractures and faultlines of a given ideological system. Like cultural materialism, new historicism has been critical of the false determinism of an Althusserian theory of ideology but also (like cultural materialism) unconvinced that agency can ever be historically or ideologically unfettered. As Anthony Giddens suggests when defining what he calls the 'concept of structuration', any ideological or other social system is fundamentally *recursive* in character:

> The concept of structuration involves that of the *duality of structure*, which relates to the *fundamentally recursive character of social life, and expresses the mutual dependence of structure and agency*. . . . the structural properties of social systems are both the medium and the outcome of those social systems. The theory of structuration, thus formulated, rejects any differentiation of synchrony and diachrony or statics and dynamics. The identification of structure with constraint is also rejected: structure is both enabling and constraining.
>
> (1979: 69)

I dwell upon Giddens in part because he and other social theorists have recently entered into some new historicists' efforts to theorize their own practices and methods (see Montrose 1989: 33 n.12, and 1990: 35–6), and in part because Giddens's emphasis on the constraining *and* enabling force of collective social structures has been a consistent focus of new historicist work, yet has been consistently ignored or marginalized in accounts of that work.

According to such accounts, which range over a wide political spectrum, from the 'red scare' tactics of Pechter (1987) to the Marxist overview of Cohen (1987), new historicism achieves a certain unanimity despite its heterogeneity. The charge is not that it revels in thickly described meaning but that it finds oppression, or cultural determination, everywhere, and denies the possibility of collective or individual agency. According to such accounts of literary studies in the 1980s, where others would find subversion, new historicists find containment.

II

In a 1981 essay entitled 'Invisible Bullets: Renaissance Authority and its Subversion', Stephen Greenblatt introduced the not-quite-binary opposition of containment and subversion. He argued that the dominant culture of early modern England did not merely *allow* certain forms of unruliness or discontent or subversive thought to be manifested; rather, 'the very condition of power' for the Tudor state rested in its capacity to *produce* forms of resistance and subversion, both in order to contain them and to use them to its own ends. Although he did not say that any or all acts of resistance or subversion are merely apparent, either the ruse and effect of power or the register of how fully contained the subjects of that power are – even when they think they are resisting it – he did suggest that much of what we embrace as subversive or radical in the period is, when examined more closely, not only 'contained by the power it would appear to threaten . . . [but also] the very product of that power' (1985: 23–4).

The essay was revised and expanded for two subsequent anthologies and most recently was included in *Shakespearean Negotiations* (Greenblatt 1988); it immediately prompted considerable debate and counter-argument among both new historicists and cultural materialists. The reaction of the latter was an interesting one, given the stakes involved for British Marxists in making their own critical practice a form of political and ideological resistance. In the introduction to *Political Shakespeare* (1985), which includes an updated 'Invisible Bullets', Jonathan Dollimore accepts Greenblatt's general criticism of previous approaches, namely that apparent radicalism in the period has often been too unquestionably embraced as genuine; he finds Greenblatt's account of the production of subversion persuasive at times – especially in the extended analysis of Thomas Harriot's colonial encounters in Virginia, from which the title is taken[11] – but questions the scope and efficacy of such ideological management and manipulation of subjects in the period. Quite rightly, he faults the overly monolithic power structure that allows Greenblatt to push his argument to the extreme (Dollimore and Sinfield 1985: 12), and which Greenblatt has subsequently qualified (Greenblatt 1988: 2–3, 65). Generally speaking, the reaction of other new historicists has been the same: ideological containment can be seen to operate in such a paradoxical and cunning fashion in some local and historically specific instances, perhaps in a great many, but not as a generalized condition of power.

The essay attempts to describe certain characteristics of early modern power in operation, not to provide a general theory of such power – although many responses to it project such a goal onto Greenblatt's argument. And as the reaction of other new historicists should suggest, neither is the essay a manifesto of new historicism, in the sense that principles, attitudes or arguments associated with it can fairly be abstracted and attributed to the movement in general. Greenblatt himself addresses both points in a more recent essay, where he contrasts his own argument in 'Invisible Bullets' with the version of that argument disseminated by critics of new historicism:

> I did not propose that all manifestations of resistance in all literature (or even in all plays by Shakespeare) were co-opted – one can readily think of plays where the forces of ideological containment break down. And yet characterizations of this essay in particular, and new historicism in general, repeatedly refer to a supposed argument that any resistance is impossible. A particularizing argument about the subject position projected by a set of plays is at once simplified and turned into a universal principle from which contingency and hence history itself is erased.
>
> (Greenblatt 1990a: 75)

I feel the need to dwell on this particular essay at some length because it has indeed served, in distorted and simplified form, as a template through which all too many commentators have viewed new historicism in general. Although such distortion is hardly unprecedented in scholarly debate, an emphatic *caveat lector* is especially in order here.

What the controversy provoked by 'Invisible Bullets' has also failed to register, moreover, is the powerful and altogether salutary effect that Greenblatt's essay, like his work in general, has had on the nature of Renaissance literary criticism and the level at which it has subsequently been conducted. Like any genuinely seminal work, Greenblatt's has introduced new topics and parameters for subsequent analysis, new terms for debate and discussion. Greenblatt's critics, like Geertz's, sometimes fail to acknowledge the degree to which their differences depend, for their very articulation, upon the transformation of the field that Greenblatt (and others) made possible. But while Greenblatt is without question one of the founding figures and ablest practitioners of new historicism, not all aspects of his work are accepted uncritically by other new historicists. To my mind, for example, Greenblatt's approach to a 'poetics of culture' tends, in its application, to obscure or homogenize a politics of culture, even when the heterogeneity of cultural forms, institutions and practices is his primary focus. Thus in his recent study of the Shakespearean theatre, focused upon the forms of cultural capital produced when objects, ideas, ceremonies and cultural practices were displaced or otherwise transferred from one cultural realm to another, his emphasis is upon a generalized 'social energy' and, in the case of the stage, the *aesthetic* empowerment produced by such circulation and negotiation. The potential ideological force of such displacements from the proper to the improper is largely ignored; circulation and acquisition are key metaphors, but appropriation is not (1988: 10–11). The category of the aesthetic in regard to Renaissance popular drama   even, perhaps especially, Shakespeare's – is itself quite problematic, given the fact that such drama was not accorded the dignity or propriety to qualify as literature or 'poesy' in the period. Greenblatt also tends to aestheticize the sites occupied by the popular playhouses – areas outside the city walls known as the Liberties – describing them as 'carefully demarcated playgrounds' (120) where the stage was 'marked off openly from all other forms and ceremonies of public life precisely by virtue of its freely acknowledged fictionality' (116). Rather than neutral zones, however, the Liberties were complexly inscribed domains of cultural contradiction, ambivalence and licence; the emergence of popular drama in them was not the escape of an artform to a sheltered retreat or preserve but rather a forceful, and forcefully felt, appropriation of a highly volatile zone in the city's spatial economy – which is indeed how the city viewed the emergence of the popular theatre (see Mullaney 1988: 1–59; Agnew 1986). Moreover, in the sixteenth century, the emergence of popular drama as a burgeoning but far from official social phenomenon and institution produced a sudden and explosive expansion of the discursive domain within which knowledge was produced and circulated – a domain that was at once a relatively closed system and one that was not strictly governed by issues of literacy. The boundary between oral and literate cultures was highly permeable, such that ideas and ideologies were disseminated not only by direct access to the printed word but also by diverse processes of representation and re-presentation, in official and unofficial forums ranging from the pulpit to the tavern, the juridical scaffold to the home or shop. Any significant expansion of this relatively closed discursive economy, any significant difference in the *degree* to which ideas and attitudes could be disseminated, threatened to become a difference in *kind* as well – altering the structure of knowledge by redefining its boundaries, contributing to the historical pressures that were forcing a transition from a relatively closed to a radically open economy of knowledge and representation. And unlike other significant expansions of the symbolic economy of the period, such as the rapid evolution of print culture and the concomitant vernacular translations of the Bible, literacy was not the price of admission to the theatre, giving the stage a currency and accessibility that was rivalled only by the pulpit.

To what degree such an expansion was or could be controlled, and by what apparatuses of a far from unified or centralized state, raises the issue of power in its ideological dimension. Although a key term in new historicist work, power is also less than adequately theorized there. An undeniable reliance upon Foucault's concept of power as 'the multiplicity of force relations' (1979: 92) in society, not primarily repressive but productive and acutely focused upon the construction of subjects and subjectivities, has led to charges that new historicists, like Foucault, foreclose all possibility of social struggle or contestation. Focusing on Greenblatt but generalizing about new historicism and Foucault, Frank Lentricchia argues that

> [Greenblatt's] description of power endorses Foucault's theory of power, preserving not only the master's repeated insistence on the concrete institutional character of power, its palpability, as it were, but also his glide into a conception of power that is elusively and literally indefinable – not finitely anchored but diffused from nowhere to everywhere, and saturating all social relations to the point that all conflicts and 'jostlings' among social groups become a mere show of political dissension, a prearranged theater of struggle set upon the substratum of a monolithic agency which produces 'opposition' as one of its delusive political effects.
>
> (1989: 235).[12]

Lentricchia's version of Foucault betrays a distressingly common selective (mis)reading, one that ignores Foucault's repeated assertions that a relational and contingent theory of power implies a relational and contingent theory of resistance:

Where there is power, there is resistance, and yet, or rather consequently, this resistance is never in a position of exteriority in relation to power. Should it be said that one is always 'inside' power, there is no 'escaping' it, there is no absolute outside where it is concerned, because one is subject to the law in any case? Or that, history being the ruse of reason, power is the ruse of history, always emerging the winner? This would be to misunderstand the strictly relational character of power relationships. Their existence depends on a multiplicity of points of resistance: these play the role of adversary, target, support, or handle in power relations. These points of resistance are present everywhere in the power network. Hence there is no single locus of great Refusal, no soul of revolt, source of all rebellions, or pure law of the revolutionary. Instead there is a plurality of resistances, each of them a special case. . . . by definition, they can only exist in the strategic field of power relations. But this does not mean that they are only a reaction or rebound, forming with respect to the basic domination an underside that is in the end always passive, doomed to perpetual defeat. Resistances do not derive from a few heterogeneous principles; but neither are they a lure or a promise that is of necessity betrayed.

(Foucault 1979: 95–6)

Foucault deconstructs the notion of autonomy rather than agency; Lentricchia and others like him fail to recognize the crucial distinction between the two.

Renaissance new historicists have necessarily but sometimes too exclusively focused upon monarchical power, oftentimes relying on Foucault's argument that an 'economy of visibility' (1977: 187) structured the power of the sovereign to emphasize that royal power existed only insofar as it manifested itself, that it was, in a sense, theatrically conceived, produced, negotiated and maintained. To what degree the royal aura, created and projected in monarchical processions and other cultural forums, succeeded in fostering 'an effective internalization of obedience' (James 1988: 358), and how such efforts were enhanced or contested in unofficial discursive and representational forums, has been the subject of wide opinion and disagreement. Greenblatt suggests that dramatic representations of monarchy on stage were, however corrosive or subversive in appearance, implicated in and contained by 'the English form of absolutist theatricality' which structured monarchical power (1988: 65), but this view has been criticized for conflating distinctly different manifestations of Renaissance 'theatricality'. Working with sixteenth-century theories of the monarchical corpus – the king's two bodies – some critics have argued that even in apparently royalist plays the effect of bringing a monarch on the dramatic scaffold, a royal figure played by a lower-class actor in borrowed robes, was inherently corrosive – that theatrical representation dismantled and derogated the carefully maintained and quasi-mystical aura of monarchical power, not simply by reproducing it but by rendering it reproducible (Moretti 1982; Kastan 1986; Mullaney 1989).

If it is misleading to collapse theatrical representation into the 'theatricality' of sovereign power, it is equally misleading to take at face value the pretensions and mystifications of sovereign presentation. In his study of the politics of literature in Jacobean England, Jonathan Goldberg draws on both Derrida and Foucault to examine the enabling contradictions of rule under James I and the degree to which poets and playwrights appropriated the radically equivocal style of Jacobean absolutism to position and sustain themselves both within and outside of the court patronage system (Goldberg 1983). The poetics and politics of Elizabethan rule have been richly and influentially examined by Louis Montrose in a series of essays that in many ways stand as exemplary instances of new historicist methodology and practice. Drawing on a wide variety of materials ranging from royal processions and proclamations to the fantasies and dreams of Elizabethan (male) subjects, Montrose provides a richly nuanced account of ways in which Elizabeth maintained her tenuous position as the female ruler of a patriarchal state, eliding the vulnerability of her own power with the vulnerability of gender and turning them both to her own advantage, styling herself as the unattainable, hence endlessly pursued, Virgin Queen, appropriating aspects of the Marian cult and the conventions of pastoral romance to restructure and manage the shape of her subjects' sexual as well as political desires. The analysis of the symbolic forms of mediation Elizabeth managed so dexterously does not preclude but rather implies and opens the way for Montrose's examination of the social, political and material realities mystified in the process (see especially Montrose 1980a, 1983a, 1983b, 1986b). Elizabethan literary works are viewed as integral and active forces in a complex process of cultural production, engaging in sometimes contestatory negotiations with and productions of Elizabethan culture, oftentimes in a manner that clarifies the male anxieties that structure and motivate traditional and historically conjunctural gender hierarchies (Montrose 1983a). Drawing explicitly on Raymond Williams's cultural theory, Montrose argues for a notion of ideology that is 'heterogeneous and unstable, permeable and processual' (1989: 22), and for a relationship between structure and subject that is both dynamic and recursive, a mutually constitutive process in which agency is neither foreclosed nor unconstrained. For Montrose, this 'process of subjectification' is also inescapably gender-specific, an *engendering* of historical subjects and subjectivities. His work with the figure of Elizabeth and the attendant cultural materials he brings to bear upon her reign have charted terrain that is in many ways crucial to an historically informed analysis of the Renaissance sex-gender system (see Newton 1989).

Although issues of gender have been a recurrent concern in new historicism, the relationship of the movement to feminist literary criticism has been an evolving one. Its emergence to a position of some prominence in the early 1980s was viewed by some feminist critics with understandable alarm and suspicion; at a juncture when feminists had begun to carve out a niche for themselves within the academy, a new movement was being embraced by the profession as something like the latest fad, threatening to displace and marginalize feminist studies and reconstruct them, in retrospect, as a passing fashion as well. That the movement in question tended to subordinate questions of feminism to those of gender and questions of gender to those of power only exacerbated suspicion. In Renaissance studies in the early 1980s – that is, the period of new historicism's emergence – feminist literary criticism was itself in a state of significant transition, or rather on the verge of such a transition. In 1980, the two most significant publications in Renaissance studies were Stephen Greenblatt's *Renaissance*

Self-fashioning and *The Woman's Part*, a collection of feminist essays on Shakespeare edited by Carolyn Lenz, Gayle Greene and Carol Neely which in many ways put the feminist study of Shakespeare on the map of literary studies. The theoretical ferment of Marxist, post-structuralist and feminist theory in the mid- to late 1970s is not significantly reflected in *The Woman's Part*, however. Centered on the interpretation of images of women in plays and strongly psychoanalytic in its approach to them – and influenced by American rather than French variants of psychoanalytic theory – the volume codified the advances of the first wave of feminist criticism in this country, but at a time when a second wave was already developing (see Cohen 1987: 22–6; Erickson 1985). British materialist feminists were in particular critical of what they viewed as an ahistorical approach to Renaissance women and dramatic characters, of a tendency to treat the latter as though they were the former, and of the essentializing model of the self applied to both (see Jardine 1983). A more materialist and historically informed feminist criticism has been emerging in this country in recent years, partially in reaction to such critiques and partially as a separate evolution of feminist literary criticism, and is evident in the work of scholars such as Jean Howard, Karen Newman, Laura Levine and others. Such work by American, British and third world feminists (see especially Belsey 1985a; Callaghan 1989; McKluskie 1989; Loomba 1989) has been influenced by new historicism and has also provided salutary and influential critiques of certain new historicist tendencies. Gender in such work is historically situated, not subordinated to an amorphous concept of power (as early versions of new historicism tended to do) but no longer the exclusive or central category of analysis (as early feminist critiques of new historicism insisted it should be); rather, in such work, gender is increasingly inscribed within a complex nexus of class, gender and race hierarchies.

New historicism has not become, as some feared, the latest orthodoxy, nor has it died away. To my mind, the record of recent years suggests it has been part of a productive, polyvocal, far from harmonious but necessary dialogue with materialist feminism, cultural materialism and other participants in the broader field of cultural studies.

III

The need for a more materialist apprehension of historical heterogeneity confronts new historicism as well as certain varieties of feminism. In one of the more cogent critiques of the movement, James Holstun (like many others) records his dissatisfaction with the various manifestations of a 'will-to-totalization' in new historicist approaches to culture. Unlike others, however, he neither attributes such totalizing tendencies to a submerged metaphysical or political agenda nor does he pretend to have in his own pocket a model of cultural criticism that does not 'explicitly or implicitly work from some model of cultural totality' (Holstun 1989: 198). Rather, he suggests that new historicism attributes an overly *logical* structure to culture – as, I would add, do both Geertz and Foucault, although in very different ways that licenses its persistent return to canonical literary works, situated as privileged texts where cultural pressures, forces and practices are more complexly and revealingly coded than elsewhere. The problem is not that new historicism totalizes culture, but that it

> totalizes prematurely by arguing that all cultural conflicts, all exercises of power and resistance necessarily register themselves inside canonical cultural artifacts. This sort of argument assumes that culture is a *logical* structure that can be captured by an artwork forming a structure homologous to it. A view of culture as a *material* entity, on the other hand, studies the relation between the way a subculture articulates itself and the way it is articulated by another subculture.
>
> (Holstun 1989: 198–9)

Holstun is concerned in particular with the radical pamphlet literature of the English revolution and the lack of attention devoted to such material, taken as evidence of 'oppositional collective self-fashioning' (1989: 209), by new historicists, despite all their talk of subversion or resistance or containment. He returns us to Raymond Williams, as it were, with a little help from Christopher Hill.

New historicism can hardly be accused of ignoring non-canonical texts, literary or otherwise, or of translating often-times compensatory articulations of dominant ideologies into the world view of a period. Nor has it been blind to the fundamental problematics that confront any socio-historical analysis. Rather than restricting itself to the articulate and articulated consciousness of the culture in question, it has sought to combine the critical analysis of such discursive records with the interpretive reconstruction, however fragmentary and even hypothetical, of more implicit, less codified modes of thought and action – to attend, in Anthony Giddens's terms, to both the *discursive* consciousness of the period (defined as that 'knowledge which actors are able to express on the level of discourse') and to the more heterogeneous realm of its *practical* consciousness (understood as those 'tacit stocks of knowledge which actors draw upon in the constitution of social activity' (Giddens 1979: 5)). However, it has tended to homogenize the latter, and here Holstun's critique is both apt and appropriate not only for the period of the English revolution.

'In a quite literal sense,' as Jean and John Comaroff have wryly observed, 'hegemony is habit forming' (Comaroff and Comaroff 1991: 23). But while the historical analysis of cultures needs to clarify the processes through which habits, ideas, meanings and subjects are indeed formed to fit the needs of hegemony, such analysis must also recognize that the fit is never certain and must attune itself to the faultlines and contradictions of social determination as well. Even where official manifestations of royal power are concerned, there is ample evidence that what might be called the intended illocutionary force of such power in operation could have an unintended illocutionary effect. Lacking the bureaucracy necessary for the policing and surveillance of its populace, early modern England was forced to rely upon a system of exemplary justice, of public and oftentimes spectacular punishment, that sought to instill the proper degree of awe and fear in the minds of its subjects. Even so eminent a figure as Sir Edward Coke was forced to recognize, however, that such a system was at best inadequate to the task – if not contrary to it:

> We have found by wofull experience that it is not frequent and often punishment that doth prevent like offenses. . . . Those offenses are often committed that are often punished, for the frequency of the punishment makes it so familiar as it is not feared.
>
> (cited in Skulsky 1964: 157)

Punishment makes familiar both the crime and its consequences, but with a crucial difference. Frequent punishment
advertises the taboo or the forbidden as a common occurrence,
and at the same time inures its audience to the spectacle of the
law taking hold of and inscribing itself upon the body of the
condemned. Exemplary power not only fails to deter, it even
produces and promulgates the very transgressions it acts upon –
by the sheer fact that it must act upon them, giving them a
currency or circulation they would not otherwise possess. What
Coke confronts is not a general 'undecidability' of meaning or
juridical effect but rather a paradoxical unpredictability and
overdetermination of affect, and one that suggests a fundamental constraint upon *any* effort to control the production of
historical meaning and subjects.

Although not as bleakly deterministic as some of its critics
have charged, new historicism would do well to recall Coke's
history lesson, to combine its analysis of the historical constraints upon individual agency with a fuller awareness of the
limits, potential or actualized, of any hegemonic power. It
would do well, in fact, to follow Roger Chartier's lead and
'reformulate the notion of appropriation and place it at the
centre of a cultural historical approach' (Chartier 1990: 13).
Such a move would allow it to realize, more fully perhaps than
it has, that cultural production is never a one-way street.
Exemplary displays of power, official and unofficial dissemina-
tions of ideas and images, even what register as 'facts', enter
into a cultural economy that is inherently dialogical; once
placed into circulation, any cultural practice, text or representation is available for and subject to appropriation, for both
licit and illicit ends.

3

Cleopatra's Seduction

CATHERINE BELSEY

I

Seduction, Jean Baudrillard maintains, is more exciting than sex. Seduction is more inventive, more subtle, a matter of nuances; it is witty and creative; it can be sublime. Seduction depends on a play of surfaces. It produces illusions, but refuses to participate in them, especially the illusion of depth. Enigmatic, enchanting, seduction defers satisfaction in order to sustain the pleasure of anticipation. It repudiates what Baudrillard calls our culture's *naturalization* of sex, its commitment to an unimaginative artlessness, and its claim at the same time to gratification as one of the human rights. Moreover, seduction refuses the sexual equivalent of the work ethic, the obligation twentieth-century Western culture so diligently promotes to put the body to good erotic use. Sex, Baudrillard argues, is quotidian, drab, referential, preoccupied by the real: seduction, which liberates us from the constraints of duty and truth-to-nature, depends on fantasy, romance, imagination. Seduction takes place at the level of the signifier (Baudrillard 1990).

Baudrillard himself, however, calls this the level of the 'sign'; and if I borrow his account of seduction here, I do so without subscribing at the same time to his anti-feminism or the apocalyptic nihilism of his vision of postmodern culture. Baudrillard's writing inhabits a world of binary oppositions –

between surface and depth, artifice and reality, illusion and truth, the sign and its referent. And in privileging the first term in each instance, he relegates the second to the status of a differentiating fiction. Faced with a supposed choice between the real and simulation, Baudrillard opts for the simulacrum. He thus remains a structuralist. His dashing prose, his undeniable powers of invention and the dazzling range of his allusion all work in the service of what amounts to a scandalous, but in the end straightforward, reversal of the conventional propositions, values and convictions of Enlightened common sense.

This makes him an easy target for those who wish to denounce the postmodern and all its works. But if Baudrillard is postmodern, he is not a post-structuralist, and if in *Seduction* he borrows from Derrida's *Spurs*, he does not emulate Derrida's fine distinctions and his rigorous precision. Derrida's work has been devoted to the deconstruction of binary oppositions, demonstrating that the other repeatedly invades the self-same. In Derrida's account, any analysis that insists on antithetical alternatives narrows the range of possibilities and excludes imaginable options. Baudrillard does much, however, to rehabilitate seduction, or at least to rescue it from a culture for which, since D. H. Lawrence, sexual activity has become an increasingly solemn obligation. Despite its theoretical limitations, Baudrillard's book has the virtue of making seduction seductive.

Fiction offers the pleasures of seduction. Fiction is frivolous. It permits fantasy and reproduces romance. Paradoxically, in a society bound closely to production, the morality of work and the making, multiplying and recycling of money, fiction proliferates. On television, at the cinema, on the bookstall, in the theatre, fiction is available on a scale unknown to previous cultures. The popular press devotes more space to entertaining stories than to hard news: knowledge, it appears, is less highly valued than pleasure. Miniature family sagas advertise cars; pocket-size soap operas sell instant coffee. Itself a mode of seduction, fiction is enigmatic, enchanting; it defers closure; it can be sublime. It is independent of the laws of truth. Fiction has no obligation to refer to a recognizable reality: only pornography, the degree zero of realism, is truly mimetic, which is to say virtually referential in its mode of address; pornography works as if it were truth (cf. Lyotard 1984: 75). At its best, by contrast, fiction, like seduction, is inventive; it depends on the play of surfaces. It is only in Literature departments and on the committees awarding literary prizes that fiction becomes solemn, weighty, a duty, a moral obligation.

Fiction can also, however, give us information about its own historical moment, not by reflection, but by producing or reproducing the images in circulation in the culture at that time. Fiction is intelligible to the degree that it draws on the representations people recognize; it is radical to the degree that it challenges or modifies those representations, but still within the limits of intelligibility. My essay in *Alternative Shakespeares* proposed that fiction permits a glimpse of an escape from the constraints of gender stereotypes. The girls, dressed as boys, played by boys, in Shakespeare's comedies registered, I tried to suggest, a dis-satisfaction with the sexual identities in the process of being set up for men and women with the emergence of Family Values. I wanted to reaffirm from a different perspective Foucault's view that there was a moment in history before sexual identities were seen as given and determining, before the binary oppositions of man and woman, or gay and straight, were firmly in place (Foucault 1979). What is more, I wanted to suggest that these new oppositions were not installed without a struggle, at least in fiction, where utopian dreams can be formulated without reprisal, and without regard to the laws of truth. Fantasy can override the oppositions cultures so busily cement.

Since then, and in the light of Lisa Jardine's account of the cross-dressed male actor as an object of homoerotic desire (Jardine 1983: 9–36), there has been a good deal of work on sexual values in Shakespeare's period. To the degree that there is a consensus, it seems to be that, while on the one hand the Puritans were eager to bring in Family Values, and the heterosexual identifications they imply, the culture at large found the love of women more threatening to male identity than homoeroticism, since female company has an effeminating effect on men (Orgel 1989; Levine 1994). Opinion varies on whether the objects of male homoerotic desire were more likely to be boys in drag, or other men.[1] And meanwhile, the quest continues for evidence of female homoerotic desire in the English Renaissance (Traub 1992a).

This work is extremely important and valuable: it deepens our understanding of historical difference, as well as bringing out the heterosexist assumptions of earlier readings. But there is an additional area of enquiry which might intensify our sense of the differences between Shakespeare's moment and our own. The nineteenth-century notions of sexual identity we have inherited depended on object-choice: heterosexual men fell in love with women, homosexual men with men, lesbian women with women, and so on. The only available alternative, apparently, was bisexuality, and there the prefix has the effect of reaffirming the idea that there are finally two possibilities, even if some people embrace them both. Not only was sexual subjectivity seen as single and univocal, but the object of desire was too. It was *either* a man or a woman (or both), even if style (butch or femme, for instance) might complicate the issue. This analysis gives us two sexes, aligned on either side of a single divide of sexual difference, and two sexual identities, gay or straight, defined by the sex of the desired object. It follows that desire is always either homoerotic or heterosexual.

Might it be that this too is a historically specific cultural construct, an Enlightenment reduction of the possibilities?[2] Is it conceivable, in other words, that what another culture finds seductive is altogether more diffuse than our quasi-scientific sexual taxonomies allow?

II

Among fictional figures, Shakespeare's Cleopatra is surely supremely seductive. Beautiful, ageless, mistress of all the arts of love, mysterious, Eastern, magical, Shakespeare's Egyptian Queen transmutes Plutarch's calculating courtesan into myth, becoming in the process the origin of a succession of recreations by George Bernard Shaw and Cecil B. de Mille, for example, as well as reinterpretations by Vivien Leigh and Elizabeth Taylor in some of the most expensive movies ever made. From the moment of her first meeting with Antony, when she rejects his invitation to supper and substitutes her own, Shakespeare's Cleopatra exercises a command over his will that proves virtually irresistible. What is at stake here is not a matter of character, the individuality of Cleopatra as an explanation of her sexual power, but the dramatic representation of seduction itself. In Plutarch she seduces Antony by her conversational skills, by participating equally with him in all his favourite diversions, and in the end by eliciting his pity. But in Shakespeare's version Cleopatra is shown consistently exploiting the lack which is the cause of desire: 'she makes hungry / Where most she satisfies' (II. ii. 247–8);[3] and she does it by promising what she frequently, but not predictably, fails to deliver, by being inconsistently *elsewhere*.

Cleopatra's most repeated seductive strategy, in other words, is not to be where Antony might expect to find her. Sometimes this is figurative, a question of her state of mind, or behaviour, as in the case where she instructs Charmian,

> See where he is, who's with him, what he does.
> I did not send you. If you find him sad,
> Say I am dancing; if in mirth, report
> That I am sudden sick . . .
>
> (I. iii. 3–6)

Earlier, she looks for him, sends for him, and then leaves as he approaches (I. ii. 90–92). When he summons her to attend him on land, she appears on water, her barge seducing the winds, the river itself and all her subjects, leaving Antony in command of an empty town:

>   The city cast
> Her people out upon her, and Antony,
> Enthron'd i'th' market-place, did sit alone,
> Whistling to th' air; which, but for vacancy,
> Had gone to gaze on Cleopatra, too,
> And made a gap in nature.
>
> (II. ii. 223–8)

By drawing everything to herself, she emblematically isolates Antony in an absence which precipitates desire. But this absence that seduces is always attended by the expectation or the offer of presence. When she lands, she promptly reverses his invitation to supper, and Antony,

> Being barbered ten times o'er, goes to the feast,
> And, for his ordinary, pays his heart
> For what his eyes eat only.
>
> (II. ii. 234–6)

Death is the ultimate absence. When Cleopatra announces her own death, she overplays her hand. Mardian's report of Cleopatra's suicide confirms Antony's own intention to kill himself, and by the time Cleopatra cancels her false message it is too late. But once again this turns out to be an absence which promises presence. Her supposed death constitutes a summons to Antony, and he imagines a triumphal entry into the Elysian world which re-enacts, this time for them both, Cleopatra's own earlier depopulation of the city:

> Where souls do couch on flowers we'll hand in hand
> And with our sprightly port make the ghosts gaze.
> Dido and her Aeneas shall want troops,
> And all the haunt be ours.
>
> (IV. xiv. 52–5)

Her actual death, meanwhile, effects the final seduction, precisely to the degree that it resembles life, as Caesar himself seems for a moment to glimpse the possibility of taking Antony's place:

> she looks like sleep,
> As she would catch another Antony
> In her strong toil of grace.
>
> (V. ii. 345–7)

It is not, in other words, Cleopatra's presence which seduces in these instances, nor simply her absence, but her imagined, promised, deferred presence. Like her supposed death which constitutes an invitation, like her real death, which emulates sleep, though without being mistaken for it, Cleopatra's seductive strategy is to exceed the alternatives of presence and absence. The play locates her *at a distance*.

But it is not only the fictional figures in the play who are seduced by Cleopatra. As the long history of her mythological status in Western culture makes clear,[4] she is also capable of seducing audiences. And here the strategy is similar: in this case it works by a kind of textual distancing. The famous account of her arrival in the barge, Shakespeare's rewriting of Plutarch, itself rewritten in due course by T. S. Eliot in *The Waste Land*, records her self-construction as a spectacle, and yet she herself is located just beyond the reach of rhetoric, even

the most elaborate rhetorical set-piece of an extraordinarily
sophisticated text:

> The barge she sat in, like a burnished throne,
> Burned on the water; the poop was beaten gold;
> Purple the sails, and so perfumed that
> The winds were love-sick with them; the oars were silver,
> Which to the tune of flutes kept stroke, and made
> The water which they beat to follow faster,
> As amorous of their strokes. For her own person,
> It beggared all description: she did lie
> In her pavilion, cloth-of-gold of tissue,
> O'erpicturing that Venus where we see
> The fancy outwork nature. On each side her
> Stood pretty dimpled boys, like smiling cupids,
> With divers-coloured fans, whose wind did seem
> To glow the delicate cheeks which they did cool,
> And what they undid did.

                                                    (II. ii. 201–15)

The rich, dense colours evoke Elizabethan aristocratic portrait-
ure at its most heraldic: the Queen of Egypt appears in a golden
vessel, polished like a throne, and rigged with crimson
('purple'). And if the speech recounts a dream of wealth and
royalty, it also presents the staging of an erotic fantasy, in which
the props are as much in love as the actors. The barge burns,
the winds are love-sick for the sails and the water thrills to the
beating administered by the oars. But when it comes to
Cleopatra's own person, the account backs away, as if overwhelmed by the impossibility of specifying a desirability so
sublime. Just as in negative theology, wherever human in-
adequacy locates God, in the ark of the covenant, in icons, in
the eucharist, he is not there, but beyond such localization, so
Cleopatra's erotic power is seen as mysteriously elsewhere,
deferred, indefinable, irreducible to language, identified only
as a transcendent and thus inevitably absent presence.

In *S/Z* Roland Barthes notes that

> Beauty (unlike ugliness) cannot really be explained: in each
> part of the body it stands out, repeats itself, but it does not
> describe itself. Like a god (and as empty), it can only say: *I
> am what I am*. The discourse, then, can do no more than assert

the perfection of each detail and refer 'the remainder' to the code underlying all beauty: Art.

(Barthes 1975: 33)

Cleopatra is like a work of art, and like Venus, goddess of love; she is like a picture of Venus, since fancy, or fantasy, can improve on nature; and yet she outdoes all these possibilities, which is to say, she outdoes divinity, nature and art. 'Left on its own,' Barthes continues,

> deprived of any anterior code, beauty would be mute. Every direct predicate is denied it; the only feasible predicates are either tautology (*a perfectly oval face*) or simile (*lovely as a Raphael Madonna, like a dream in stone,* etc.); thus, beauty is referred to an infinity of codes: *lovely as Venus*? But Venus lovely as what? As herself?. . . . There is only one way to stop the replication of beauty: hide it, return it to silence, to the ineffable, to aphasia, refer the referent back to the invisible.
>
> (Barthes 1975: 33–4)

Returned to ineffability, rendered invisible by the description of a spectacle in which she constitutes the absent centre, Cleopatra thus escapes definition, gets away, enchants the audience, like Antony, at a distance, from elsewhere (cf. Derrida 1979: 49).

The account declares itself to be a representation. It is part of a story, the narrative of the first meeting between Antony and Cleopatra, and it seduces at least partly as fiction, as romance. 'I will tell you', Enobarbus begins, in response to Agrippa's reference to the report he has heard of the occasion, and what follows is explicitly a 'telling'. Much of Cleopatra's seduction depends on such third-person accounts: 'Age cannot wither her, nor custom stale / Her infinite variety' (Enobarbus, II. ii. 245–6); 'she looks like sleep, / As she would catch another Antony' (Caesar, V. ii. 345–6); 'Now boast thee, Death, in thy possession lies / A lass unparalleled' (Charmian, V. ii. 314–15). It is one of the strategies of Shakespeare's text that our attention to Cleopatra is filtered in this way, so that her image appears deflected, oblique. In consequence, the signifier which defines her, or rather fails to define her, also pushes her away, supplants her, takes her place, relegating her to the same mysterious distance. Cleopatra *herself* is what is lacking from the representations of her seductive power; she is the element that is by definition subtracted from what it is possible to say.

III

This fictional strategy of defining Cleopatra obliquely, in the third person, is required, of course, by the conditions of performance on Shakespeare's stage. Cleopatra cannot be made present at the Globe Theatre because she is the most beautiful woman the world has ever known, because she is supremely, mythically seductive, but also because she is played by a boy. She herself indirectly draws attention to this when she determines not to submit to the humiliation of a Roman triumph, and the passage is famous beyond the confines of the play, because it is part of the evidence for the fact that women on the Jacobean stage were commonly played by boys rather than grown men:[5]

> The quick comedians
> Extemporally will stage us and present
> Our Alexandrian revels; Antony
> Shall be brought drunken forth; and I shall see
> Some squeaking Cleopatra boy my greatness
> I' th' posture of a whore.

(V. ii. 215–20)

By naming her imagined future impersonator as a boy and as a travesty, Shakespeare's Cleopatra distances herself from her present impersonator on the stage of the Globe. The fictional figure we are invited to imagine, the object of the audience's fantasy, thus separates herself from the conditions of the possibility of her representation in the theatre, and this separation is crucial if Cleopatra is to seduce the audience as a woman. The gap between the future performance that Cleopatra imagines and fears on the one hand, and the play we are watching on the other, invites us to suppose that the figure before us now is the real, authentic Cleopatra. Ironically, however, the speech also invokes the boy-actor it repudiates. There is no disavowal which does not draw attention to the very thing that is disavowed. The audience is reminded of the difference between the fiction and the performance, the imagined Cleopatra and her impersonation, even as it is invited to suspend its awareness of that distinction in its attention to the gap between this performance and its projected parody.

Cleopatra's story, the seductive romance of Antony and Cleopatra, exists outside the performance that the audience is witnessing. The play depends on this recognition. And indeed, this is self-evidently the case: the story had already been told by Chaucer, as well as Plutarch, and in Daniel's *Tragedy of Cleopatra*, reissued in revised form in 1607. But the project of Shakespeare's Cleopatra in obliquely claiming for herself an existence beyond Shakespeare's text is surely not to reinsert herself into some prior *text*, not even a classical text with the authority of Plutarch's. On the contrary, it is to affirm her mythological, metaphysical existence beyond textuality itself, her presence as an Idea in the consciousness of the audience independent of representation. 'Piece out', the figure on the stage seems indirectly to say, in an unspoken echo of the opening Chorus of *Henry V*, 'Piece out our imperfections with your thoughts', investing this inadequate image, which is no more than representation (re-presentation) by a boy, with the 'imaginary puissance' of the most seductive of women. By this means Shakespeare's Cleopatra lays claim to the sublimity of a concept which cannot be made present (cf. Rackin 1972).

But this claim is itself precisely metaphysical. Cleopatra owes her mythological seductive power not to an idea but to texts, and supremely to Shakespeare's own text. This was not in print in Shakespeare's lifetime, and we have no means of knowing what form it took, whether as a series of speeches for distribution to the actors, or as a continuous manuscript; nor do we know the degree to which it resembled the play we have, first printed, with whatever modifications, in the Folio of 1623, and altered as a result of subsequent editorial accretion. And this lost text, in turn, was merely the script for a perfomance which involved a boy-actor. Shakespeare's Cleopatra cannot be made present in the play, but she is not present independent of the performance either. The nearest thing there has ever been to a realization of Shakespeare's Cleopatra incorporates the boy-actor she so decisively disavows.

What are the implications for our understanding of Cleopatra's seduction of this explicit incorporation of youthful ('squeaking') masculinity into the representation of a figure we might have been inclined to describe as precisely *all woman*? Is it a disruption, or does it constitute, improbably enough, an enhancement of Cleopatra's erotic appeal? It is possible to see the Cleopatra who is played by a boy as somehow androgynous, both things to both sexes, bisexually seductive. But more radically, perhaps there is an element in her seductiveness which exceeds the binary opposition we tend to take for granted between men and women, or masculine and feminine. If so, there was a moment in history when an erotic appeal so intense as to claim metaphysical status evidently involved a complexity beyond the binary classifications that current common sense allows.

IV

Cleopatra is not present in the account of her appearance in the barge, whether as a person or as a body, though the text concedes that she has 'delicate cheeks'. What takes her expected place in the culminating moment of Enobarbus's description is a reference to 'pretty dimpled boys'. These figures have flesh: it is 'dimpled'; they themselves are seductive: 'pretty'; and presumably, like everything else which is named in the speech, they are there either as objects or as subjects of desire. Their inclusion in the speech is vindicated by the reference to the artful spectacle of Cleopatra as out-picturing Venus: they are Cupids, who might well be expected to appear in paintings of their mother in the European Renaissance tradition. It is perhaps worth considering some of these visual putti, not necessarily because they influenced Shakespeare (though who knows what he might have seen or heard about in Renaissance London, especially among the theatre's aristocratic patrons?[6]), but because they constitute analogues which might possibly illuminate the seductive role of the pretty dimpled boys in Cleopatra's barge.

'The Rokeby Venus' of Velazquez offers one of the most delightful examples of a widespread convention (National Gallery, London; Figure 1). This painting probably dates from forty years after the play (1647–51), but the poses of the figures, the mirror and the crimson drapery allude indirectly to any number of Titians', familiar in Spain from the previous century, since Philip II was one of Titian's main patrons. Cupid is crucial to the painting. Not only does he hold the glass, which

shows Venus's face at the centre of the picture, her expression misty, not sharply defined, and at one remove – at a distance – because reflected. He also completes the symmetry of the composition, his head matching hers, his wing echoing the shape of her elbow. Even the colours match: the grey and white of the wing pick up the colours of the satin she lies on. The flesh displayed in the picture, his and hers, is almost continuous, a narcissistic semicircle of nudity. The putto also contributes to the charm of the image: he is naive, disarming, precisely *lovable*. Cupid evidently admires Venus, but if the picture hints at infant sexuality, it also implies an eroticism without threat or danger.[7] The suggestion is not, of course, that he offers a direct sexual invitation, or that the picture invokes the abuse of children. But charm is part of the seductive process: the appeal to the spectator is to take pleasure in the joint image of a naked woman and an engaging little boy, who is also naked.

Poussin could hardly put brush to canvas in his mythological paintings without depicting a good many little loves. *The Triumph of Flora* (c. 1627, Louvre Museum, Paris) includes eleven. Venus dances with four in attendance; behind her, one is putting a chaplet of hyacinths on the head of Adonis. Two more are pulling the chariot, an indication of the lightness and delicacy of Flora. In the foreground, one is picking flowers, and another is offering them to the goddess. And two flutter above her, crowning her with a wreath. (There are no girls.) The motif of the triumph indicates a classical origin, of course, and these putti are in one sense copied from the antique figures of Eros or Amor. But they display a vitality and energy which belongs very specifically to the Renaissance. The flirtatiousness they represent[8] is active and uninhibited compared with the solemn behaviour of the grown-ups: even Venus dances in a very stately manner. This is an Ovidian picture, innocently erotic in a generalized way, but the little boys do not come from the *Metamorphoses*. They are descended from classical art, but they are equally and unmistakably a product of the seventeenth century.

Seven years later six Cupids, their wings derived from birds or butterflies indiscriminately, fly above the goddess of love in Poussin's *Birth of Venus* (Philadelphia Museum of Art; Figure 2). They scatter flowers, and fire arrows at Neptune as he rises from the waves. One carries a torch, like Lechery in medieval allegory, but with more charm and less menace. Venus comes

2 Nicolas Poussin, *The Birth of Venus*, Philadelphia Museum of Art: The George W. Elkins Collection

in from the sea, her shell drawn by dolphins, surrounded by Nereids and Tritons. The efforts of the attendant figures, and the gaze of the admiring Neptune, are all fixed on the goddess. But at the front of the scene, in the centre directly below her, a putto on a dolphin's back gazes serenely out of the canvas, as if content to be an object of the spectator's enchanted gaze.[9]

In Titian's *The Worship of Venus* little loves have taken over almost the whole of the pictorial space (1516–18, Prado, Madrid; Figure 3). The goddess, represented in stone, is marginalized by the composition. Austere, aloof, remote, she remains an object of adulation: love, we are to understand, can be sacramental. Meanwhile, living flesh belongs to the putti, who tumble over each other energetically: one climbs a tree; two are certainly kissing one another; at the centre of the group one is involved with a hare in a way that is not sharply specified. The spectator is invited to suppose that they're having a good time in a slightly salacious, broadly mischievous way, and to find them pretty, dimpled and quite irresistible. These little boys represent all that is uninhibited, playful and pleasurable in the process of seduction.

By the first half of the sixteenth century the tradition was established in Northern Europe as well. Cranach's *Cupid Complaining to Venus* shows bees stinging the little boy, who has stolen a honeycomb from their hive (National Gallery, London; Figure 4). He appeals to his mother for help because he evidently has no sense that the punishment is in any way deserved: he is without shame. And this lawlessness is characteristic of the Renaissance Cupid: he represents love as anarchic. Whereas in the medieval tradition, in the *Romance of the Rose*, for example, the God of Love is an adult and delivers a set of commandments to the Dreamer, the Renaissance Cupid, like his Hellenistic predecessor, inhabits a world prior to Law:[10] he escapes the prohibitions that constrain grown-up behaviour. He seems to know nothing about propriety or morality: the love he stands for is playful, irresponsible; it seeks pleasure without consideration of the consequences.[11]

Cleopatra also inhabits a space outside moral and civil law. She has no sense of regal or feminine propriety. She hops in the streets (II. ii. 239); she drinks as much as Antony; she dresses him up in her clothes and wears his sword; she teases him with a dead fish (II. v. 15–23); she lies without remorse; and she beats

3 Titian, *The Worship of Venus*, Prado, Madrid

innocent messengers. She enters into direct competition with
Antony's wives, without any sense of guilt, or any apparent
recognition of the respect conventionally due to marriage. The
primary Orientalism of this play consists in locating the East
beyond the reach of Law, a realm of pleasure where everything
is permitted, where waiting women talk frankly about sex,[12]
and even eunuchs think what Venus adulterously did with
Mars (1. v. 18–19). Seduction is indifferent to moral constraints:
it cares nothing for obligation or duty.

Correggio's *School of Love* (c. 1523, National Gallery, London)
shows Mercury, one of Cupid's putative fathers, trying to teach
him to read. The implication is that it's a waste of time: Cupid
is not amenable to discipline. Sonnet 17 of Sidney's *Astrophil*

4 Lucas Cranach the Elder, *Cupid Complaining to Venus*, reproduced by
courtesy of the Trustees, The National Gallery, London

and Stella also depicts a family group with Cupid at the centre, but this one is more fractious. Astrophil recounts how Venus got angry with her son because he failed to keep up the assault on Mars with his arrows, so that her lover was becoming less attentive. Cupid, however, refused to shoot, for fear that Mars would beat him. Venus, in a rage, broke Cupid's bow and arrows. But Nature came to the rescue by making better bows out of Stella's eyebrows, and infinite numbers of arrows from her eyes. Cupid is delighted:

> O how for joy he leapes, o how he crowes,
>   And straight therewith, like wags new got to play,
>   Fals to shrewd turnes, and I was in his way.
>
> (Sidney 1962: 173)

The image again is of an irrepressibly mischievous child, who acts purely from self-interest. He repudiates his mother's cruelty, not out of compunction, but only because of a deeper fear of Mars. And his dangerous weapons are toys in his hands. Astrophil is seduced because he happens to be in Cupid's quite arbitrary line of fire.

Spenser includes little boys in the Bower of Bliss, *The Faerie Queene*'s most detailed allegory of seduction. The famous fountain covered with golden ivy, which C. S. Lewis exposed as art, not nature, and therefore inimical to true love, is evidently a perfect example of Italian Renaissance sculpture:

> Most goodly it with curious imageree
> Was over-wrought, and shapes of naked boyes,
> Of which some seemd with lively jollitee,
> To fly about, playing their wanton toyes,
> Whilest others did them selves embay in liquid joyes.
>
> (Spenser 1980: II. xii. 60)

'Wanton' perfectly indicates the ambiguity of the putti. As a noun, wanton can be a term of endearment, as well as of contempt: dear little thing, or wicked little thing (*OED* B1 and 2); as an adjective it means amorous (*OED* A2), sportive and merry (*OED* A3), in addition to 'naughty' or 'unruly' (*OED* A1). The 'wanton toyes' of Spenser's putti are engaging, probably morally dubious, frivolous, pleasurable, precisely *seductive*.

In the mythology of the period the archetypal seduction took place in the Garden of Eden: the serpent seduced Eve and Eve seduced Adam. Conventional representations of the Fall make evident the sexual component of the whole episode in the nudity of the central figures, and sometimes in their gestures as well. The serpent, meanwhile, sustains the erotic reference: sometimes the snake is overtly phallic; alternatively, it often has the face of a woman, to show how sexual desire endangers men. But unusually, in Titian's version of the Fall (Prado, Madrid), the tempter is a pretty dimpled boy, whose serpentine tail virtually disappears among the branches of the Tree of Know- ledge. Eve reaches up towards the boy; Adam reaches up towards Eve, echoing her gesture. When Rubens copied Titian, although he introduced minor variations, including a parrot, he left the temptation in the hands of a little boy: evidently the idea made sense, or at least did not seem inappropriate. This putto is not merely decorative: he plays a central part in the process of seduction (1628–9, Prado, Madrid; Figure 5).[13]

The garden which encloses Spenser's Bower of Bliss is a parody of the Garden of Eden: the poem refers to it ironically as a 'Paradise' (II. xii. 70). The events that take place there are clearly not innocent; and the central female figure is not Eve but a witch. Just as the Fall transforms Adam and Eve, however, reducing them to a lower level than they held when they were created in the image of God, so that they become sinful, unhappy, mortal, Acrasia transforms the men she seduces into beasts, taking them one link lower still on the chain of being. At the heart of the Bower of Bliss, Acrasia's lover sleeps, after 'long wanton joyes'. There are boys there too:

> Whilst round about them pleasauntly did sing
>   Many faire Ladies, and lascivious boyes,
> That ever mixt their song with light licentious toyes.

(II. xii. 72)

In all these instances the putti are more than pretty decoration, and considerably more than innocent bystanders; they are part of the process of seduction, actively participating in it.

The boys in Cleopatra's barge are also active. They hold, Enobarbus says, 'divers-coloured fans, whose wind did seem / To glow the delicate cheeks which they did cool, / And what they undid did'. The meaning of these unheralded oxymorons, on the basis of the syntax, seems to be that the fans both cool Cleopatra's cheeks and make them blush. Is this a question of

5 Peter Paul Rubens, *Adam and Eve*, Prado, Madrid

reflection – the various colours in the fans reflected in her delicate skin? That makes a kind of sense, perhaps. Or is there rather a metonymic relation between the fans and the Cupids, so that by implication the boys both cool and heat Cleopatra, fan her and make her blush? Are we invited to understand that they are seductive to her, that their licentiousness not only reflects on her but excites her too?

In Titian's *Venus and Cupid* (*c*.1548, Prado, Madrid) it is the infant, his arm grasping hers, his hand resting just above her naked breast, who distracts Venus's attention from the unmistakably admiring musician. Certainly in Bronzino's *Allegory* of love Cupid plays a remarkably active role in the proceedings, though the goddess of love does not seem to need much persuasion (1540, National Gallery, London; Figure 6).[14] Here Venus holds an apple. The fruit is not Eve's: it is the prize awarded to Love by Paris in the contest between the three goddesses. In return, Venus gave him Helen and caused the Trojan war. This apple comes from pagan mythology, but since it too brings death into the world, and a great deal of woe, no Renaissance iconographer could have missed the connection with the Fall. The painting is moral – or perhaps has been heavily moralized by the critical tradition. The little boy with the flowers is thought to be Pleasure, and behind him Deceit has a beautiful female face, but a body which is part animal, part reptile. The tormented figure in the background to the left of Venus and Cupid was once thought to be Jealousy, but has more recently been identified as Syphilis (Conway 1986). Meanwhile, Oblivion at the top tries to draw a veil over the activities in the foreground, but he is prevented by Father Time, who puts the scene on display in order to indicate the mutability of earthly delights. But however hard art history works to find a serious moral justification for looking at sexy pictures, there is no mistaking, it seems to me, the appeal to a spectator of the central image. Whose gaze is solicited here, if not ours? Who is seduced by Titian's paintings? And by Enobarbus's speech, so widely quoted, anthologized, rewritten?

This reopens the question of fiction itself as seductive. In Poussin's *Inspiration of the Poet* the central figure is, appropriately enough, Apollo, the god of poetry with his lyre (before 1630, Louvre Museum, Paris; Figure 7). The poet is taking dictation from the god, while a putto flies past with a laurel wreath

6 Bronzino, *An Allegory with Venus and Cupid*, reproduced by courtesy
of the Trustees, The National Gallery, London

representing the poet's public recognition. Another putto carries a second wreath, and a completed epic. But is that the end of the story? The female figure is probably Euterpe, the Muse of lyric poetry, with a flute. But she is also a woman with a naked breast, and in that capacity too, it seems to me, she constitutes an element in the inspiration of the poet. And if so, is it not possible that the pretty dimpled boys indicate one of the sources of poetry, as well as the bearers of its rewards? Aren't they too among the images Poussin's poet creates, as well as the evidence of his success? The little boys, and the pleasures they both represent and enact, are included, I have been suggesting, in the material of poetry at its most seductive.

V

If this argument proves in any way persuasive, it implies that for more than a century, all over Europe, boys were involved, implicated, somehow incorporated into female seductiveness. The tradition more or less disappears by the nineteenth century (the Victorians seem to have been more interested in little girls), so the duration of this extraordinary state of affairs, however long, is historically limited. The inference I draw is that at that time seduction was apparently a more complex process than any system of sexual identification which is based on object choice and dependent on binary oppositions allows, or makes space for. If the offer of the paintings and of Enobarbus's speech is to seduce the spectator, then who is the spectator assumed to be? A homosexual man? Evidently not, since the central figure in each case is female. A heterosexual man, then? But what would the term 'heterosexual' mean, if a pretty dimpled boy was part of the process of his seduction? The distinctions between gay and straight do not in this context make sense. And what about women, whether heterosexual or lesbian? Isn't there a narcissistic element in seduction, as well as a response to charm? Are we not seduced too, even if not in quite the same way? After all, images of beautiful women in fashion magazines currently induce some of us to part with money in the hope of becoming more seductive by imitation. But in addition, the magazines themselves can also prove curiously seductive, in my experience, the images proffering a pleasure of their own.

7 Nicolas Poussin, *The Inspiration of the Poet*, Louvre Museum, Paris

The frame of Enobarbus's portrait of Cleopatra in the barge (with boys) is Antony's marriage to Octavia. Antony has affirmed his commitment publicly, in a reference to the Elizabethan marriage service, only forty-five lines earlier in the same scene: 'May I never, / To this good purpose that so fairly shows, / Dream of impediment!' (II. ii. 152–4). Caesar leads Antony off to meet Octavia, and Enobarbus, Agrippa and Maecenas are left behind to discuss the impediment in question. When Enobarbus has finished his tale, they revert to the marriage issue: 'If beauty, wisdom, modesty can settle / The heart of Antony, Octavia is / A blessed lottery to him', Maecenas piously declares (II. ii. 251–3). The audience, in the light of the barge speech, knows better. Beauty, wisdom and modesty are all good things, but they have nothing whatever to do with seduction.

They have a good deal, on the other hand, to do with the new model of marriage that emerged in early modern culture, though it was left to the Victorians to crystallize the general hope that the love of a good woman would prove redemptive. As the new basis of marriage in the sixteenth century, true love was in due course to domesticate desire and outlaw seduction. At the same time, it was to line up sexual preferences as either acceptable or perverse, and in the process to naturalize sexual identities in a pattern of binary oppositions from which we are still only beginning to escape.

When *Antony and Cleopatra* was first staged this process was already well under way. We have no access to the experiences of our ancestors, but Enobarbus claims that in art fantasy is able to outdo nature. Perhaps even then it was only in fiction and in painting that the imagination was able to construct representations of seduction not yet entirely subject to the emerging cultural norms. We still live in the shadow of the Victorian desire to make binary oppositions stick: between men and women, sexual dispositions, objects of desire. Some of the texts and pictures of the European Renaissance suggest, however, that at the very moment when desire was being brought under the control of the Law and confined within heterosexual marriage, it was still possible to recognize as seductive images that were more heterogeneous than the resulting taxonomies have been willing to allow.

Imprints: Shakespeare, Gutenberg and Descartes

MARGRETA DE GRAZIA

I Metaphysics

Why wax?

In the *Meditations*, Descartes alone in his study, sitting by the fire, wrapped in his cloak, resolves to make a clean sweep of all his old opinions – among them, the opinion that external objects are more real than consciousness itself. In order to examine this opinion, he needs a representative thing or body. He chooses wax. 'Let us consider . . . one particular body. Let us take, for example, this piece of wax' (Descartes 1993b: 20). My question is, with a world of objects to choose from, why wax?[1]

It is generally assumed that he chooses the object most noted for mutability.[2] Wax waxes. As he notes, it has already undergone two transformations – from flower to honeycomb – before reaching him. And when put before the fire, it suffers a whole gamut of additional changes, one for each of the senses: shape, but also colour, flavour, smell, feel, even sound (when he raps it). That he still, despite these permutations, knows the object to be wax, demonstrates that, contrary to his old opinion, perception of the wax does not depend on the wax itself but on 'the intellect alone' (22).

It is not just wax in the abstract that Descartes contemplates, but a particular piece of wax: '*this* piece of wax' [my italics].

He not only observes this piece of wax: he handles, whiffs, licks, knocks it. It is at hand; why at hand? Because it is on the top of the desk where he is writing (Hertz 1992: 175). Until replaced by self-adhering and gummed envelopes (before envelopes even), return addresses, individuating signatures and a national postal service, wax belonged on every well-equipped desk, as indispensable as paper, pen and ink. As the editors of his eight volumes of letters point out, Descartes – in self-imposed exile for most of his life – was a prolific letter writer (Descartes 1991: viii). Every letter he sent, he must have sealed. (If we had receipts for purchase of wax, we could approximate the number of letters he wrote and sent.[3]) What must be noted, however, is that Descartes makes no mention of the instrument that was used to make the imprint on wax: the signet. Indeed, he seems to be teasing us with its absence. Warming the wax by the fire was part of the sealing routine: the wax was first melted and then imprinted. But Descartes softens the wax not so that it will receive the signet's defining form but so that it will go formless.

Descartes had good reason to dismantle this little piece of standard desk-top equipment. It was the traditional metaphor for how knowledge is acquired and retained. A common household item, the signet/wax apparatus symbolized the mystery of how the outside world entered the mind and stayed there. As the mirror received reflections, so the wax received impressions. Unlike reflections, however, impressions remained – as memory or fantasy. To repeat, then, my opening question: why wax? Why did Descartes choose wax as the representative object? It was not, after all, the only mutable object at hand: he might have reached for a sheet of paper from his desk, for example, and crumpled, ripped, stained, burned it to ashes; he might have taken frost from the window pane. I would like to suggest that his choice of wax was a choice of wax-without-signet. To feature wax alone was to dismantle the apparatus which, as we shall see, was key to those old opinions he determined to clear from his mind. It was critical, for example, to Plato's epistemology and Aristotle's metaphysics, as well as to Descartes's own earlier philosophy.

The model of the signet and wax figures centrally in the Platonic dialogue generally considered to have defined epistemology as a separate science from ontology, knowing as a separate domain from being. In the *Theaetetus*, Socrates asks Theaetetus to 'imagine that our minds contain a wax block' (Plato 1988: 99), the scriptive surface used in classical times before papyrus, vellum and paper (Rouse and Rouse 1990: 1–13). It is on this wax block that impressions were made of perceptions and of ideas, 'as if we were making marks with signet-rings' (Plato 1988: 100), says Socrates. Knowledge and memory depend upon these imprints: 'We remember and know anything imprinted, as long as the impression remains in the block; but we forget and do not know anything which is erased or cannot be imprinted.' The quality of a man's intelligence depends on the state and upkeep of his mental wax block. Those whose wax block is 'deep, plentiful, smooth and worked to the right consistency. . . are called clever'; while those in whom it is 'dirty, with impurities in the wax . . . or too moist or too hard . . . are said to be in error about things and to be ignorant' (104–5).[4]

The same graphic device returns in Aristotle's *De anima*, again in relation to cognition, with emphasis on a new detail: 'as the wax takes the sign from the ring without the iron and gold – it takes that is, the gold or bronze sign, but not *as* gold or bronze', so too sense receives the forms of the objects it perceives but not their matter (Aristotle 1986: 187). In both processes, efficient and material causes remain distinct. These figural imprints constitute sense impressions which register in the mind as memory, 'just as when men seal with signet rings' (Aristotle 1935: 287); both remembering and thinking draw on these images. Their durability depends on the quality of the surface: a diseased or aged memory, for example, retains no more imprint than if a 'seal were impressed on flowing water'. The metaphor of imprint on wax continues well into the middle ages and beyond, in discussions of mnemonic devices which derive the metaphor from the anonymous *Ad Herennium* as well as from Quintilian and Cicero (Yates 1994: 49–50).

In his earlier *Rules for the Direction of the Mind* (1628), Descartes called upon the same device to describe perception: 'sense-perception occurs in the same way in which wax takes on an impression from a seal' (Descartes 1993a: 40). Descartes insists that this statement is to be taken literally: 'It should not be thought that I have *a mere analogy in mind here*' [my italics]; and he proceeds to explain how the surface of our sentient bodies is literally changed by the perception of an object, 'in exactly the same way as the shape of the surface of the wax is altered by the seal'. It is not just touch that depends on impressions made on skin, but the other senses as well, for each is wrapped in thin, skin-like membranes which are malleable but not permeable: 'in the ears, nose and the tongue, the first membrane which is impervious to the passage of the object thus takes on a new shape from the sound, the smell and the flavour respectively'.

Even vision depends on physical impressions, for an 'opaque membrane receives the shape impressed upon it by multi-coloured light'. To illustrate how colour impresses the eye, Descartes reproduces three imprints representing white, blue and red (Figure 8). The figures illustrate the abstract form in which extended things, *res extensae*, like colour, might enter the brain as thought, *res cogitans*. The imprint made by the object on the eye is in turn imprinted on the internal surface of the brain.[5] There is no perception that could not be reduced to a similar imprint: 'The same can be said about everything perceivable by the senses, since it is certain that the infinite multiplicity of figures is sufficient for the expression of all the differences in perceptible things' (41).

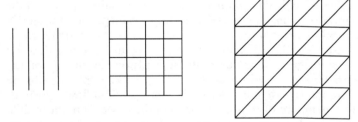

8 Imprints of white, blue and red; R. Descartes, *Rules for the Direction of the Mind* (1628)

The senses relay such imprints first to the common sensibility (the internal sense, which receives and coordinates impressions delivered by the external senses) and then to the imagination (or memory). At each stage, the transmission takes place 'in exactly the same way as the shape of the surface of the wax is altered by the seal' (40). The triple relay of imprints finishes in the brain or 'cognitive power'. Unlike the passive senses, common sensibility and imagination, the brain functions like both parts of the instrument: now passive, now active: 'sometimes resembling the seal, sometimes the wax'. But now we *are* in the realm of mere analogy: 'But this should be understood merely as an analogy, for nothing quite like this power is to be found in corporeal things'(42). What was literally true in relation to the senses is in relation to the mind no more than a figure of speech.

Ten years later, when Descartes writes the *Meditations*, the apparatus is not even useful as analogy. The device has been disassembled: wax stands alone. Signet and wax had represented the process by which objects in the world became objects of knowledge; wax by itself, however, suggests an autonomous consciousness, dependent on its own innate ideational resources. The absence of the signet is conspicuous too in a letter Descartes wrote on 2 May 1644 in which wax returns as an analogue for the brain, not because it receives imprints, but because it assumes different shapes (Descartes 1991: 232).[6] Paired with the signet, wax worked as something of an epistemic talisman, guaranteeing a correspondence between inner and outer, mind and bodies. Apart from it, mind is thrown back on its own devices – its innate ideas – the most salient of which is the idea of God itself, 'as it were, the mark of the craftsman stamped on his work' (1993a: 35).

II Genetics

The signet/wax apparatus presided over another area of classical enquiry besides epistemology. It was repeatedly evoked to illustrate a similarly mysterious phenomenon: not only how world entered mind to produce thought, but also how man penetrated woman to produce children. The gendering of the two parts of the apparatus was predictable: the form-giving seal was male and the form-receiving wax female. The male bearing down on the female left a foetal imprint (Figures 9 and 10). The analogy supported the theory that the foetus was from the moment of conception complete, its parts and organs fully formed and therefore undergoing no development, only enlargement.[7] Early modern engravings suggest how easily this theory

10 Female figure 2; C. Estienne, *La disséction des parties du corps humain* (1546), copyright British Library

lends itself to the wax/signet analogy. In Figure 9, for example, the womb of the woman before impregnation is represented as a blank armorial seal awaiting the imprint that is blazoned on the pregnant womb of Figure 10, a flat surface imprinted with a completely formed child. The signet and wax apparatus, then, served to illustrate both processes of *conception*: the having of thoughts and the having of children.

The double designation appears as ancient as the technique itself, existing in both Greek and Latin, activated in several of Plato's dialogues.[8] In the same dialogue that features the wax block, Socrates discusses learning in terms of giving birth, brainchildren as children of loins, using the language of fertility, barrenness, gestation, labour, delivery and childbirth to describe the arduous and protracted process by which ideas are generated in the mind (Plato 1988: 25–9). In addition to introducing these obstetrical terms, Socrates assigns himself the role of midwife: 'my midwifery has all the standard features, except that I practise it on men instead of women, and supervise the labour of their minds, not their bodies' (27).

Socrates's identification of himself with midwife seems calculated to replace (and neutralize) his identification in *Symposium* with lover or *eros* (1989: xxiii, 177D). In ancient Athens, relationships between older men and younger boys were conventionally erotic and instructive, pederastic and pedagogic (xiv–xv); bodies as well as minds were seduced and inseminated in the process. The continuity between the two is established by the priestess Diotima in *Symposium*. In her famous disquisition, she explains how 'the ladder of love' begins with love of a beautiful boy and extends by gradations to love of wisdom. By casting himself as midwife rather than lover, Socrates removes learning from the realm of volatile desire so empowering to the teacher. There is a special urgency to this refiguring of the teacher's role, for the dialogue ends with Socrates departing to face charges of having corrupted the youth of Athens. The claim to midwifery seems calculated to disarm his accusers: an obstetrician, an innocent by-stander (*obstare*), has no power to corrupt, unlike the seductive and inseminating teacher.

In Aristotle's *De generatione*, the seal/wax mechanics proves as apt in describing generation as it had perception, both types of conception depending on form giving imprint to matter. The

homologous relation between the male and female reproductive organs could itself be imaged as the relation between
the depressed image on the signet and the raised image on the
wax, the female genitalia an inversion of the male.[9] The
apparatus was also useful in representing generation itself: the
foetus is formed when male seed imparts form to female seed,
when male generative principle (the efficient cause) imposes
perfection upon female matter (the material cause): 'The
female always provides the material, the male that which
fashions it, for this is the power we say they each possess, and
this is what it is for them to be male and female' (Laquer 1990: 30).

In his much less respected theories of generation, as in his
epistemology, Descartes dispenses with the signet/wax mechanics. Foetus and mind stand alone and autonomous, like the
wax. In *Meditations*, he makes the seemingly offhand remark
that his parents had a negligible part in creating what he
identifies as himself: 'insofar as I am a thinking thing, [my
parents] did not even make me; they merely placed certain
dispositions in the matter which I have always regarded as
containing me, or rather my mind, for that is all I now take
myself to be' (Descartes 1993b: 35). He has no more connection
to his progenitors than his ideas do to the objective world. In
his later physiological work, *Description of the Human Body*
(1647/8), Descartes includes a section describing the formation
of the foetus or, as he terms it, 'the seminal material' (Descartes
1993a: 321). Here too, as innate ideas are independent of the
external world, so the foetus bears no imprint of world or
parent. Indeed, for him, there is no moment of inception in
which matter receives definitive form but rather a protracted
process in which parts and organs gradually come into being.[10]
Nor are two distinct sexes involved, active fashioning passive;
instead two not very different fluids commingle initially to
produce not a foetus but 'a disorganized mixture of two fluids'
(322), an impossibility for Aristotle since the mixture of male
and female semen would confuse efficient and material causes.
These fluids interact upon one another to generate a mutual
heat which in turn sets off a process of fermentation, 'as a
kind of yeast':

> We may observe how old dough makes new dough swell, or
> how the scum formed on beer is able to serve as yeast for
> another brew; and in the same way it is easy enough to accept

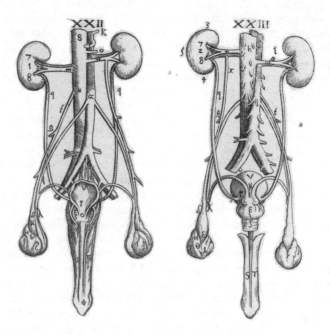

11 Organs of generation; A. Vesalius, *Vivae imagines partium corporis humani* (1572), copyright British Museum

that the seminal material of each sex functions as a yeast to that of the other, when the two [male and female] fluids are mixed together.

(Descartes 1993a: 322)

The Cartesian foetus is thus produced by a self-activating internal process (like Cartesian innate ideas) rather than by stimuli from the outside (like pre-Cartesian ideas).[11]

As this brief account has indicated, the signet/wax apparatus has been of tremendous importance to theories of both knowledge and generation, illustrating the critical interactions that were otherwise imperceptible between world and thought and between father and child. If there were no conformity between world and thought, there would be no truth (only error, fantasy and madness), no basis in the world for thought. If there were

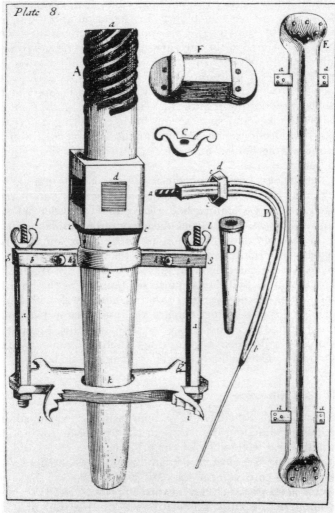

Plate 8.

A The Spindle (p. 66)
B The Bar (p. 71)
C The Female Screw (p. 71)
D The Wooden Handle
E The Ribs (p. 73)
F The Cramp Irons (p. 74)

12 Printing press parts; J. Moxon, *Mechanick Exercises* (1683–4) by permission of Oxford University Press

no conformity between parent and child, there would be no blood lines, no basis in biology for social organization. The mechanics of the signet/wax apparatus demonstrated what could not be seen at the site either of cognition (*in mentis*) or of impregnation (*in utero*). In order to clear the mind of all its old opinions (about epistemology, about physiology), Descartes does away with that little apparatus, pulling it apart in the *Meditations*, omitting it altogether in *Description of the Body*. His solipsistic ideas and spontaneous births, requiring no contact with the outside, rendered the apparatus obsolete as a metaphoric and mechanical guarantee of both metaphysical thought and physical birth.

Though not quite altogether: having taken it apart at the beginning of the Second Meditation, Descartes puts it back together in its concluding line. He repairs it in order describe imprints that come, not from outside but from inside, not from world but from mind: 'I should like to stop here and meditate for some time on this new knowledge I have gained, so as to fix [*imprime*] it more deeply in my memory' (1993b: 23; 1953: 283). Here the mind itself has assumed the function of the imprint-making signet, impressing its own mnemonic wax with knowledge. In this concluding sentence, the titular act of meditation is represented as a kind of psychic self-imprinting. Meditation involves a self-reflexive impressing, another fantasy of pure autonomy – like original thought and autogenetic birth.

III Metaphorics

In the English Renaissance, comparisons of mechanical and sexual reproduction, imprints and children, seem to multiply, as if the new technology of the printing press revitalized the ancient trope.[12] A cluster of infantilizing tropes anticipates the nineteenth-century term for early printed books, *incunabula* (from *cunabula*, cradle). The textual imprint as child recurs in preliminaries to early modern books, putting into play the semantics shared by biological and textual reproduction: of issue, generation, copying, duplication, multiplying, engraving and gravidity; of textual and sexual inscriptions that survive the grave through enduring ideas and successive children; of two types of lines, scripted and genealogical which promise to extend the parent/author beyond death.

Dedication pages abound in which imprinted children complain of having been disowned, orphaned, discredited and abused, often as spurious or illegitimate. Without parental protection of any kind, they seek patronage, a patron or foster father who would adopt and support. The preliminaries to the 1623 Folio edition of Shakespeare's plays attempt to procure surrogate guardians or fathers (in the Earls of Pembroke and Montgomery) for the 'orphanes' or playtexts gathered by the volume (de Grazia 1991: 37–9). A patron was to protect the textual dependent from various misfortunes, plagiarism among them. It is thought that the poet Martial coined the term – *plagiarus*, literally a kidnapper – to protest against another poet's having claimed Martial's verses as his own (White 1935: 16).

The trope in reverse is also pervasive: the child as imprint as well as the imprint as child, the imprint of the father, as Aristotle would lead us to expect. Thus Hermia is, 'but as a form in wax, / [by her father] imprinted' (*A Midsummer Night's Dream* I. i. 50), and Aaron's son is his 'stamp' and 'seal', his 'seal . . . stamped in his face' (*Titus Andronicus* IV. ii. 69, 127). With all stamping techniques – whether of wax, coins or paper – there is always the possibility of forgery. Posthumus, convinced of the infidelity of all women, concludes that his father's whereabouts were unknown, 'When [he] was stamped. Some coiner with his tools / Made me a counterfeit' (II. v. 5). The changeling child might be substituted for the legitimate child as easily as the counterfeit coin for the true, or – as in the case of Hamlet – the forged letter for the authentic. Hamlet succeeds in substituting his own forgery for his uncle's commission because he has his father's authorizing signet. 'How was it seal'd?' (V. ii. 47), asks Horatio. Once Hamlet gave it 'th'impression' (52) of his father's signet, 'The changeling [was] never known' (53).[13]

Shakespeare's Sonnets use the trope in both directions. The children the poet enjoins the fair youth to beget would be his imprints: '[Nature] carved thee for her seal, and meant thereby / Thou shouldst print more, not let that copy die' (Shakespeare 1986: 11). And the poetic imprints the poet produces would be surrogate children. Early on in the collection, the scheme for dynastically reproducing the youth yields to the project of poetically reproducing him, inked verse lines substituting for generational loins or lineage, preserving the young man's image for posterity, obliterating thereby Time's disfiguring engravings, the 'lines and wrinkles' (63) of old age (de Grazia 1994: 46).

In these instances, the connections between offspring and imprints are metaphorical: the book without a patron is *like* an orphan; the legitimate child is *like* the father's seal. But the same semantic overlappings acquire a more material dimension in practices such as pedagogy and obstetrics, learning and engendering, the reproduction of knowledge and the reproduction of children. Boys are capable of learning for the same reason that women are capable of engendering: because they are impressionable, like wax. That the analogy was more than mere metaphor is demonstrated by the importance of temperature control to both processes. Because a cold pupil could be intractable, schoolmasters are advised to save the most arduous writing exercises until one o'clock in the afternoon (Brinsley 1612: 32). Midwifery manuals maintain that a matrix needs to be kept warm in order to avoid barrenness, just as wax needs warming before receiving on impression (Everden 1993).

Of boys, it is said that teaching them before the age of seven is futile because, 'that which printed is therein / It holds as sure as water graved with pin' (Whythorne 1962: 7). But once the surface is firm enough, the imprinting process can begin: through mimetic or copying practices, from letters to *exempla* to precepts, so that the child himself will be able to reproduce them, like a 'mint of phrases' (*Love's Labour Lost* I. i. 165).[14] Up to the late middle ages, these lessons were routinely impressed on wooden tablets covered with wax (Rouse and Rouse 1990); but they could also be inscribed on paper with pen. A material inscription would ideally register in the mind as well as the writing surface, seeping through the surface via the writing hand or the reading eye into memory itself, from a graphic to a psychic register (Goldberg 1990: 159–60; 1988: 316). Receptive to pedagogic and stylistic imprints, boys often serve as *pages*, taking in their master's lessons, like Shakespeare's generic pupil William Page.[15]

In all these instances, the line between education and seduction tends to blur, just as it does in Plato's *Theaetetus* and *Symposium*, so that pedagogy slips into pederasty. Falstaff, like Socrates, is alleged to be a great corrupter of youth as well as a philanderer. His great weight makes him a natural maker of imprints; he is called a 'bed presser' (*1 Henry IV* II. iv. 242), the bed of the printing press being the surface on which the forme is laid. It is suggested that he will imprint anything that takes an impression – with the possible exception of Mistress Quickly, who, like an otter, is neither fish nor flesh, a man knows not where to have her – whether it be his own boy page in *2 Henry IV* given to him by Hal, who might himself have similarly served him (Goldberg 1995: 56–7) or Mistress Page and Mrs Ford. To the last two, Falstaff sends duplicate love letters to each wife, second editions, each wife assumes, a good thousand having already been printed. Textually and sexually indiscriminate, he 'cares not what he puts in press' (*The Merry Wives of Windsor* II. i. 78).[16]

In addition to boys and women, Falstaff also impresses men. In *2 Henry IV*, we observe him impressing men into the King's service, drafting or conscripting them, by writing their names on his list (enlisting them), what he calls 'pricking' them. Men in the military are much more susceptible to martial pricking – to the peppering of gun shot and knife points – but also to sexual pricking: 'I have mis*us'd* the king's *press* damnably'(*1 Henry IV*, IV. ii. 12; my italics), admits Falstaff, suggesting sexual coercion as well as monetary extortion. This is the basis of Falstaff's joke at the expense of Feeble, the woman's tailor, Shallow asks, 'Shall I prick him?' (III. ii. 142), doubting whether the tailor used to making holes in women's petticoats, will be any good at making holes in the enemy's coats, and Falstaff quips, 'If he had been a man's tailor he would have pricked you' (III. ii. 153), though both Feeble's and Shallow's names suggest limitations in that area. In this context, it is hard not to see the thigh wound Falstaff obscenely gives the dead Hotspur as another instance of his indiscriminate bent for pricking and impressing bodies, male and female, young and adult, dead and alive.

Martial pricking or scoring has venerable precedents among the Ancients – both the Greek, Patroclus and Achilles and the Roman, Coriolanus and Aufidius. Coriolanus, for example, bears a sword that marks men with 'death's stamp' (*Coriolanus* II. ii. 107). Embarrassed by his own scars, he prefers to publicize wounds he has given his enemies, particularly the stripes he has 'impressed' (V. vi. 107) upon Aufidius in the 'encounters' (IV. v. 123) that are the subject of the latter's fantasies. Aufidius admits as much at a telling moment: while embracing Coriolanus as passionately as he did his virginal bride.

The impress of the law makes itself felt in time of peace as well as war, through penal rather than military inscriptions, the lashes, wounds and scars of corporeal punishment. These disciplinary markings are not altogether unpedagogical. Law impresses itself on the body that will not take in its lessons in any other form. Branding letters on the flesh – the S for Sedition, for example – is intended as a warning to the public, to be sure, but also as a final lesson to the criminal, as if to imprint on the body the instructive cipher resisted by the mind. Caliban is whipped (receives what Shakespeare elsewhere calls 'the impression of keen whips', *Measure for Measure* II. iv. 101), according to Prospero, because resistant to more literate forms of instruction, 'which any print of goodness will not take' (*The Tempest* I. ii. 352). So too boys in Tudor schoolrooms were subjected to the schoolmaster's rod. In fact, Erasmus notes that in many cases, 'the school is, in effect, a torture chamber' (Halpern 1991: 26). The lettered, however, are spared the law's most extreme imposition. The death sentence could be avoided by demonstrating literacy with the reading of the 'neck clause'. It was not until the very end of the seventeenth century that women gained the full benefit of clergy, but before this they could plead for a benefit of another kind: pregnancy instead of literacy.[17] The same logic seems to underlie these two special dispensations, as if both inseminated women and male seminarians were spared because of their reproductive or generational capacity for children and letters respectively.

Impregnation, as our attention to Aristotle would lead us to expect, is also described as an imprinting technique, as when in *The Taming of the Shrew* Lucentio is told to take the woman he intends to marry, '*Cum privilegio ad imprimendum solum*' – an inscription appearing on title-pages signifying that the printer had the sole right to print (IV. iv. 93). In other words, Lucentio should impress Bianca with his inseminating imprint before she loses to another man's mark the whiteness or virginity proclaimed by her immaculate page-like name. Beatrice's fantasy takes a similar form when she imagines herself and Benedict between folded sheets, bed sheets and folio sheets, with Benedict, one assumes, on top, imprinting her with his issue. Submission is not always voluntary, as in the case of Lucrece; indeed, she bases her self-defence on women's constitutional inability to resist male disfiguration: 'Women [have] waxen minds' that take on 'th'impression of strange kinds' (1242), with no more culpability 'than wax . . . Wherein is stamp'd the semblance of a devil' (1245–6).

In coining, the impression is made on molten metal, like wax and paper a surface capable of receiving graphic and sexual imprints. The unstruck metal was called a *blank*, like the unmarked page Blanches and Biancas are named after in honour of their virginity (or, ironically, their promiscuity). Ophelia's lap as well as Gertrude's is made of this metal, and Hamlet finds the maid's more magnetic than the matron's: 'here's metal more attractive' (III. ii. 108). His next question pushes the word further: 'Lady, shall I lie in your lap? . . . I mean, my head upon your lap' (110–11, 114). Despite Hamlet's disclaimer, the request to lie head in/on lap *does* mean '*count*ry matters' (my italics) – the kind of copulative lying that would transform blank metal to a medal or medallion stamped with the head of the father. Isabella's complaint in *Measure for Measure* that women 'are credulous to false-prints' (II. iv. 130) refers specifically to the seducing imprint threatened by the man who bears the name of a coin, Angel, whose 'metal/ mettle' had the great figure of the Duke 'stamp'd upon it' (I. i. 49–50) before it was tested. The stamp Juliet receives is also precipitous, for Claudio impregnates or imprints her with 'too gross' charactering before their union has been fully legitimized (I. ii. 154).

Counterfeit coining, like usury, is frequently associated with sodomitic sex.[18] Imprints can be made on both sides of the body, *verso* as well as *recto*, just as they can on both side of a page or a coin. Jove lavishly drops his seminal coins on the right or front side of Danae but on the inverse or backside of Ganymede, another *page*. Ganymede, in Henry Peacham's emblem book (1612), is emblematized as both sodomite and counterfeiter, guilty, says the gloss, of the 'crime of false coin', a sexual and economic violation.[19] It is he himself who is the counterfeit coin, an example of base metal stamped with the image of the Olympian king, circulating among numismatic nobles, sovereigns, crowns and royals. But he is base metal too because pressed on the backside or bottom, struck from behind (Fischer 1985: 95). Social and anatomical inversions both run counter to nature and are therefore unproductive of either progeny or profit. The association between sodomy and counterfeiting unfolds in the surprising etymology of the term 'queer': used from the seventeenth century as a cant term for counterfeit money ('queer money'), before centuries later it was applied to aberrant sex (Fisher 1994).

The sexual and mechanical interconnections so prevalent in the period's semantics can also be traced in its graphic representations. In Figures 9 and 10, for example, the womb is represented before and after conception: first as *tabula rasa* and then as emblazoned seal. The woodcut of the woman is a reworking of a reclining Venus, with an important modification: a rectangle around the abdominal wall has been left open, to be filled in with a woodblock of the gynaecological section. This *factotem* was a labour-saving device, enabling the printer to use the same model in illustrating different views of the womb. But it was a device, too, that in the printer's hand graphically enacted the generational trope of male imprinting female. Two independent woodblocks have been impressed on the womb of the female models: of a blank heraldic crest on Figure 9 and of a monogramatic foetus on Figure 10. The foetus looks like an insignia, incised on the flat abdominal wall, not unlike the letters cut into the stone plinth beneath the woman's crotch. The figural foetus has been imprinted by the male into the material body of the female, whose womb here serves to showcase the little pictograph. Inception is clearly the formative moment rather than gestation. The foetus from the start is fully formed and independent of the womb which provides it only with temporary lodging, like the loggia enclosing the spectacled male in the upper left corner.

In generation as well as in education, the two types of conceptual powers (mental and corporeal) could become confused. As the pupil's body could be impressed as well as his mind, so too the woman's mind could be impressed as well as her body; and simultaneously, though not necessarily by the same male. In a mid-seventeenth century collection of questions and answers attributed to Aristotle, the question arises:

> Wherefore doth the imagination of the mother, which *imagineth* of an Ethiopian or Blackmore, cause the mother to

bring forth a black child, as Albertus Magnus reporteth of a Queen, who in the act of carnal copulation *imagined* of a Blackmore which was painted before her, and so brought forth a Moor?

(Aristotle 1647: D4)

And the philosopher responds that in this instance, 'the childe born followeth her imagination, and not his power of forming and shaping'. The picture of the Moor pre-empts the imprint of the father, the ocular impression subverts the venereal. The reverse happens in *Titus Andronicus*: white overshadows black not in Aaron's child who bears his father's black stamp, but in his kinsman Mulietus's child who is fair enough to pass for the Emperor's heir.

Imprinting metaphors surface repeatedly around issues of virginity and chastity, rape and adultery. Editors explain in glossing Malvolio's exclamation upon breaking the seal of the letter he believes from Olivia – 'By your leave wax. Soft! And the Impressure, her Lucrece with which she uses to seal' (*Twelfth Night* II. iv. 93) – that Lucrece must have been engraved on Olivia's seal. To stop there is to miss the ugly joke. Women are sealed in two states: virginity and chastity. The hymenal seal is broken in marriage; the marital seal is broken by either rape or adultery. Lu*crece*'s very name connects her to this sealing process, for it suggests two types of *creases*. There are epistolary creases like those made by Lucrece herself in the letter she sends her husband, folded (1311) and sealed (1331).[20] And there are labial creases, like those of Lucrece's 'sweet lips fold' and those of their vaginal counterparts; the one sealed with kisses, the other by sexual consummation, both ideally conjugal. The raped Lucrece is like a letter whose seal has been tampered with – and she imagines that one violated seal will be as detectable as the other. The two seals also overlap in *King Lear*: Edgar's bold ripping of Goneril's epistolary seal – 'Leave, gentle wax' (IV. vi. 256) – is warranted by its contents: proof of her adulterous breaking of the sacramental seal. One broken seal deserves another. The reverse happens in *The Winter's Tale*. Leontes receives a letter from Delphos, has his messengers swear they 'have not dared to break the holy seal' (III. ii. 128), and after breaking it himself reads that his wife's seal (that is, *his* seal on her) was also never violated, 'Hermione is chaste' (131).

Violated chastity and adulterous fornication lead to questions of bastardy and paternity, and once again to imprinting devices. Leontes strains to see himself in his son Mamillius just as he begins to doubt his paternity. He looks at him for a miniature portrait of himself, the only possible confirmation besides women's suspect words. He refuses to see such signs in the daughter he has convinced himself he did not sire, though Paulina insists she is 'Copy of the father' – her features, like so many incisions and recesses in an incised surface, duplicating her father's: 'The trick of's *frown*; his forehead; nay, the *valley*, / The pretty *dimples* of his chin and cheek, his *smiles*' (*The Winter's Tale* II. iii. 100–3; my italics). What Leontes doubts in his own children, he recognizes immediately in Polixenes's son: 'Your mother was most true to wedlock, *prince*, / For she did *print* your *royal* father off, / Conceiving you' (V. i. 123–5). The trope is from both coining and printing, for a *royal* is both a coin and a size of printing paper (as well as the books made from it: royal octavo, royal quarto, etc.). The *prince* is like both a numismatic and bibliographic *print* of his royal father.

IV Mechanics

As the examples from Shakespeare have demonstrated, the mechanics of the imprint – of seal, stamp, coin or woodblock – worked itself into the semantics of the period, wending its way through discourses beyond the literary, into pedagogy, anatomy, law, finance. But it was not simply that these reproductive machines generated reproductive metaphors. Reproductive metaphors structured reproductive machines, at least one machine: that huge, epochal, imprinting machine – *the printing press*. The press is after all a machine which, like the seal, makes impressions. Or rather it is an aggregate of seals or signets: so many typebodies to be set and locked into a chase and pressed mechanically to produce an imprint, on absorbent paper instead of malleable wax.[21]

The astonishing thing about this machine was the degree to which it materialized or mechanized the metaphorics of the signet and wax. It was made and made to function as a generational or reproductive system: made up of sexualized parts, it performed virtual copulative acts. It is not just that textual reproduction shared with sexual reproduction a vocabulary of generating issue, propagating copy, like begetting like. It materialized and mechanized that vocabulary.

Both the text and diagrams of the earliest full description that we have of the construction and workings of the printing press, Joseph Moxon's *The Mechanick Exercises on the Whole Art of Printing* (1683–4), suggest the extent to which the printing press was constructed as a sexually gendered generational apparatus (Figure 12 above). The various pieces of equipment – the chase, the mold, the dressing block, the ribs of the press itself – were held together by gendered pieces: '*Male-Duftails* are fitted into *Female-Duftails*' (Moxon 1978: 43); 'The *Female Block* is such another *Block* as the *Male Block*, only, instead of a *Tongue* running through the length of it, a *Groove* is made to receive the *Tongue* of the *Male-Block*' (181); 'The Office of the *Male-Gage* is to fit into, and slides along the *Female Gage*' (140); '*Male-screw* is fitted into a square Nut with a *Female-screw* in it' (72). These mechanical pairs – the male and female duftails, blocks, gages and screws – are the mechanical counterparts to Galen's sexual organs. According to his model, there was basically one sex: the female reproductive system was simply an inverted, interior and inferior version of the male, as numerous anatomical drawings attest (Laqueur 1990: 32–5, Figures 20–37). That the one-sex model should have endured so long, from the fourth century B.C. to the Enlightenment, and despite mounting empirical refutations, is hard to explain (150–54). But surely its holding power had something to do with its power to hold: the best way of holding objects and bodies together – of joining wood and coupling bodies – is the mechanics (and erotics) of the plug and the hole.[22]

Put together with copulating parts, the press operated when the force of the press and the press-man bore down on the forme (smeared with viscous oil-based ink) to imprint the absorbent and retentive page. Called a 'horse' and later a 'bear', the press-man must have been Falstaffian in his corpulence, and so he appears in a late sixteenth-century engraving of the printing-house (Figure 17 below). Of course, all presses – wine presses, olive presses, paper presses – might be said to suggest the same sexual act of 'bearing down'. The press of the printing press was unique, however, in that it applied not just pressure but a figure of some kind: an imprint. So too did all reproductive apparatuses, from the signet on wax, to the stamp

The true Effigies of **Iohn Guttemberg** *Delineated from the Original Painting at* **Mentz** *in Germanie.*

13 Gutenberg with punch; A. Thevet, *Vies et portraits des hommes illustres* (1587) by permission of Oxford University Press

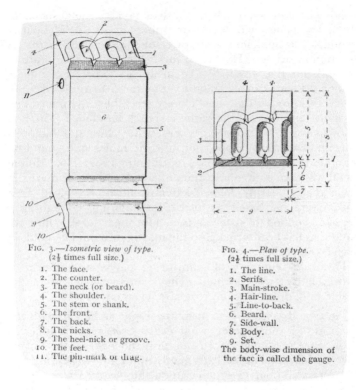

FIG. 3.—*Isometric view of type.*
(2½ times full size.)

1. The face.
2. The counter.
3. The neck (or beard).
4. The shoulder.
5. The stem or shank.
6. The front.
7. The back.
8. The nicks.
9. The heel-nick or groove.
10. The feet.
11. The pin-mark or drag.

FIG. 4.—*Plan of type.*
(2½ times full size.)

1. The line.
2. Serifs.
3. Main-stroke.
4. Hair-line.
5. Line-to-back.
6. Beard.
7. Side-wall.
8. Body.
9. Set.
The body-wise dimension of
the face is called the gauge.

14 Diagram of type; L. A. Legros and J. C. Grant, *Typographical Typing Surfaces* (1916)

on coin, to the woodblock on paper and textiles. All these techniques involved, like the act of copulation itself, inverse commensurate parts, either in relief or *intaglio*, raised or sunken, the reproduced image an inside-out version of the reproduced original: 'what is inside women, likewise sticks out in males' (Laqueur 1990: 133).

The feature that distinguished the printing press from all other modes of reproduction – movable type – was made by a process that also required gendered conjoining. The process began with a punch or patrix – a sleek tapered metal shank (of about 1¾ inches) with letters or ciphers on its tip. The patrix or punch was 'sunk into' a soft piece of wood called a *matrix*. (A question arises, 'viz. How deep the *Punches* [or patrices] are to be Sunk into the *Matrices?*'. The answer is, 'a thick space deep, though deeper to an n would be yet better' (Moxon 1978: 154). It was this process that most closely resembled the imprinting of signet and wax, as the earliest French handbook (1567) on print specified: 'la matrice . . . n'est autre chose que l'imprés-sion du charactère frappé, non plus ne moins que quand on margue un cachet dedans la cire' (Plantin 1567: 236). Molten metal was then poured into and impacted against the matrix in order that a sharply defined letter would be produced. In a 1587 engraving based on an earlier painting, Gutenberg is depicted holding the patrix or punch for the letter A in his right hand that has been struck into the matrix or mould he holds in his left (Figure 13).

From this coupling of imprinting patrix and imprinted matrix letters were formed. They were removed from the mould and 'dressed' with great care, even tenderness:

> the type dresser goes as near the Light as he can with the *Letters* . . . and examins what *Letters Come not well* either in the Face or shanck. . . . Then with the *Balls* of the fingers of both his Hands, he Patts gently upon the *Feet* of the *Letter*, to press all their *Faces* down upon the *Tongue*; which having done, he takes the *Mallet* in his right-Hand, and with it knocks gently. . . Then with a small piece of *Buff* or some other soft *Leather*, he rubs a little upon the Feet of the Letter to smooth them.
>
> (Moxon 1978: 184, 187)

The letters were treated like newborns. And indeed they do look astonishingly humanoid, with human anatomies: a body (stem of metal) standing on 'feet' with 'shoulders' supporting a face whose physiognomy is literally its character, a legible face (Figure 14). The anthropomorphic quality of typebodies has not gone unremarked:

> For purposes of nomenclature typefounders and printers have always regarded the single movable type character as a human being standing erect, each type having a body, a face, beard, neck, shoulder, back, belly, and feet. These parts fall

into three divisions: the shank, the shoulder, and the face; the shoulder and shank together comprising the body.

(Thomas 1936: 17)

As the mechanical letter has face and body, so too the anatomical man has letters: in Geofrey Tory's anatomy, 'L'homme letré' (Figure 15) is 'insinuées et intimées' (Tory 1529: XXIIIv) with the twenty-three letters of the Attic (Roman) alphabet, programmed for virtuous words and deeds.

Issuing from copulative mechanical exercise, letters could themselves be quite sexy, as they are in sixteenth-century embodied alphabets in which the body of the letter is represented by lusty human bodies in seductive poses and erotic positions, intended to inspire a love of letters (Figure 16) (Goldberg 1990: 226–8). And their inseminating power was suggested by the name of the receptacle in which they were held when not in use, (upper and lower) *cases* (Moxon 1978: 27–32) (Figure 17, left], the same name given the seed-carrying scrotum and uterus, which also possessed upper and lower cases (Parker 1987: 27–31). It is because the letters have such anthropomorphic traits and drives that the Star Chamber orders that offending presses and letters be 'defaced', 'battered' and 'broken' (Greg 1930: 161, 240, 243). Once dismembered, its broken parts are returned, like the scattered bones of a saint. A *male* saint, it must be emphasized, for the imprinting typbodies, true to Aristotle, were decidedly male, each one possessing that determining marker of masculinity – a beard.[23]

Like the letters, the printing-house was gendered male.[24] The printers' guild, the Brothers of the Stationers' Company, was unusual in excluding female apprentices.[25] This cannot have been because of the physical and messy nature of printers' work, for female apprentices were routinely admitted in the early modern centuries to such 'unfeminine' crafts as wheelwrighting, masonry and blacksmithing (Snell 1984: 274–5). It was not until 1666, however, that the first girl was indentured to the Stationers' guild (Blagden 1960: 162). It is true that printers' widows not uncommonly became members of the Company in the sixteenth century. However, that remarriage outside the Company entailed the forfeiture of membership (95, 162) suggests that it was conferred upon them not in their own right but as surrogates for their deceased husbands. Even as late as the nineteenth century with the large influx of women

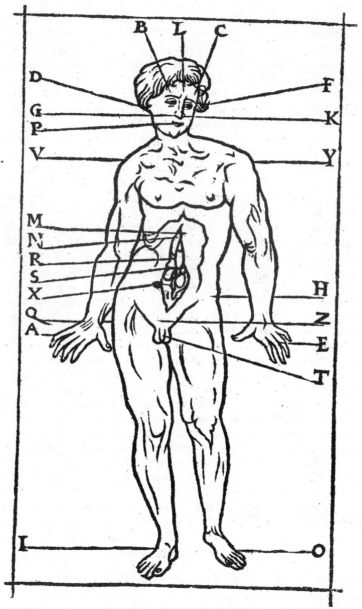

15 Lettered man; G. Tory, *Champ Fleury* (1529), copyright British Museum

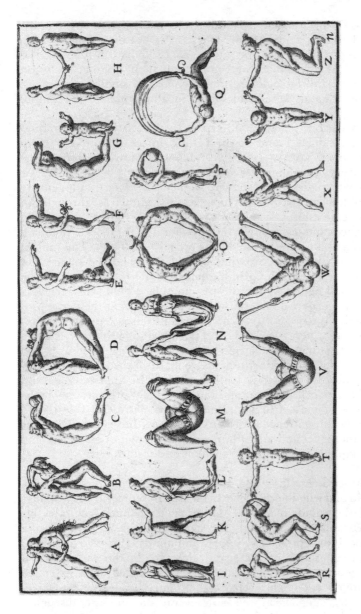

16 Alphabet; T. and I. de Bry, *Alphabeta et Characteres* (1596), copyright British Library

into the printing industry, they were mainly barred from print-making machine and type and assigned to the manufacturing and stitching of print-taking pages (Cockburn 1991: 23–6). Nor was this assignment any more than their original exclusion dictated by biological difference, for, if anything, women's smaller hands were better suited for the nimble work required by type-setting.

A curious female counterpart to the masculinist printing-house can be found in the birthing-place (Figure 18). Until midwives' hands were replaced by man-midwives' forceps, the delivery of children was an exclusively female occupation.[26] As recent studies have shown, women in seventeenth-century London received their training as midwives through an apprenticeship system made up only of women; so too, the licences and testimonials required for practising were obtained through a female network (Everden 1993: 9–26). The mutual exclusivity of the two sites upheld the gendered binaries of signet and wax: the printing-house doing the printing of the notional figural signet, the birthing-place doing the receiving of the corporeal material wax. The belief that the two repro-ductive processes were incompatible also kept the realms discrete. There is evidence in French printing shops of fear lest menstruating women ruin metal machinery, 'rust iron and brass, dull cutting instruments, jeopardize the already hazard-ous process of casting, and the like.'[27] In England generally, midwives called for the assistance of male surgeons only if the foetus or mother or both had died (Eccles 1982: 109–18). In this deeply entrenched division of labour, the gendered binaries of the signet and wax still prevail, directing not only ideas and metaphors but machines, customs and institutions.

This essay has discussed how imprinting devices – seal, stamp, coin and woodblock – have been used to represent the workings of the mind and body. From ancient times, reproductive mechanisms, particularly the signet and wax, have provided a model for reproductive bodies and minds – for the conception and generation of ideas and children. In the early modern period, these connections were elaborated and extended through a complex semantic circuitry, traceable in Shake-speare's language as well as in several contemporary discursive sites and practices. Yet the transposition between the mechan-

ical and human worked in more than one direction: not only
from machine to man to mechanized man, but also from man
to machine to humanized machine – as the example of the
printing press suggests. With its anthropomorphic reproductive
parts and processes, the copying machine was a kind of
copulating body.

A copulating body *with a difference*, that is, and not just in size
or capacity. The difference pertained to the imprint-making
mechanism itself: uniform in all other imprinting apparatuses,
it was multiform in the press. A signet or stamp could produce
only one insignia; the forme of the press, however, made up of
variable and movable letters, could produce a virtually infinite
number of impressions. Even in the course of a single working
day, the forme was assembled and disassembled, often repeatedly. On a bad day, letters might even spill out onto the floor (and
the compositor would be fined for each one dropped). It may
be quite misleading, then, to assume that *fixity* was the printing
press's great effect on Western culture. The innovation was,
after all, *movable* type. While perhaps more fixed than *cursive*
script, it was certainly less stable than *stamp, block* or *signet*.

The movable imprint of the press made for a more efficient
and flexible reproductive technology, to be sure. But what
happened to the epistemic and genetic theories that once
conformed with the fixed imprint of the signet? Were knowledge and generation imagined differently? Was the new mechanics of the press attended by transformations in how thought
and sex were construed?

It is fair to raise such huge questions at the end of this study
only because it may well be that recent Shakespeare studies
have been in the process of anticipating answers. Textual
scholars are no longer tyrannized by the Fixity of Print, the
assumption that typography worked to standardize, regularize
and stabilize texts. It is generally recognized now that mal-
leability and provisionality characterize the Shakespearean text
to such a degree that it is not clear whether certain texts should
be regarded as single or multiple (de Grazia 1995: 1–7). As our
sense of what kind of textual imprints the early modern press
produced has changed, so may have our assumptions about
knowledge and sexuality. We are sceptical of claims like
Hamlet's that plays constitute 'the very form and pressure' of
the age (III. ii. 24). The discursive complexes in which the plays

17 Printing-house; J. van der Straet, *Nova reperta* (1600), copyright British Museum

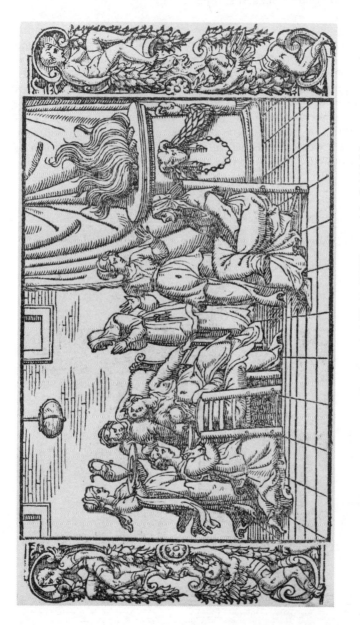

18 Birthing-place; L. Dolce, *Trensformationi d'Ovido* (1555), copyright British Museum

are enmeshed are mimetic of no prior and independent reality, historical or empirical. Nor is the binary model of imprinting male and imprinted female any longer adequate for plays that are now seen to stage a range of polymorphous fits and mis-fits. In approaching body, mind and text, Shakespeare studies appear to be dispensing with the binaries once mechanized by the signet and wax. It may be that the combinatorial possibilities of movable type on page are more in line with our present expectations, as we ourselves move from one form of reproductive technology to another.

5
L[o]cating the sexual subject
BRUCE R. SMITH

As an object of academic inquiry, sexual behaviour in early
modern England has been approached, by and large, from two
converging directions: via deconstruction and via new historicism. Each of these methodologies implies a different model
for *articulating* sexual behaviour, for dividing it into parts
and turning it into words. Appropriating the principles of
Sausurrean linguistics, deconstruction asks us to read sexual
behaviour in terms of binaries. Acknowledging differences in
the construction of sexuality from culture to culture, new
historicism asks us to read sexual behaviour as a continuum. In
practice if not in theory, the two approaches are comple-
mentary: if all sexual identities are made by marking binary
differences, then particular identities can be plotted along a line
of possible variations. I propose to consider these two models
one by one, to assess their strengths and weaknesses and to offer
a third model in their place.[1] But first we should take a sceptical
look at 'sex' and 'sexual' as objects of enquiry. 'Sex' was not,
after all, a conceptual category for any of the constituent
cultures of early modern England, even for the religious and
academic institutions that supplied the dominant culture with
its justifying ideology. The *OED* corroborates Foucault's claim
that the notion of 'sex' as something more than genital coding
dates only from the end of the eighteenth century (Foucault

1979: 115–31). For us, 'sex' is an idea, an abstraction. What I wish to address here is something more immediate, more physical than that. In the words of Sonnet 129, the subject at hand is 'lust in action' – something that is seen, heard, touched, smelled and tasted before it is remembered, read, studied, analysed and talked about.

In addition to Saussure, the binary model has early modern ideology to recommend it. Ethical discourse about sexual behaviour in early modern England proceeds along lines of the permitted and the not permitted – in an anthopologist's terms, along lines of 'totem' and 'taboo'. To give oneself up to lechery is to upset the rational order of the cosmos – and not only by placing body above spirit. Take, for example, John Earle's characterization of 'A lascivious man' in his character book *Micro-cosmographie: Or, a Peece of the World Discovered; In Essayes and Characters*: 'A lascivious man* is the servant he sayes of many Mistresses, but all are but his lust: to which onely hee is faithfull, and none besides, and spends his best blood, and spirits in the service. His soule is the Bawde to his body, and those assist him in this nature, the neerest to it' (Earle 1629: sigs G12–G12v). Earle's talk of 'servant', 'mistresses' and 'bawd', all in the same breath, indicates that binaries other than body and spirit are at work in ethical discourses about sexual behaviour. The lascivious man exchanges the role of master for servant as well as the role of male for female. In general, Puritan attacks on the theatre conflate sexual licence with gender confusion – and both with social subversion (Orgel 1989; Howard 1994a: 22–46). For a common player to impersonate a nobleman was an outrage; for a boy-actor to play a noblewoman was a double outrage. The boy-actor who played Lady Anne opposite Richard III, for example, was twice over a malefactor. Ultimately, however, Puritan objections to the stage are about ontology, as Jonas Barish insists:

> The prejudice seems too deep-rooted, too widespread, too resistant to changes of place and time to be ascribed entirely, or even mainly, to social, political, or economic factors. It bestrides too many centuries, it encompasses too many different climes and cultures. It wells up from deep sources. . . . It belongs to an ethical emphasis in which the key terms are those of order, stability, constancy, and integrity, as against

a more existentialist emphasis that prizes growth, process, exploration, flexibility, variety, and versatility of response. In one case we seem to have an ideal of stasis, in the other an ideal of movement, in one case an ideal of rectitude, in the other an ideal of plenitude.

(Barish 1981: 116–17)

In the terms set down by Plato, the fundamental binary is nothing less than Being versus Becoming. The body, gender, social class, one's very state-of-being; all these differences are implicated in each other.

In the binary opposition of 'licit'/'illicit', sexual behaviour does not have a fixed place. Rather, it functions as a sign or metaphor for other kinds of concerns. Control the sexual body and, according to one line of logic, you control the body politic. The politics of difference-marking help to explain the importance of the binary model both to feminism and to queer theory Historically, one notable result of this binary way of looking at sexual behaviour has been to cast women as scapegoats for male anxieties: about the body, about social stability, about the order of the cosmos. Those anxieties find a convenient focus in sexual behaviour, as Coppélia Kahn (1981), Jeanne Roberts (1991) and Jean E. Howard (1994a), among many others, have argued. The political consequences of binary thinking likewise explain why queer theory has founded its critical platform on deconstruction. Unlike Puritan objectors to early modern theatre, who are interested in affirming binaries, practitioners of queer theory set out to destabilize binaries, to expose their arbitrariness and challenge their political authority. Forceful examples are to be found in the work of Gregory Bredbeck (1991) Jonathan Dollimore (1991) and Jonathan Goldberg (1992).

As important as this work has been in dislodging prejudice, the game of 'binary trump' entails certain epistemological hazards, as indicated by the troubled relationship that has emerged between queer theory and feminism. First, in fixing attention on the semiotic process of meaning-making, queer theory runs the risk of turning women into the disembodied absences they often occupy in early modern texts. Carried to its logical conclusion, queer theory deconstructs the *femina* that gives feminism its very reason for being. If all conceptual categories are inherently unstable, is there, after all, anything *there* to study? What remains *un*questioned are 'sex' and 'sexuality' as categories of knowledge. They are privileged in ways that subsume gender, as Judith Butler astutely observes: 'Sexual difference, irreducible to "gender" or to the putative biological disjunction of "female" or "male," is rhetorically refused through the substitution by which a unitary "sex" is installed as the proper object of study' (Butler 1994: 4). Second, queer theory reinforces the binary thinking that served to marginalize women in the first place. In the process, it runs the risk of replicating in political terms the exclusionary boundary-marking that it purports to be attacking in semiotic terms. Critical movements may begin in polyglossia, but they tend to end in monologia. In place of the old binary 'male'/'female', queer theory imposes a new master binary: 'correct'/'incorrect'.

The Puritan example alone should make us wary of the reactionary potential present in *all* binaries, not just those we happen not to approve of. The notion of sexual behaviour as a continuum is a more liberally appealing idea and one that I endorsed in *Homosexual Desire in Shakespeare's England* (1991). If the binary model asserts *either/or*, the continuum model insinuates *both/and*. Once again, there is plenty of evidence from early modern England to recommend such a model. When it came to sodomy, for example, ethical treatises and legal statutes may have set in place clear dichotomies, but social practice suggests a much less certain state of affairs. The capital punishment prescribed for sodomites in the statute 5 Elizabeth, Chapter 17, was invoked only in extraordinary circumstances – circumstances that had as much to do with the abuse of private property in the form of someone else's cow, sheep, servant, apprentice or prepubescent child (as witness the indictment hearings recorded for the Home Counties between 1559 and 1602), with race (as witness 'Domingo Cassedon Drago a negro' arraigned for sodomy in 1647), or with religion and politics (as witness the Earl of Castlehaven convicted in 1631 for committing sodomy with his male servants and abetting one of them in the rape of Lady Castlehaven) as it did with specific sexual acts.[2]

If sexual behaviour presents itself not as a binary but as a continuum, what marks the extremes? In early modern England, as now, the criterion seems clear enough: it is, in

Gramsci's terms, political hegemony.[3] Whatever served to undergird patriarchal authority in early modern England fell within the range of permitted behaviour. In certain circumstances, that might involve sexual relations among men. Indeed, the oxymoronic images of embracing and fisting in Aufidius's welcome to Coriolanus in IV. v. 102–36 would suggest that homoerotic desire served to fuel the patriarchal enterprise: it strengthened the male bonds that kept patriarchy in place. In terms of political utility, the ends of the continuum, I would argue, are marked by two figures: the sodomite and the whore. Although one end of the continuum is thus gendered 'male' and the other 'female', the issue that places the two figures is the same: power. When a man engages in sexual behaviour that somehow compromises patriarchal power-structure, he becomes a sodomite. When a woman assumes power over her own body, she becomes a whore. Thomas Gainsford is eloquent on the subject in *The Rich Cabinet Furnished with varietie of Excellent Discriptions, exquisite Charracters, witty discourses, and delightful Histories, Devine and Morrall* (1616): 'A whore hath many significant names, as filth, curtisan, queane, strumpet, puncke, light-huswife, concubine, leman, love, mistresse, and infinite other fictions, according to mens fantasies; but all concluding, breach of chastity, and contempt of loyaltie, either to virginitie or mariage' (Gainsford 1616: 164v). 'Chastity' and 'loyalty' are concepts that make sense only with reference to men: a whore makes a 'breach' in male privilege, she shows 'contempt' for male priorities.

If the sodomite leers at the male end of the continuum we might suspect that something equivalent to a lesbian might occupy the other end. But that is not the case. Valerie Traub (1992a) has showed how the primacy of gender as a marker of erotic difference has the effect of making invisible any representation of female/female desire in early modern texts. To state it as baldly as possible: it seems to have been impossible for males in Shakespeare's time to imagine a female sexuality that did not include them. To say that are no representations of female/female sexual *acts* does not mean that there can be no representations of female/female *passion*. Traub finds an unmistakable eroticism in the way several pairs of Shakespeare's female characters – Helena and Hermia, Titania and her Indian votress, Emilia and Flavinia – speak of their feelings for one another in bodily terms. Paradoxically, what seems to make these speeches possible is the absence of bodily acts that are perceived to be threatening to men. Men's control of men's bodies is one thing; women's control of their own bodies is something else again. It is precisely the issue of control that separates the whore from the sodomite. Aufidius's servants may conflate the two – 'Our general himself makes a mistress of him,' they say of Aufidius and Coriolanus (IV. v. 199–200) – but the ends of the continuum remain distinct. At the 'male' end, sexual offence is very narrowly defined; at the 'female' end, it could hardly be broader. In early modern England it was very hard for a male to be branded as a sodomite, but it was very easy for a woman to be branded as a whore.

For all its flexibility, the continuum model preserves two indispensible binaries: male/female and subject/object. Indeed, it tends to conflate the two by positing a desiring male subject on the one hand and a desired female object on the other. In this respect, the model is only following the dictates of early modern genres and early modern speech. Suffolk's wooing of Margaret in *1 Henry VI* reveals at an early stage in Shakespeare's career just how the performance dynamics of 'lust in action' operate on the stage. '*Enter Suffoke with Margaret in his hand*,' says the F1 stage direction to the scene marked V. iv. in modern editions (Shakespeare 1623: 469). 'Be what thou wilt, thou art my prisoner.' Then comes the direction '*Gazes on her.*'

> O fairest beauty, do not fear nor fly,
> For I will touch thee but with reverent hands,
> And lay them gently on thy tender side.
>
> (V. iv. 1–4)

In the dialogue that follows, Suffolk is given a series of confidential asides in which he confesses his passion to the audience; Margaret is scripted to speak only to Suffolk. What the audience seems to be witnessing is an objectification of the desired body (Margaret's) and a subjectification of the desiring body (Suffolk's) via soliloquy. The same dynamic operates in scenes that are less obviously seductions. Othello's preparations to smother the sleeping Desdemona in V. ii appear to be just such a scene of subject/object relations in which the spectators' complicity is solicited on behalf of the desiring subject. So, too, does Aufidius's welcome to Coriolanus in IV. v. The objectification of the desired body seems to be be confirmed by the reticence, if not downright silence, imposed upon it by the speaking subject's declaration of desire. It was Laura's prerogative only to say no, or at least to remain silent, otherwise Petrarch would have had no occasion to write 366 *canzoniere*. Aufidius says erotically charged things to Coriolanus, but what does Coriolanus say in return? In Shakespeare's plays, as presumably in early modern English society, a man can say without shame that he desires to conjoin his body with the body of another male. Achilles does; Aufidius does; the Antonio of *Twelfth Night* does. What a man can*not* say without shame is that he wants to be so desired. The objects of Achilles's desire, of Aufidius's desire, of Antonio's desire are never scripted to say yes. Early modern English confirms this apparent objectification. It is significant that contemptuous slang words existed only for the supposedly passive object of male homoerotic desire – 'minion', 'ganymede', 'ingle' – and not for the desiring subject. Early modern English had still another name for this erotic object: 'boy'. When Coriolanus and Aufidius fall out with one another at the end of the play, the terms of estrangement are no less erotic – and no less violent – than the terms of endearment were before. The words of contempt that Aufidius hurls at his sometime enemy sometime ally provoke Coriolanus to cry out, 'Hear'st thou, Mars?' To which Aufidius replies, 'Name not the god, thou boy of tears' (V. vi. 100–1). In effect, Aufidius emasculates Coriolanus, turning subject into object, male into female.

In the very act of challenging, and in some cases inverting, these dynamics of gender representation, feminist criticism has helped to keep in place a set of binaries that may or may not inform 'lust in action' on the early modern stage. Take, for example, Suffolk's wooing of Margaret. Early modern ethical discourse persistently views desire itself as effeminate. An 'effeminate' man is one who desires women only too much – or, rather, he experiences sexual desire, gender of the object unspecified – in just the extreme terms that women supposedly do. The situation suggests a disjunction, not a congruence, between gender and subject position. Does Suffolk play the female in succumbing to desire? What about male listeners who attend to Suffolk's asides? What about female listeners who attend to Suffolk's asides? Do male listeners assume the subject position only of male speakers? Do female listeners assume the subject position only of female speakers? The complexities of theatrical performance suggest that even a continuum of sexual behaviours anchored in male/female distinctions may not, in the last analysis, be the most inclusive model. The grid lines separating male/female and subject/object are not absolute. In practice if not in theory, the continuum model tends to be complicit with its historical object of study. It replicates the power structure and the genre conventions of early modern England by leaving out all sorts of contingencies: women desiring women, women desiring men, men being desired by women, men being desired by men.

The problems with both the binary and the continuum models, as I see them, are three: (1) they reify sexuality as an object of study in terms anachronistic to the seventeenth century; (2) in practice if not in theory they accept gender as a 'master principle'; and (3) they endorse a distinction between the desiring and the desired that in effect denies status to the desired as a subject. All three problems pose particularly significant consequences for women. In pursuit of something different, let us mark off an open space.

'Lust in action' requires three things: bodies, place and time. Each of these three factors has received critical attention in its own right. Stephen Greenblatt (1988), Thomas Laqueur (1990) and Gail Kern Paster (1993) have anatomized the early modern body in terms radically different from the postmodern body. If early modern men and women understood their bodies in culture-specific terms, then surely their experience of 'lust of action' was dictated by those terms. If, for example, female genitalia were understood to be the inverse of male genitalia and the ovaries were understood to be inverted testicles, then female 'ejaculation' must have been consciously present, both to men and women, as a necessary condition for procreation. Concerning place, Stephen Mullaney (1988) has taken a census of the social geography of early modern London and directed us to see contiguities among brothels, bear-baiting pits and public theatres that are radically different from the linkages we ourselves would make. Of the three factors, time may be the most elusive, despite the fact that Stephen Hawking (1990) has popularized the idea that time has a history. To understand

'lust in action' in terms specific to early modern England, we
need to need to take account of bodies, place and time as
cultural variables. Our goal is a typology that would let us
position certain bodies in certain places at certain times. In a
phenomenologist's terms, we are isolating 'lust in action' and
'bracketing' it, setting it off from other kinds of experience and
trying to understand it on its own terms. We can begin the
project in approved new historicist fashion by reading representations of 'lust in action' in Shakespeare's plays and poems
against other kinds of texts: diaries, ethical treatises, medical
writings. To complete the project, however, we shall need to
configure these readings in terms more attuned to bodies,
places and times than to printed texts.

Concerning bodies, early modern writers communicate most
persistently a sense of estrangement, a sense that one's self and
one's person may occupy the same place at the same time, but
that they do not constitute one entity. James I is reported to
have made such an observation part of his 'ordinary discourse':

> God made one part of man of earth, the basest element[,] to
> teach him humilitie; his soul proceeded from the bosome of
> Himself, to teach him goodnesse; so that if he looks down-
> ward nothing is viler, if he cast his eyes to heaven he is of a
> matter more excellent then Angels; the former part was a
> type of *Adam*, the second of Christ, which gives life to that
> which was dead in itself.

> (James I 1643: 8)

One's self, that is to say, has an 'above' and a 'below'. For
women at least, Lear marks a precise point of division: 'Down
from the waist they are Centaurs, / Though women all above'
(*King Lear* IV. vi. 126–7). Under the sign of the Centaur lodge
ideas about the wandering womb ('Hysterica passio! down,
thou climbing sorrow! / Thy element's below' [*King Lear* II.
iv. 57–8]), about blood as the seat of lust ('When daffodils begin
to peer, / With heigh! the doxy over the dale, / Why then
comes in the sweet o'the year, / For the red blood reigns in the
winter's pale' [*The Winter's Tale* IV. iii. 1–4]), about humoral
affinities between lust and violence ('If the balance of our lives
had not one scale of reason, to peise another of sensuality, the
blood and baseness of our natures would conduct us to most
preposterous consclusions. But we have reason to cool our

raging motions, our carnal stings, our unbitted lusts' [*Othello* I. iii. 326–32).[4]

Under the sign of the Centaur also lodges 'filth'. 'Filth' hangs like a dirty fog in the diction of an unbroken series of plays from Shakespeare's mid-career: *Measure for Measure* (1603), *Othello* (1604), *All's Well That Ends Well* (1604), *Timon of Athens* (1605), *King Lear* (1605) and *Macbeth* (1606).[5] As a term of opprobrium, 'filth' has two valences, social and sexual. It is, presumably, the literal dirtiness of common people that prompts Sir William Cornwallis to use the term when he describes 'earthlings' gathered around a ballad-singer on the street and straining to hear 'a filthy noise' (Cornwallis 1600: sig. 117v) or Falstaff to boast to his cohorts, 'And I have not ballads made on you all, and sung to filthy tunes, let a cup of sack be my poison' (*1 Henry IV* II. ii. 43–5) (Greenblatt 1990b). The more powerful valence, however, is sexual. Gainsford in *The Rich Cabinet* makes the application viscerally immediate:

> Lechery is a filthinesse of such beastly varietie, that men may sinne with men, women with women: man may sinne by himselfe, by and with his owne wife, with beasts in abhominable prostitutions: with their own blouds and kinred in incestuous maner: with other mens wives in adulterous copulation: with all sorts in filthy licenciousnesse: and in all, both abuse GOD, and confound themselves in body and soule.
>
> (Gainsford 1616: 82v–83)

It is 'filthy vices' perpetrated by the likes of Claudio that Angelo presumes to police in *Measure for Measure* (II. iv. 42) – vices of which he himself becomes guilty, as Isabella tells Claudio, in an appropriation of Angelo's very words: 'His filth within being cast, he would appear / A pond as deep as hell' (III. i. 92–3). The filthiest filth of all is sodomy. Anyone who raises moral charges against poets, Sidney declares, ought to do the same against philosophers, 'as likewise one should do that should bid one read *Phaedrus* or *Symposium* in Plato, or the discourse of love in Plutarch, and see whether any poet do authorize abominable filthiness, as they do' (Sidney 1966: 58). The concatenation of social–sexual–sodomitical makes it hard to know just which sense of 'filth' is being invoked when Paroles describes Lafeu behind his back as a 'scurvy, old, filthy, scurvy lord' (*All's Well*

That Ends Well II. iii. 234), or when Mariana says of Paroles's solicitations on Bertram's behalf, 'a filthy officer he is in those suggestions for the young earl' (III. iv. 16–17), or when Prospero complains to Caliban, 'I have us'd thee, / Filth as thou art, with human care; and lodged thee / In mine own cell, till thou didst seek to violate / The honour of my child' (*The Tempest* I. ii. 347–50). In terms of one's own body, 'lust in action' is, in more ways than one, an *abandonment*, a movement from 'above' to 'below'. The 'below' toward which most of these speeches gesture is not the vagina but the anus. In terms of someone else's body, 'lust in action' is, as John Donne knows, polydirectional: 'Licence my roving hands, and let them goe / Behind, before, above, between, below' (Donne 1965: 15).

The impulse to *place* 'lust in action', to give it a local habitation and a name, can be witnessed in a gazetteer of the new found land to which Donne alludes in the elegy 'To his Mistris Going to Bed'. 'The City on the Hill' demands a Sodom on the plain (Warner 1994) – an ontological need that has dutifully been supplied in the original Atlantic coast colonies of the United States of America. No fewer than thirty-one places carry to this day the stigma of Puritan spiritual geography: Massachusetts has five sites, North Carolina five, Pennsylvania four, Connecticut three, Maine three, New York three, Vermont three, Rhode Island two, Georgia one, New Hampshire one, New Jersey one and West Virginia (originally part of Virginia) one. Beyond the colonies settled in the seventeenth and early eighteenth centuries there are only twelve localities named Sodom in the entire United States, only two of them west of the Mississippi River.[6] In early modern London 'lust in action' was likewise a place – or, rather, a ring of places, all of them just outside the City walls. The sexual geography of London, like that of all cities, was shaped by the intersection, or perhaps the overlay, of three factors: 'material forces, the power of ideas and the human desire to ascribe meaning' (Knopp 1995: 151). We can read that geography in the pamphlet celebrating the first performance of *The Comedy of Errors* during the Gray's Inn Christmas revels of 1594. *Gesta Grayorum* takes census of the fictional domain of the 'Prince of Purpool' who reigned over the festivities. Among the prince's tributaries are a number of taverners and at least one brothel-keeper:

Lucy Negro, Abbess *de Clerkenwell*, with the Lands and Privileges thereunto belonging, of the Prince of *Purpoole* by Night-Service in *Cauda*, and to find a Choir of Nuns, with burning Lamps, to chaunt *Placebo* to the Gentlemen of the Prince's Privy-Chamber, on the Day of His Excellency's Coronation.

(*Gesta Grayorum* 1968: 17)

Like her fellow subjects from Holborn, St Giles, Tottenham, Bloomsbury, Paddington, Islington, Kentish Town and Knightsbridge, Lucy of Clerkenwell occupies a position outside the City walls. Since 'Black Lucy' maintains title to her holdings 'by Night-Service in *Cauda*' (i.e. 'in the tail', with a pun on the legal obligation of 'entail'), her 'nuns' may have specialized in the filthy pleasure that self-proclaimed pornography like Aretino's *I modi* casts as the most titillating of all.[7] The sexual geography of *Gesta Grayorum* replicates that of built London and the fictional Vienna of *Measure for Measure* by consigning brothels to the outer reaches of civic space. In doing so it also situates Lucy and her cohorts socially and economically. In early modern London, as in most cities outside post-industrial North America, geographic centrality coincided with social centrality. To reach Clerkenwell Green from Gray's Inn one had to negotiate Fleet Ditch, notorious for its pestilential filth. Within the fictional realm of *Gesta Grayorum*, class differences, along with gender differences, are distanced, eroticized and assigned a commerical value. Like the body, the place of 'lust in action' is *classified* knowledge.

In addition to the impressions he recorded of performances of four of Shakespeare's plays, the astrologer Simon Foreman kept careful notes about just when, and on a few occasions just where, he managed to seduce women, some of whom had come to him for medical advice. '*Halekekeros harescum tauro*' ('fuck like a bull with a rabbit'?) is Foreman's private code for 'lust in action'. When Foreman does specify a place in his year-by-year self-chronicle, it is not a bedchamber but a garden. Avis Allen, a married woman who provoked an interminable series of fallings out and makings up, is the occasion of one such example in 1596: 'The 12th of March, Friday p.m. 30 past 5, I went to garden, where I found Avis Allen; we became friends again and I did halek, etc., cum illa' (Rowse 1974: 294). Not surprisingly, it was in a garden that Foreman had his most

adventurous sexual experience, an erotic dream about Queen
Elizabeth (Montrose 1988: 32–3). As places for erotic encounters, gardens had plenty to recommend them: the Fall of
Man in Genesis, the licence of pastoral poetry, the respites in
blissful bowers of romantic epic, and the exigencies of early
modern social life. Foreman's notes bear out Lena Orlin's
argument (1994a) that, aside from the long galleries of country
houses, gardens were the only places in which two people could
find conversational privacy in crowded early modern house-
holds. For people lacking gardens of their own, there were the
gardens of better-situated friends or the gardens attached to
cakes-and-ale houses just outside the City walls. The bed-trick
arranged by the Duke in *Measure for Measure* takes place in
just such a *hortus conclusus*, 'a garden circummured with brick'
(IV. i. 27).

To the spaces beyond garden walls – to the woods outside
Athens, to the Forest of Arden, to Illyria, to Mytilene – belong
the most extravagant erotic fantasies of all. Stubbes reserves
for the greenwood a description even more lurid than for the
theatre:

> Against *May, Whitsonday,* or other time, all the yung men and
> maides, old men and wives, run gadding over night to the
> woods, groves, hils, & mountains, where they spend the night
> in plesant pastimes; & in the morning they return, bringing
> with them birch & branches of trees, to deck their assemblies
> withall. . . . I have heard it credibly reported (and that *viva
> voce*) by men of great gravitie and reputation, that of fortie,
> threescore, or a hundred maides going to the wood over
> night, there have scarcely the third part of them returned
> home againe undefiled.
>
> (Stubbes 1877: 149)

The people Stubbes is talking about here are not the likes of
you and me, of course, but the filthy rabble, and the offenders
he singles out for special opprobrium are not the local young
men but the local maids. In place, as in body, 'lust in action'
involves a dislocation. As with the body, that dislocation
involves gender identity and class status. Jeanne Roberts has
imagined early modern Culture-with-a-capital-C as 'a central
Citadel defined by and for males', beyond which stretch three

overlapping reaches of the Wild: the animal Wild, the barbarian Wild and the female Wild (Roberts 1991: 26).

Taken altogether, this imaginative evidence challenges our own assumption that sexual acts belong to the privacy of one's own bedroom. As Lena Orlin (1994b) has demonstrated in great detail, attitudes toward privacy in early modern England were highly conflicted. Foreman's diary and Stubbes's fulminations, not to mention the settings of Shakespeare's comedies, suggest that the imaginative place of 'lust in action' was much larger than a private chamber. A circuit of images that begins in bed but ranges out through gardens and forests finds physical embodiment in several surviving sets of bed-hangings from the late sixteenth century. There are two elements to these hangings: horizontal valences stretched along the tester at the top of the bed and vertical curtains hung from the tester to the floor. The curtains, typically embroidered with repeated motifs of leaves, stalks and flowers, often in circular coils, can be drawn to enclose the sleepers in a space not unlike a bower. Sometimes embroidered on the valence are events that might take place within such a space – events that are as startlingly violent as erotic. Sets of valences preserved in the Victoria and Albert Museum depict Venus's fumblings with Adonis (T.879–1904) and Myrrha's incestuous designs on her father (T.879A–1904); another set, displayed in a loan exhibition at the Metropolitan Museum of Art, shows the story of Philomel, including a panel of the raped and mutilated Philomel working at a sixteenth-century embroidery frame. Lucrece's banquet is the subject of a bed cover in the Victoria and Albert. In a densely leaved bower, Lucrece is shown entertaining her soon-to-be ravisher along with another noble couple. In all these examples, tones of blue, green and yellow establish the verdant background against which the red of lust (uniformly faded now to a pale brown) performs its violent deeds.[8] The fact that these hangings were usually the product of female labour – sometimes the labour of the lady who slept in the bed – should warn us that the gender of the desiring subject, even in acts of sexual violence, need not always be male. Suburban brothel, garden, forest, curtained bed: the one thing these diverse spaces have in common is the fact that all are, in some sense, spaces *beyond*. 'Lust in action' asks not for a particular locale but for some kind of barrier – a wall, a ditch, a screen, a set of curtains –

that separates the *here* of ordinary experience from the *there* of sexual passion.

Because it lacks the physical presence of bodies and places, time may be the most elusive of the cultural coordinates of 'lust in action'. There are, so to speak, two faces or aspects to time, one external and one internal. The external signs, like the numerals on the face of a clock, can be plotted easily enough; the internal experience of time can be surmised from these external place-markers. However vague he may have been about *where*, Foreman was remarkably precise about *when*, usually specifying not only the day of the week but the hour and the minute of each '*halekekeros harescum tauro*'. The afternoon was, by far, his favoured hour. Only once does he record a turn at night, and that was with his wife. However typical or atypical Foreman's experiences may have been, Shakespeare echoes Stubbes in consigning 'lust in action' to the night. 'What hast thou been?' Lear asks 'Tom O'Bedlam'. 'A servingman, proud in heart and mind; that curl'd my hair, wore my gloves in my cap, serv'd the lust of my mistress' heart, and did the act of darkness with her' (*King Lear* III. iv. 84–8). If 'deeds of darkness' demand night, it is because they entail a breaching of distinctions and hierarchies that keep the daylight world in order – not least of all the hierarchies and distinctions that separate one's own person from others. Arthur Little (1993) and Kim Hall (1995) have showed how blackness – unfathomable, lustful, Other – works as a marker or reference point for constructing normative identity in early modern culture. Night covers the dislocations of *A Midsummer Night's Dream* and the bed-tricks of *Measure for Measure* and *All's Well That Ends Well*.

The time of 'lust in action' is not ordinary time. Morning, afternoon or night: peculiar to 'lust in action' is not a certain time *when* but a sense of time *out*. The external marks of that distinction have their internal counterparts. Scenes of *aubade*, the dawn leave-taking of lovers, stress again and again the disruption of time effected by a night of sexual passion. 'Night hath been too brief,' says Cressida. 'Beshrew the witch!' cries Troilus. 'With venomous wights she stays / As tediously as hell, but flies the grasps of love / With wings more momentary-swift than thought' (*Troilus and Cressida* IV. ii. 11–14). For Juliet, the night she has spent with Romeo will transform the ensuing time, turning minutes into days, hours into years (*Romeo and*

Juliet III. v. 43–7). The diurnal rhythm of *Romeo and Juliet,*
*A Midsummer Night's Dream, Troilus and Cressida, Measure for
Measure* and *All's Well That Ends Well* is day → night → day. This
external rhythm has its internal counterpart in an experience
of time that is slow → fast → slow. The compression of 'lust in
action' is effected against the restraints that precede that action
and the relaxation that follows it. Mistress Quickly, like 'Black
Lucy', makes time fast.

What we have managed to bracket here is a culture-specific
configuration of time, place and body: time *out,* place *beyond,*
body *below, around, on, from, with, within, without.* The shape of
the space we have isolated is neither binary nor linear. It is a
space that allows for the interplay of all sorts of contingencies.
Unlike the binary model, it does not privilege one set of
determinants over another. *Above/below, within/beyond, in time/
time out* are, to be sure, binaries, but they have signifying power
only in relationship to one another. Unlike the continuum
model, which treats sexual behaviour as a text, the space we
have created situates the sexual subject within physical coordinates, within a series of spatial prepositions. What we have,
as these spatial reference points suggest, is a perceptual space,
defined by the horizons of seeing, hearing, touching, tasting
and smelling. What we have is a circle.

Circles exclude; they simultaneously include. By bracketing
bodies, place and time we have been able to set off 'lust in
action' from other kinds of experience outside the circle. If we
grant a certain autonomy to experience inside the circle, in
what terms can we read it? Just what does the circle inscribe?
There are several ways of considering the matter. One answer
is implied by the play on ring and vagina with which Graziano
nervously brings *The Merchant of Venice* to a close: 'Well, while
I live I'll fear no other thing / So sore, as keeping safe Nerissa's
ring' (V. i. 306–7). In Graziano's view the circle is – or *should*
be – a thoroughly controlled space, the sphere of the known,
the familiar, the orderly. It is a domain of male privilege and
social hierarchy, assured through marriage. In Barish's terms,
the circle inscribes 'an ideal of stasis'. In terms of contemporary
critical theory, this is just the kind of space that new historicism
hopes to chart. It is a space made up of cultural variables,
interacting in complicated and elusive ways, but a space that

none the less includes documentary 'facts', positive data that can be known and mastered.

On the other hand, the circle may be a frighteningly *empty* space, just as Graziano fears. As such, it is the domain of the unspeakable. What Shakespeare's characters, even his female characters, *can* say when it comes to 'lust in action' had become a social embarrassment within a generation of Shakespeare's retirement.[9] Mercutio knows all about such licence. Looking in vain for his lovestruck friend, Mercutio makes fun of Romeo: 'Now will he sit under a medlar tree, / And wish his mistress were that kind of fruit / As maids call medlars when they laugh alone' (*Romeo and Juliet* II. i. 34–6). In just such bawdy terms do Shakespeare's maids sometimes talk, for example Julia and Lucetta in *Two Gentlemen of Verona* II. vii. On occasion, female characters exchange bawdy jests one for one with male characters, as Desdemona does with Iago in *Othello* II. i. 117–66 and Helen with Paroles in *All's Well That Ends Well* I. i. 104–82. Only one sexual act seems to have been truly unspeakable – or at least unprintable. 'O *Romeo* that she were, ô that she were / An open, or thou a Poprin Peare' (Shakespeare 1599: sig. D1v): Jonathan Goldberg (1992) has demonstrated how the 'open, or' of the 1599 quarto of *Romeo and Juliet*, like the 'open *Et Caetera*' of the play's first printing two years earlier, conceals the 'open arse' that modern editors have accepted into the text – an opening that undoes all the anachronistic heterosexual assumptions that have secured *Romeo and Juliet* a place in high school textbooks.

If anal intercourse seems to be the one inadmissible form of sexual behaviour in Shakespeare's scripts, there are several reasons why. In physiological terms, the anus figures as the ultimate site of the body's fleshly materiality, its fundamental filthiness. In terms of gender, the anus is, furthermore, disturbingly *un*gendered. David Halperin (1992) has observed how the Adonis-figure, so often the focus of erotic attention in Renaissance painting and Renaissance verse, fetishizes specific body-parts – flashing eyes, rosy lips, a smooth chin, a white neck and ripe young buttocks – that can be found both in maidens and prepubescent boys. In social terms, anal intercourse is the very thing that early modern sodomy laws were set up to police. Sir Edward Coke's formula for sodomy indictments insists on '*res in re*', on 'the thing inside the thing'

(Coke 1660: 60). In epistemological terms, finally, the anus is a void, a dark vortex that leads into decay and annihilation: the anus is the fissure of deconstruction par excellence. Gainsford catches this threat of annihilation in one of his witty turns on whores: 'A whore cannot be better compared then to deep pits, from whence it is easier to keep oneself from falling than, once fallen, to recover out' (Gainsford 1616: 165–165v). 'Lust in action', no less than the desire that motivates it, is always the deferred signified (Belsey 1994: 42–71). Darkness, marginality, the body 'below' are a chain of signifiers that gesture toward a certain space, but they do not fill that space: they circumscribe it.

If not the fact-filled space investigated by new historicism, if not the empty space implied by deconstruction, the configuration of time, place and body that we have been bracketing here constitutes a performative space – the kind of space inhabited by phenomenology as a critical method. As such, it is not so much a cognitive space as a specular and oracular space. We need, then, to qualify the original question: who, *in these particular circumstances*, is the sexual subject? Within the circle of 'lust in action' there is not one configuration of time, place and bodies but three: one that contains the characters within Shakespeare's fictions, one that contains the original consumers of those fictions, and one that contains us as observers of the other two. If the circle as a model for reading 'lust in action' has any heuristic power, that power derives from an appreciation of the differences in body, place and time that set these three sets of subjects apart from each other. Let us examine the three configurations one by one and speculate on the relationships among them.

Within Shakespeare's fictions, 'lust in action' is something heard about or read about, not something seen directly. *The Rape of Lucrece* is not, strictly speaking, about rape at all: the sexual act itself is signified by a blank space between stanzas at lines 686 and 687 and by an abrupt shift from present tense to present perfect: 'But she hath lost a dearer thing than life, / And he hath won that he would lose again' (687–8). In the sonnets, sexual acts likewise belong to the province of present perfect. Onstage, to be sure, bodies are scripted to touch bodies in present tense: to grab, to clasp, to kiss, to smother, to strangle, to stab. And Shakespeare's verbal bawdy comes very much from *this* side of Freud's sexual unconscious. But 'sex' itself is much less *there* in Shakespeare's texts than either the binary or the continuum models might lead us to suppose. On the stage, in manuscript, on the printed page, 'lust in action' is represented obliquely, through gestures toward an offstage, off-the-page reality. If not the absence of the signified, 'lust in action' is the absence of the signifier. Thomas Nashe catches the situation exactly in the boast he makes before the most infamous pornographic poem in early modern English, 'The Choice of Valentines':

> Complaints and praises everyone can write,
>   And passion-out their pangs in stately rhymes,
>   But of love's pleasures none did ever write
> That hath succeeded in these latter times.
>
> (Nashe 1972: 458)

That is to say, most love poetry is all about the *before*, not the *during*. The usual temporal, spatial and corporeal parameters of 'lust in action' are specified in sonnet 129: 'Before, a joy propos'd; behind, a dream.' In Shakespeare's plays and poems 'lust in action' is always a matter of synecdoche.

It is tempting to talk about 'before' and 'behind' in terms of liminality, to isolate the kind of social and psychological work that may be going on during the 'time out' of sexual passion, and to ask whether that work is subversive or constitutive of the social order. In phenomenological terms, however, the important thing is the *beforeness* and the *behindness* of the experience. What happens before and what happens after seem much too contingent for a pat structuralist answer. Amid these contingencies one thing is certain: 'before' and 'behind' happen to coincide with the only aspects of 'lust in action' that are representable. Bodies in certain postures constitute an object-ive fact, but lust is a subjective experience. 'Lust in action' is something felt, not seen. The trope of 'before' finds its most obvious instances in comic endings that point toward a sexual consummation that will take place just outside the frame of the fiction. 'Proceed, proceed. We will so begin these rites, / As we do trust they'll end, in true delights' (*As You Like It* V. iv. 196–7): the couplet with which Duke Senior closes *As You Like It* plays one variation on a coy pattern that is repeated in the final scenes of *Two Gentlemen of Verona*, *The Taming of the Shrew*,

A Midsummer Night's Dream, Much Ado About Nothing, Twelfth Night, Measure for Measure, All's Well That Ends Well and *Pericles*. Even within the fiction, seduction always points to an action that will happen in another time and another place.

Valerie Traub (1992a) has pointed out how 'lesbian' desire in early modern texts is always already over, while in my own work I have stressed how pastoral provides a device for distancing the homoerotic desires of male adolescence (Smith 1991: 79–115). This *behindness* may, in fact, be characteristic of *all* representations of erotic experience. Certainly that is the case for the reader or spectator, who witnesses the present re-enactment of a fictionally past experience. Stage representation of the passion of Antony and Cleopatra demonstrates how 'behind' can be every bit as powerful as 'before'. The play begins with the couple's passion as an accomplished fact: 'Nay, but this dotage of our general's / O'erflows the measure' (I. i. 1–2) are the first words in the play. What the audience hears and sees thereafter is an extended series of variations on scenes of parting. The one scene in the play that most patently plays out the trope, Antony's arming to go off to battle in IV. iv, reveals the immense differences in time, place and body that separate these scenes of *aubade* from their youthful counterparts in *Romeo and Juliet* III. v. and *Troilus and Cressida* IV. ii. As ways of framing 'lust in action', 'before' and 'behind' refuse, however, to retain their separateness. One is always implicated in the other. 'Behind' makes emotional sense only in terms of 'before'; 'before' can anticipate an inevitable 'behind'. Interplay between 'before' and 'behind' is especially remarkable in the scenes of erotic posturing between weary Orsino and earnest 'Cesario'.

> Now, good Cesario, but that piece of song,
> That old and antic song we heard last night;
> Methought it did relieve my passion much,
> More than light airs and recollected terms
> Of these most brisk and giddy-paced times.
> Come, but one verse.
>
> (*Twelfth Night* II. iv. 2–7)

The song figures as a token of erotic exchange between Orsino and 'Cesario', far in advance of any such exchange in body – an exchange that takes place, true to form, just outside the fiction. As a means to 'relieve' his passion, the song is recalled by Orsino – and shared with 'Cesario' – just as if it were an erotic memory. That the song turns out to be a song about death, 'Come away, come away death, / And in sad cypress let me be laid', complicates 'before' by insinuating an even more distant 'behind'. Orsino's desire is a verbal tissue of night, violence, memory and anticipation. For the characters in Shakespeare's fictions, 'lust in action' is something that is yet to happen, has happened already – or both. But the action itself is not present in the fiction.

Hence, perhaps, its attraction to the original consumers of the fiction. With respect to *Antony and Cleopatra*, Jonathan Dollimore locates the rhetorical power of Cleopatra's final speeches precisely in the absence of Antony (Dollimore 1984: 207). Why should that be so? For the theatre, for the manuscript culture in which the sonnets were first circulated, for the printed books in which *Venus and Adonis* and *The Rape of Lucrece* were first published the key question is how the configuration of place, time and bodies *within* the fiction might be transposed *outside* the fiction in such a way that listeners, spectators and readers could read the synecdoche of 'lust in action' and supply the imagined whole for the inscribed part. Let us begin with the body. The consumer's body is not below, around, on, from, with, within, without, but *opposite*: she remains on *this* side of the barrier that marks the erotic 'beyond'. In the theatre the spectator stands or sits opposite the represented action; with printed book or manuscript the reader touches the representing medium with his body but keeps it, literally, at arm's length.

The simultaneous transparency and opacity of illusion that we can readily see in the theatre – the illusion's quality of being *there* but *not* there at the same time – is also true of the book. The book in hand is a material thing, just as the bodies of actors in the theatre are material things, but, as Susan Stewart observes, the book as an object

> has a life of its own, a life outside human time, the time of the body and its voice. . . . The book stands in tension with history, a tension reproduced in the microcosm of the book itself, where reading takes place in time across marks which have been made in space. Moreover, because of this tension, all events recounted within the text have an effect

of distancing, an effect which serves to make the text both transcendent and trivial and to collapse the distinction between the real and the imagined.

(Stewart 1993: 22)

With respect to time and place, then, the act of reading is no less an experience *within* a set of physical coordinates than the act of watching and hearing a play. Nor is reading less of a social experience. Crammed into the theatre, or isolated with the book, the consumer's body is not only opposite but *among*. The three modes of communication – theatre, print and manuscript – would seem to imply increasing degrees of privacy and intimacy, from the inclusiveness of the theatre through the relative selectivity of print to the exclusivity of shared manuscripts. And yet all three modes of imagining 'lust in action' involve a tension between the individual and the group, between 'mine' and 'ours'. Mary Hobbs (1992) and Arthur F. Marotti (1995) have demonstrated how the commercial success of print transformed manuscript culture into a way for subcultures like universities, political factions and religious sects to affirm their identity and maintain a sense of community. Shakespeare's 'sugar'd sonnets among his private friends' would, by this measure, have spoken as much about 'us' as about 'him' the poet or 'me' the reader. *Venus and Adonis* and *The Rape of Lucrece* declare their affinity with the culture of the inns of court through their similarity to Ovid-inspired works more explicitly associated with young gentlemen of the inns of court, works like Middleton's *The Metamorphosis of Pygmalion's Image* (Finkelpearl 1969: 3–80; Smith 1991: 102–3). In the inns of court, if anywhere, was to be found the 'community of readers' posited by reader-response criticism (Fish 1980). In a sense, then, the reading of 'lust in action' is always a group activity. With respect to place, 'public' and 'private' might usefully be thought about, not as separate entities, but as states of being that, in varying degrees, are co-present in one another: psychologically in manuscript and on the printed page, physically as well as psychologically in the theatre.

When we configure body, place and time for the consumer against body, place and time for characters in the fiction, we confront the consumer's privileged position as a sexual subject: omniscient, omnipresent, omnifarious. Tricking the drunken

Christopher Sly into thinking he is a lord, the conspirators in *The Taming of the Shrew* offer their dupe a roster of visual pleasures from which he can choose – and in the process set in place a paradigm of voyeuristic pleasure that informs *all* representations of 'lust in action':

> SECOND SERVING MAN
> Dost thou love pictures? We will fetch thee straight
> Adonis painted by a running brook,
> And Cytherea all in sedges hid,
> Which seem to move and wanton with her breath
> Even as the waving sedges play with wind.
> LORD
> We'll show thee Io as she was a maid,
> And how she was beguiléd and surpris'd,
> As lively painted as the deed was done.
> THIRD SERVING MAN
> Or Daphne roaming through a thorny wood,
> Scratching her legs that one shall swear she bleeds,
> And at that sight shall sad Apollo weep,
> So workmanly the blood and tears are drawn.
> *(The Taming of the Shrew, Induction ii. 50–61)*

Sly will get to enjoy not just a representation of Daphne but of Apollo watching Daphne, not just a representation of Adonis but of Venus watching Adonis. Apollo and Venus, the desiring subjects in the fiction, become themselves the desired objects of Sly, the desiring subject outside the fiction. The voyeur thus becomes the subject in two senses: he finds points of reference within the fiction with which he imaginatively identifies at the same time that he objectifies the entire fiction. In a sense, Sly can be both in the fiction and outside it. That is an especially comfortable position to be in when the representation at hand breaches taboos, as for example when a play solicits the spectators' complicity in homoeroticized violence (Smith 1995). As Lynda Boose observes about the death-scene in *Othello* – the first erotic bed-scene on the early modern stage: 'while the action accuses, the picture seduces' (Boose 1987a: 142).

Rather than thinking of subject and object as fixed entities set in opposition to one another, we might more usefully think of them in a dialectical relationship. Merleau-Ponty's investigation of 'The Body in its Sexual Being' locates individual consciousness in just such a dialectic. As the possessor of a body, I can become the object of someone else's gaze; I can also assert my subjecthood by gazing upon that person's body, turning it into an object. But neither alternative is entirely satisfying:

> this mastery is self-defeating, since, precisely when my value is recognized through the other's desire, he is no longer the person by whom I wished to be recognized, but a being fascinated, deprived of his freedom, and who therefore no longer counts in my eyes. Saying that I have a body is thus a way of saying that I can be seen as an object and that I try to be seen as a subject, that another can be my master or my slave, so that shame and shamelessness express the dialectic of the plurality of consciousnesses, and have a metaphysical significance. The same might be said of sexual desire. . . . What we try to possess is not just a body, but a body brought to life by consciousness.
>
> (Merleau-Ponty 1962: 167)

That is to say, the sexually desiring subject needs the subject-hood of the desired object. Within the fiction, that need entails constantly shifting relations between subject and object, master and slave. Outside the fiction, it entails constantly shifting relations between the consumer and the points of identification within the fiction. Opportunity for the spectator/listener/reader to shift positions seems, in fact, to be one of the distinguishing features of representations of 'lust in action'. As a poem written by a male poet but offering its readers a subject position that is female, *Venus and Adonis* provides numerous moments when the gender identity of the reading subject is susceptible to metamorphosis. The opportunity is especially ripe in passages where Adonis is effeminized as passive and pale:

> Full gently now she takes him by the hand,
> A lily prisoned in a jail of snow,
> Or ivory in an alabaster band;
> So white a friend engirds so white a foe.
>   This beauteous combat, wilful and unwilling,
>   Showed like two silver doves that sit a-billing.
>
> (361–6)

Who is the sexual subject here and what is its gender? Do we
have a male (the reader) watching a female (Venus) watching
a male (Adonis)? A male (the reader) watching a male (the
narrator) watching a male (Adonis)? A male (the reader)
watching a female (Venus) watching a female (Adonis as
androgynous body)? A female (the reader) watching a female
(Venus) watching a female (Adonis as androgynous body)? A
female (the reader) watching a male (the narrator) watching a
male (Adonis?) A female (the reader) watching a female (Venus)
watching a male (Adonis)? Within the fiction, the voyeur/
reader is neither subject nor object   and yet both. The only
check on her freedom is the gaze of another – a gaze that may
come from left, right or behind but never from the fictional
bodies that are opposite. Hence the consumer's licence to know
omnisciently, to move omnipresently, to exist omnifariously.

With respect to bodies, place and time, *we* as sexual subjects
occupy a position different yet again from sexual subjects
within the fiction and sexual subjects as consumers of the
fiction. Time for us is not the compressed time of sexual union
or the two hours' traffic of the stage or the time it takes to read
the 1855 lines of *The Rape of Lucrece* or 154 sonnets but the
malleable, tractable time of analytical thought. The place we
occupy is not the crowded public space of the Globe or even
the intimate space that separates the reading eye from the book-
holding hand, but the calibrated distance that separates eyes
and hands from the computer monitor. The bodies we call our
own are not the estranged, filthy bodies of Protestant theology
but the medicalized, psychologized, politically radicalized
bodies of postmodern culture. The circle within which we
perform as academics and students is much more adept than
the theatre at denying its contingency. And the knowledge we
produce is not about 'lust in action'. In this regard, Merleau-
Ponty draws a useful distinction between 'comprehension' and
'understanding':

> Erotic perception is not a *cogitatio* which aims at a *cogitatum*;
> through one body it aims at another body, and takes place
> in the world, not in consciousness. A sight has a sexual
> significance for me, not when I consider, even confusedly, its
> possible relationship to the sexual organs or to pleasurable
> states, but when it exists for my body, for that power always

available for bringing together into an erotic situation the stimuli applied, and adapting sexual conduct to it. There is an erotic 'comprehension' not of the order of understanding, since understanding subsumes an experience, once perceived, under some idea, while desire comprehends blindly by linking body to body.

(Merleau-Ponty 1962: 157)

Academic discourse about sexuality – however self-reflexive it may be about the gap of time and cultural difference that separates postmodern analysis from early modern text, however attentive it may be to historical constructions of the body, however committed it may be to a contemporary politics of the body – assumes a very different relationship with the body than fictional discourse does: academic discourse turns the body into an object, an entity that exists apart from the perceiver. In Merleau-Ponty's words, 'to thought, the body as an object is not ambiguous; it becomes so only in the experience which we have of it, and pre-eminently in sexual experience, and through the fact of sexuality' (1962: 167). The circular model asks us to talk about sexual experience, not *on* the body, but *through* the body.

The sexual subject in Shakespeare belies the definite article: there exists not one subject, but three subjects, each occupying a different performative space. The circular model attends to these differences. To the polarities of the binary model the circle adds an experiential dimension. The sexual subject may be positioned according to the difference-marking of various discourses, but that position is experienced in terms of prepositions: below, around, on, from, with, within, without, beyond, out, before, behind. Within the circle, the constructions of the continuum model become subject to all sorts of contingencies: sexual behaviour is seen, not as a prescribed given, but as a range of possibilities that can be called into play under certain circumstances. Unlike the binary and the linear models, which turn sexuality into an object of cerebral knowledge, the circular model *subjectifies* sexuality. It attempts to see it, hear it, touch it. Finally, unlike the other two models, which insist on a rigid distinction between subject and object, the circular model investigates ways in which objects of 'lust in action' can become subjects; and subjects, objects – especially when the 'subject' in question is a detached observer of someone else's subjectivity. If such an approach is phenomenological criticism, it belongs not to a superseded moment in critical dialogue of the 1950s and 1960s but to a dialectical move beyond post-structuralism – a move that incorporates the political lessons of the past twenty years. It is concerned, not with the-*author*-in-the-work, as earlier phenomenological criticism was, but with the-looking-hearing-reading-*subject*-in-the-work. What the circle model inscribes is both politics and poetics.

6
How to read *The Merchant of Venice* without being heterosexist
ALAN SINFIELD

It has been recognized for a long time that *The Merchant of Venice* is experienced as insulting by Jewish people, who constitute a minority in Western Europe and North America. So powerful, though, is the reputation of Shakespeare's all-embracing 'humanity' that this scandal has often been set aside. Nevertheless, in 1994 a newspaper article entitled 'Shylock, Unacceptable Face of Shakespeare?' described how directors were acknowledging that the text requires radical alterations before it can be produced in good faith.[1] David Thacker at the Royal Shakespeare Company was changing some of Shylock's most famous lines and moving scenes around. And Jude Kelly at the West Yorkshire Playhouse was presenting a Portia ready to embrace racist attitudes in her determination to be worthy of her father and a Jessica weeping inconsolably at the end as she laments her loss of her Jewish heritage.

For some commentators, it is a sign of the deterioration of our cultures that minority out-groups should feel entitled to challenge the authority of Shakespeare. Christopher Booker, writing in the *Daily Telegraph* in 1992, complained bitterly about an English Shakespeare Company production of *The Merchant* set in 1930s Italy, with Shylock as a suave, sophisticated modern Jewish businessman confronted by fascists. 'In other words,' Booker writes, 'the producer had given up on any distasteful (but Shakespearean) idea of presenting Shylock as an archetypal cringing old miser. He really had to be more sympathetic than the "Christians".' To Booker this was 'bleatings about racism', whereas 'Shakespeare so wonderfully evokes something infinitely more real and profound . . . a cosmic view of human nature which is just as true now as it was in his own day' (Booker 1992).

The problem is not limited to Jewish people. The Prince of Morocco is made to begin by apologizing for his colour – 'Mislike me not for my complexion,' he pleads (II. i. 1), taking it for granted that Portia will be prejudiced. And he is right, for already she has declared her distaste: 'if he have the condition of a saint, and the complexion of a devil, I had rather he should shrive me than wive me' (I. ii. 123–5); and after Morocco has bet on the wrong casket she concludes: 'Let all of his complexion choose me so' (II. vii. 79). And how might gay men regard the handling of Antonio's love for Bassanio, or the traffic in boys that involves Launcelot, the disguised Jessica, the disguised Nerissa and the disguised Portia?

The question of principle is how readers not situated squarely in the mainstream of Western culture today may relate to such a powerful cultural icon as Shakespeare. In a notable formulation, Kathleen McLuskie points out that the pattern of 'good' and 'bad' daughters in *King Lear* offers no point of entry to the ideas about women that a feminist criticism might want to develop; such criticism 'is restricted to exposing its own exclusion from the text' (McLuskie, 1985: 97).[2] This challenge has caused some discomfort: must exclusion from Shakespeare be added to the other disadvantages that women experience in our societies? But it has not, I think, been successfully answered. In this essay I pursue the question as it strikes a gay man.

I Antonio vs. Portia

As W. H. Auden suggested in an essay in *The Dyer's Hand* in 1962, the *The Merchant of Venice* makes best sense if we regard Antonio as in love with Bassanio (Auden 1963; see also Midgley 1960). In the opening scene their friends hint broadly at it. Then, as soon as Bassanio arrives, the others know they should leave the two men together – 'We leave you now with better company. . . . My Lord Bassanio, since you have found

Antonio / We two will leave you' (I. i. 59, 69–70). Only Gratiano is slow to go, being too foolish to realize that he is intruding (I. i. 73–118). As soon as he departs, the tone and direction of the dialogue switch from formal banter to intimacy, and the cause of Antonio's sadness emerges:

> Well, tell me now what lady is the same
> To whom you swore a secret pilgrimage –
> That you to-day promis'd to tell me of?
>
> (I. i. 119–21)

Bassanio moves quickly to reassure his friend and to ask his help: 'to you Antonio / I owe the most in money and in love' (I. i. 130–1). The mercenary nature of Bassanio's courtship, which troubles mainstream commentators who are looking for a 'good' heterosexual relationship, is Antonio's reassurance. It allows him to believe that Bassanio will continue to value their love, and gives him a crucial role as banker of the enterprise.

Whether Antonio's love is what we call sexual is a question which, this essay will show, is hard to frame, let alone answer. But certainly his feelings are intense. When Bassanio leaves for Belmont, as Salerio describes it, he offers to 'make some speed / Of his return'. 'Do not so,' Antonio replies:

> And even there (his eye being big with tears),
> Turning his face, he put his hand behind him,
> And with affection wondrous sensible
> He wrung Bassanio's hand, and so they parted.
>
> (II. viii. 37–8, 46–9)

The intensity, it seems, is not altogether equal. As Auden observes in his poem 'The More Loving One', the language of love celebrates mutuality but it is unusual for two people's loves to match precisely:

> If equal affection cannòt be,
> Let the more loving one be me.
>
> (Auden 1969: 282)

Antonio the merchant, like Antonio in *Twelfth Night* and the Shakespeare of the sonnets, devotes himself to a relatively casual, pampered younger man of a higher social class.

In fact, Antonio in the *Merchant* seems to welcome the chance to sacrifice himself: 'pray God Bassanio come / To see me pay his debt, and then I care not' (III. iii. 35–6). *Then* Bassanio would have to devote himself to Antonio:

> You cannot better be employ'd Bassanio,
> Than to live still and write mine epitaph.
>
> (IV. i. 117–18)

As Keith Geary observes, Antonio's desperate bond with Shylock is his way of holding on to Bassanio (Geary 1984: 63–4); when Portia saves Antonio's life, Lawrence W. Hyman remarks, she is preventing what would have been a spectacular case of the 'greater love' referred to in the Bible (John 15:13), when a man lays down his life for his friend (Hyman 1970: 112).

That theme of amatory sacrifice contributes to an air of homoerotic excess, especially in the idea of being bound and inviting physical violation. When Bassanio introduces Antonio to Portia as the man 'To whom I am so infinitely bound', she responds:

> You should in all sense be much bound to him,
> For (as I hear) he was much bound for you.
>
> (V. i. 135–7)

At the start, Antonio lays open his entire self to Bassanio:

> be assur'd
> My purse, my person, my extremest means
> Lie all unlock'd to your occasions.
>
> (I. i. 137–9)

Transferring this credit – 'person' included – to Shylock's bond makes it more physical, more dangerous and more erotic:

> let the forfeit
> Be nominated for an equal pound
> Of your fair flesh, to be cut off and taken
> In what part of your body pleaseth me.
>
> (I. iii. 144–7)

In the court, eventually, it is his breast that Antonio is required to bear to the knife, but in a context where apparent boys may be disguised girls and Portia's suitors have to renounce marriage altogether if they choose the wrong casket, Shylock's penalty sounds like castration. Indeed, Antonio offers himself to the knife as 'a tainted wether of the flock'; that is, a castrated ram (IV. i. 114).

The seriousness of the love between Antonio and Bassanio is manifest, above all, in Portia's determination to contest it. Simply, she is at a disadvantage because of her father's casket device, and wants to ensure that her husband really is committed to her. The key critical move, which Hyman and Geary make, is to reject the sentimental notion of Portia as an innocent, virtuous, 'Victorian' heroine. Harry Berger regards her 'noble' speeches as manipulations: 'Against Antonio's failure to get himself crucified, we can place Portia's divine power of mercifixion; she never rains but she pours.' Finally, she mercifies Antonio by giving him back his ships (Berger 1981: 161–2; see Hyman 1970; Geary 1984).

Antonio's peril moves Bassanio to declare a preference for him over Portia:

> Antonio, I am married to a wife
> Which is as dear to me as life itself,
> But life itself, my wife, and all the world,
> I would lose all, ay sacrifice them all
> Here to this devil, to deliver you.

Portia, standing by as a young doctor, is not best pleased:

> Your wife would give you little thanks for that
> If she were by to hear you make the offer.
>
> (IV. i. 278–85)

It is to contest Antonio's status as lover that Portia, in her role of young doctor, demands of Bassanio the ring which she had given him in her role of wife. Antonio, unaware that he is falling for a device, takes the opportunity to claim a priority in Bassanio's love:

> My Lord Bassanio, let him have the ring,
> Let his deservings and my love withal
> Be valued 'gainst your wife's commandement.
>
> (IV. ii. 445–7)

The last act of the play is Portia's assertion of her right to Bassanio. Her strategy is purposefully heterosexist: in disallowing Antonio's sacrifice as a plausible reason for parting with the ring, she disallows the entire seriousness of male love. She is as offhand with Antonio as she can be with a guest:

> Sir, you are very welcome to our house:
> It must appear in other ways than words,
> Therefore I scant this breathing courtesy.
>
> (V. i. 139–41)

She will not even admit Antonio's relevance: 'I am th'unhappy subject of these quarrels', he observes; 'Sir, grieve not you, – you are welcome not withstanding', she abruptly replies (V. i. 238–9). Once more, self-sacrifice seems to be Antonio's best chance of staying in the game, so he binds himself in a different project: *not* to commit his body again to Bassanio in a way that will claim a status that challenges Portia:

> I once did lend my body for his wealth,
> Which but for him that had your husband's ring
> Had quite miscarried. I dare be bound again,
> My soul upon the forfeit, that your lord
> Will never more break faith advisedly.
>
> (V. i. 249–53)

Portia seizes brutally on the reminiscence of the earlier bond: 'Then you shall be his surety' (V. i. 254). Antonio's submission is what she has been waiting for. Now she restores Bassanio's status as husband by revealing that she has the ring after all, and Antonio's viability as merchant – and his ability to return to his trade in Venice by giving him letters that she has been withholding.

A gay reader might think: well, never mind; Bassanio wasn't worth it, and with his wealth restored, Antonio will easily find another impecunious upper-class friend to sacrifice himself to. But, for most audiences and readers, the air of 'happy ending' suggests that Bassanio's movement towards heterosexual relations is in the necessary, the right direction (like Shylock's punishment, perhaps). As Coppélia Kahn reads the play, 'In Shakespeare's psychology, men first seek to mirror themselves in a homoerotic attachment . . . then to confirm themselves through difference, in a bond with the opposite sex – the marital bond' (Kahn 1985: 106). And Janet Adelman, in a substantial analysis of male bonding in Shakespeare's comedies, finds that 'We do not move directly from family bonds to marriage without an intervening period in which our friendships with same-sex friends help us to establish our identities'

(Adelman 1985: 75). To heterosexually identified readers this might not seem an exceptional thought, but for the gay man it is a slap in the face of very familiar kind. 'You can have these passions,' it says, 'but they are not sufficient, they should be a stage on the way to something else. So don't push it.'

To be sure, Kahn points out that 'it takes a strong, shrewd woman like Portia to combat the continuing appeal of such ties between men' (1985: 107). And Adelman remarks the tendency towards casuistical 'magical restitutions' and the persistence of 'tensions that comedy cannot resolve' (1985: 80). So hetero-patriarchy is not secured without difficulty or loss. None the less, when Adelman writes 'We do not move directly . . . to marriage', the gay man may ask, 'Who are "We"?' And when Kahn says 'men first seek to mirror themselves in a homoerotic attachment', the gay man may wonder whether he is being positioned as not-man, or just forgotten altogether. If Antonio is excluded from the good life at the end of the *Merchant*, so the gay man is excluded from the play's address. The fault does not lie with Kahn and Adelman (though in the light of recent work in lesbian and gay studies they might want to formulate their thoughts rather differently). They have picked up well enough the mood and tendency of the play, as most readers and audiences would agree. It is the Shake-spearean text that is reconfirming the marginalization of an already marginalized group.

II Property and sodomy

The reader may be forgiven for thinking that, for a comment-ator who has claimed to be excluded from the *Merchant*, this gay man has already found quite a lot to say. Perhaps the love that dared not speak its name is becoming the love that won't shut up. In practice, there are (at least) two routes through the *Merchant* for out-groups. One involves pointing out the mechan-isms of exclusion in our cultures – how the circulation of Shakespearean texts may reinforce the privilege of some groups and the subordination of others. I have just been trying to do this. Another involves exploring the ideological structures in the playtexts – of class, race, ethnicity, gender and sexuality – that facilitate these exclusions. These structures will not be the same as the ones we experience today, but they may throw light upon our circumstances and stimulate critical awareness of how our life-possibilities are constructed.[3]

In *The Merchant*, the emphasis on the idea of being boun displays quite openly the way ideological structures work. Through an intricate network of enticements, obligations and interdictions – in terms of wealth, family, gender, patronage and law – this culture sorts out who is to control property and other human relations. Portia, Jessica and Launcelot are bound as daughters and sons; Morocco and Arragon as suitors; Antonio and Bassanio as friends; Gratiano as friend or dependant, Nerissa as dependant or servant, and Launcelot as servant; Antonio, Shylock and even the Duke are bound by the law; and the Venetians, Shylock rather effectively remarks, have no intention of freeing their slaves (IV. i. 90–8).

Within limits, these bonds may be negotiable: the Duke may commission a doctor to devise a way round the law, friendships may be redefined, servants may get new masters, women and men may contract marriages. Jessica can even get away from her father, though only because he is very unpopular and Lorenzo has very powerful friends; they 'seal love's bonds new-made' (II. vi. 6). Otherwise, trying to move very far out of your place is severely punished, as Shylock finds. It is so obvious that this framework of ideology and ·coercion is operating to the advantage of the rich over the poor, the established over the impotent, men over women and insiders over outsiders, that directors have been able to slant productions of the *Merchant* against the dominant reading, making Bassanio cynical, Portia manipulative and the Venetians arrogant and racist.

The roles of same-sex passion in this framework should not be taken for granted (I use the terms 'same-sex' and 'cross-sex' to evade anachronistic modern concepts). For us today, Eve Sedgwick shows this in her book *Between Men*, homosexuality polices the entire boundaries of gender and social organization. Above all, it exerts 'leverage over the channels of bonding between all pairs of men'. Male–male relations, and hence male–female relations, are held in place by fear of homosexuality by fear of crossing that 'invisible, carefully blurred, always-already-crossed line' between being 'a man's man' and being 'interested in men' (Sedgwick 1985: 88–9; see Dollimore 1992: chs 17–18). We do not know what the limits of our sexual potential are, but we do believe that they are likely to be disturbing and disruptive;

that is how our cultures position sexuality. Fear even of thinking homosexually serves to hold it all in place. So one thing footballers must *not* be when they embrace is sexually excited; the other thing they mustn't be is in love. But you can never be quite sure; hence the virulence of homophobia.

If this analysis makes sense in Western societies today, and I believe it does, we should not assume it for other times and places. As Sedgwick observes, ancient Greek cultures were different (1985: 4). In our societies whether you are gay or not has become crucial – the more so since lesbians and gay men have been asserting themselves. An intriguing thought, therefore, is that in early modern England same-sex relations *were not terribly important*. In *As You Like It* and *Twelfth Night*, homoeroticism is part of the fun of the wooing ('Ganymede', the name taken by Rosalind, was standard for a male same-sex loveobject); but it wouldn't be fun if such scenarios were freighted with the anxieties that people experience today. In Ben Jonson's play *Poetaster*, Ovid Senior expostulates: 'What! Shall I have my son a stager now? An engle for players? A gull, a rook, a shotclog to make suppers, and be laughed at?' (Jonson 1995: I. ii. 15–17).[4] It is taken for granted that boys are sexual partners (engles) for players; it is only one of the demeaning futures that await young Ovid if he takes to the stage. Moralists who complained about theatre and sexual licence took it for granted that boys are sexually attractive.

'Sodomy' was the term which most nearly approaches what is now in England called 'gross indecency'; it was condemned almost universally in legal and religious discourses, and the penalty upon conviction was death. Perhaps because of this extreme situation, very few cases are recorded. Today, staking out a gay cruising space is a sure-fire way for a police force to improve its rate of convictions. But in the Home Counties through the reigns of Elizabeth I and James I – sixty-eight years – only six men are recorded as having been indicted for sodomy. Only one was convicted, and that was for an offence involving a five-year-old boy.[5]

In his book *Homosexual Desire in Shakespeare's England*, Bruce R. Smith shows that while legal and religious edicts against sodomy were plain, paintings and fictive texts sometimes indicate a more positive attitude. This derived mainly from the huge prestige, in artistic and intellectual discourses, of ancient Greek and Roman culture where same-sex passion is taken for granted (Smith 1991: 13–14, 74–6 *et passim*). Smith locates six 'cultural scenarios': heroic friendship, men and boys (mainly in pastoral and educational contexts), playful androgyny (mainly in romances and festivals), transvestism (mainly in satirical contexts), master–servant relations' and an emergent homosexual subjectivity (in Shakespeare's sonnets). Within those scenarios, it seems, men did not necessarily connect their practices with the monstrous crime of sodomy – partly, perhaps, because that was so unthinkable. As Jonathan Goldberg emphasizes, the goal of analysis is 'to see what the category [sodomy] enabled and disenabled, and to negotiate the complex terrains, the mutual implications of prohibition and production' (1992: 20; see Bray 1982: 79). The point is hardly who did what with whom, but the contexts in which anxieties about sodomy might be activated. So whether the friendships of men such as Antonio and Bassanio should be regarded as involving a homoerotic element is not just a matter of what people did in private hundreds of years ago; it is a matter of definition within a sex-gender system that we only partly comprehend.

Stephen Orgel asks: 'why were women more upsetting than boys to the English?' That is, given the complaints that boy-actors incite lascivious thoughts in men and women spectators, why were not women performers employed – as they were in Spain and Italy? Orgel's answer is that boys were used because they were less dangerous; they were erotic, but that was less threatening than the eroticism of women. So this culture 'did not display a morbid fear of homosexuality. Anxiety about the fidelity of women, on the other hand, does seem to have been strikingly prevalent' (Orgel 1989: 8, 18). Leontes and Polixenes lived guiltlessly together, we are told in *The Winter's Tale*, until they met the women who were to be their wives (I. ii. 69–74). The main faultlines ran through cross-sex relations.

Because women may bear children, relations between women and men affected the regulation of lineage, alliance and property, and hence offered profound potential disruptions to the social order and the male psyche. Same-sex passion was dangerous if, as in the instance of Christopher Marlowe's *Edward II*, it was allowed to interfere with other responsibilities.

Otherwise, it was thought compatible with marriage and perhaps preferable to cross-sex infidelity. The preoccupation, in writing of this period, is with women disturbing the system – resisting arranged marriages, running off with the wrong man, not bearing (male) children, committing adultery, producing illegitimate offspring, becoming widows and exercising the power of that position. In comedies things turn out happily, in tragedies sadly. But, one way or the other, Shakespearean plays, as much as the rest of the culture, are obsessively concerned with dangers that derive from women.

'We'll play with them the first boy for a thousand ducats', Gratiano exclaims, betting on whether Nerissa or Portia will bear the first boy-child (III. ii. 213–14). As Orgel remarks, patriarchy does not oppress only women; a patriarch is not just a man, he is the head of a family or tribe who rules by paternal right (1989: 10). To be sure, women are exchanged in the interest of property relations in Shakespearean plays, as in the society that produced them. But the lives of young, lower-class and outsider men are determined as well. In *The Merchant*, as everywhere in the period, we see a traffic in boys who, because they are less significant, are moved around the employment–patronage system more fluently than women. Class exploitation was almost unchallenged; everyone – men as much as women – had someone to defer to, usually in the household where they had to live. The most likely supposition is that, just as cross-sex relations took place all the time – Launcelot is accused, in passing, of getting a woman with child (III. v. 35–6) – same-sex passion also was widely indulged.[6]

Traffic in boys occurs quite casually in *The Merchant*. Launcelot is a likely lad. He manages to square it with his conscience to leave his master, Shylock, but it is unclear where he will go (II. ii. 1–30). He runs into his father, who indentured Launcelot to Shylock and is bringing a present for the master to strengthen the bond. Launcelot persuades him to divert the gift to Bassanio, who is providing 'rare new liveries', for the expedition to Belmont (II. ii. 104–5). The father attempts to interest Bassanio in the boy, but it transpires that Shylock has already traded him: 'Shylock thy master spoke with me this day, / And hath preferr'd thee' (II. ii. 138–9). Nor is Launcelot the only young man Bassanio picks up in this scene: Gratiano presents his own suit and gets a ticket to Belmont conditional upon good behaviour. And when Jessica assumes the guise of a boy, the appearance is of another privileged young man, Lorenzo, taking a boy into his service and giving him new livery: 'Descend, for you must be my torch-bearer. . . . Even in the lovely garnish of a boy' (II. vi. 40, 45). When the young doctor claims Portia's ring from Bassanio for services rendered, therefore, a pattern is confirmed.

My point is not that the dreadful truth of the *Merchant* is here uncovered: it is really about traffic in boys. Rather, that such traffic is casual, ubiquitous and hardly remarkable. It becomes significant in its resonances for the relationship between Antonio and Bassanio because Portia, subject to her father's will, has reason to feel insecure about the affections of her stranger-husband.

III Friendly relations

Heroic friendship is one of Smith's six 'cultural scenarios' for same-sex relations (1991: 35–41, 67–72, 96–9, 139–43). In Shakespeare, besides the sonnets, it is represented most vividly in the bond between Coriolanus and Aufidius in *Coriolanus*:

> Know thou first,
> I lov'd the maid I married; never man
> Sigh'd truer breath; but that I see thee here,
> Thou noble thing, more dances my rapt heart
> Than when I first my wedded mistress saw
> Bestride my threshold.
>
> (IV. v. 114–19).[7]

Unlike Portia, Aufidius's wife is not there to resent him finding his warrior-comrade more exciting than she.

In his essay 'Homosexuality and the Signs of Male Friendship in Elizabethan England', Alan Bray explores the scope of the 'friend' (Bray 1990). Even as marriage was involved in alliances of property and influence, male friendship informed, through complex obligations, networks of extended family, companions, clients, suitors and those influential in high places. Claudio in *Measure for Measure* explains why he and Juliet have not made public their marriage vows:

> This we came not to
> Only for propagation of a dower
> Remaining in the coffer of her friends,
> From whom we thought it meet to hide our love
> Till time had made them for us.
>
> (I. ii. 138–42)

On the one hand, it is from friends that one anticipates a dowry; on the other hand, they must be handled sensitively. Compare the combination of love and instrumentality in the relationship between Bassanio and Antonio: the early modern sense of 'friend' covered a broad spectrum.

While the entirely respectable concept of the friend was supposed to have nothing to do with the officially abhorred concept of the sodomite, in practice they tended to overlap (see Bray 1990). Friends shared beds, they embraced and kissed; such intimacies reinforced the network of obligations and their public performance would often be part of the effect. So the proper signs of friendship could be the same as those of same-sex passion. In instances where accusations of sodomy were aroused, very likely it was because of some hostility towards one or both parties, rather than because their behaviour was altogether different from that of others who were not so accused.

The fact that the text of the *Merchant* gives no plain indication that the love between Antonio and Bassanio is informed by erotic passion does not mean that such passion was inconceivable, then; it may well mean that it didn't require particular presentation as a significant category. What is notable, though, is that Portia has no hesitation in envisaging a sexual relationship between Bassanio and the young doctor: 'I'll have that doctor for my bedfellow', she declares, recognizing an equivalence (V. i. 33). She develops the idea:

> Let not that doctor e'er come near my house –
> Since he hath got the jewel that I loved,
> And that which you did swear to keep for me.
>
> (V. i. 223–5)

The marriage of Bassanio and Portia is unconsummated and 'jewel' is often genital in Shakespearean writing: the young doctor has had the sexual attentions which were promised to

Portia. 'Ring', of course, has a similar range, as when Gratiano says he will 'fear no other thing / So sore, as keeping safe Nerissa's ring' (V. i. 306–7; see Partridge 1955: 135, 179). Portia's response to Bassanio (allegedly) sleeping with the young doctor is that she will do the same:

> I will become as liberal as you,
> I'll not deny him anything I have,
> No, not my body nor my husband's bed.
>
> (V. i. 226–8)

Notice also that Portia does not express disgust, or even surprise, that her husband might have shared his bed with a young doctor. Her point is that Bassanio has given to another something that he had pledged to her. Nor does she disparage Antonio (as she does Morocco). Shylock, for the social cohesion of Venice, has to be killed, beggared, expelled, converted or any combination of those penalties. Same-sex passion doesn't matter nearly so much; Antonio has only to be relegated to a subordinate position.

Bray attributes the instability in friendly relations to a decline in the open-handed 'housekeeping' of the great house. Maintaining retinues such as those Bassanio recruits – young men who look promising and relatives who have a claim – was becoming anachronistic. So the social and economic form of service and friendship decayed, but it remained as a cultural form, as a way of speaking. The consequent unevenness, Bray suggests, allowed the line between the intimacies of friendship and sodomy to become blurred (1990: 12–13). Don Wayne, in his study of Ben Jonson's poem 'To Penshurst' and the country-house genre, relates the decline of the great house to the emergence of a more purposeful aristocracy of 'new men' who 'constituted an agrarian capitalist class with strong links to the trading community'; and to the emergence, also, of 'an ideology in which the nuclear, conjugal family is represented as the institutional foundation of morality and social order'. We associate that development with the later consolidation of 'bourgeois ideology', but 'images and values we tend to identify as middle class had already begun to appear in the transformation of the aristocracy's own self-image' (Wayne 1984: 23–5).

The Merchant of Venice makes excellent sense within such a framework. Portia's lavish estate at Belmont is presented as a fairy-tale place; in Venetian reality Bassanio, an aristocrat who already cultivates friends among the merchant class, has to raise money in the market in order to put up a decent show. At the same time, Portia's centring of the matrimonial couple and concomitant hostility towards male friendship manifests an attitude that was to be located as 'bourgeois'. This faultline was not to be resolved rapidly; Portia is ahead of her time. Through the second half of the seventeenth century, Alan Bray and Randolph Trumbach show, the aggressively manly, aristocratic rake, though reproved by the churches and emergent middle-class morality and in violation of the law, would feel able to indulge himself with a woman, a young man or both.[8]

If I have begun to map the ideological field in which same-sex passion occurred in early modern England and some of its points of intersection in *The Merchant*, I am not trying to 'reduce' Shakespeare to an effect of history and structure. I do not suppose that he thought the same as everyone else – or, indeed, that *anyone* thought the same as everyone else. First, diverse paths may be discerned in the period through the relations between sexual and 'platonic', and same-sex and cross-sex passions. These matters were uncertain, unresolved, contested – that is why they made good topics for plays, satires, sermons and so on. Second, playtexts do not have to be clear-cut. As I have argued elsewhere, we should envisage them as working across an ideological terrain, opening out unresolved faultlines, inviting spectators to explore imaginatively the different possibilities. Anyway, readers and audiences do not have to respect closures; they are at liberty to credit and dwell upon the adventurous middle part of a text, as against a tidy conclusion (Sinfield 1992: 47–51, 99–106). As Valerie Traub remarks, whether these early comedies are found to instantiate dissidence or containment is a matter of 'crediting *either* the expense of dramatic energy *or* comedic closure' (1992b: 120; see Smith 1992).

Generally, though, there is a pattern: the erotic potential of same-sex love is allowed a certain scope, but has to be set aside. The young men in *Love's Labour's Lost* try to maintain a fraternity but the women draw them away. In *Romeo and Juliet* Mercutio has to die to clear the ground for Romeo and Juliet's grand passion. In *Much Ado About Nothing* Benedick has to agree to kill Claudio at his fiancée's demand. *As You Like It* fantasizes a harmonious male community in the forest and intensifies it in the wooing of Orlando and Ganymede, but finally Rosalind takes everyone but Jacques back into the old system. Yet there are ambiguities as well. In the epilogue to *As You Like It* the Rosalind/Ganymede boy-actor reopens the flirting: 'If I were a woman, I would kiss as many of you as had beards that pleased me, complexions that liked me, and breaths that I defied not' (V. iv. 214–17; see Traub 1992b: 128). And Orsino in *Twelfth Night* leaves the stage with Viola still dressed as Cesario because, he says, her female attire has not yet been located. Even Bassanio can fantasize: 'Sweet doctor', he says to Portia when she has revealed all, 'you shall be my bedfellow, – / When I am absent then lie with my wife' (V.i.284–5).

And why not? Was it necessary to choose? Although the old, open-handed housekeeping was in decline, the upper-class household was not focused on the marital couple in the manner of today. Portia welcomes diverse people to Belmont; Gratiano and Nerissa for instance, whose mimic-marriage reflects the power of the household. *The Two Gentlemen of Verona* starts with the disruption of friendship by love for a woman, but ends with a magical reunion in which they will all live together: 'our day of marriage shall be yours, / One feast, one house, one mutual happiness' (Shakespeare 1969: V. iv. 170–1). In a discussion of *Twelfth Night* elsewhere, I have suggested that Sebastian's marriage to a stranger heiress need not significantly affect Antonio's relationship with him (Sinfield 1992: 73). They might all live together in Olivia's house (as Sir Toby does); she may well prefer to spend her time with Maria and Viola (who will surely tire of Orsino) rather than with the naive, swashbuckling husband whom she has mistakenly married. So Antonio need not appear at the end of *Twelfth Night* as the defeated and melancholy outsider that critics have supposed; a director might show him delighted with his boyfriend's lucky break.

This kind of ending might be made to work in the *Merchant*. R. F. Hill suggests it, and Auden reports a 1905 production which had Antonio and Bassanio enter the house together (Hill 1975: 86; Auden 1963: 233). However, Portia plays a harder game than Rosalind and Viola. She doesn't disguise herself, as they do, to evade hetero-patriarchal pressures, but to test and limit her husband. When disguised as a boy she does not, Geary observes, play androgynous games with other characters or the audience (1984: 58). Antonio is invited into the house only on her terms.

Overall in these plays, Traub concludes, the fear 'is not of homoeroticism *per se*; homoerotic pleasure is explored and sustained *until* it collapses into fear of erotic exclusivity and its corollary: non-reproductive sexuality' – a theme, of course, of the sonnets (Traub 1992b: 123, 138–41). The role of marriage and child-(son-)bearing in the transmission of property and authority is made to take priority. If (like me) you are inclined to regard this as a failure of nerve, it is interesting that the *Merchant*, itself, offers a comment on boldness and timidity. 'Who chooseth me, must give and hazard all he hath' – that is the motto on the lead casket (II. ix. 21). Bassanio picks the right casket and Portia endorses the choice but, as Auden points out, it is Shylock and Antonio who commit themselves entirely and risk everything; and in the world of this play there are penalties for doing that (Auden 1963: 235).

IV Subcultures and Shakespeare

Traub notes a reading of *Twelfth Night* that assumes Olivia to be punished 'comically but unmistakably' for her same-sex passion for Viola. But 'to whom is desire between women funny?' Traub asks (1992b: 93). This was my initial topic: must Shakespeare, for out-groups such as Jews, feminists, lesbians, gays and Blacks, be a way of re-experiencing their marginalization? I have been trying to exemplify elements in a critical practice for dissident readers. Mainstream commentators on the *Merchant* (whether they intend to or not) tend to confirm the marginalization of same-sex passion. Lesbians and gay men may use the play (1) to think about alternative economies of sex–gender; (2) to think about problematic aspects of our own subcultures. But (the question is always put): Is it Shakespeare? Well, he is said to speak to all sorts and conditions, so if gay men say 'OK, this is how he speaks to us' – that, surely, is our business.

With regard to the first of these uses, the *Merchant* allows us to explore a social arrangement in which the place of same-sex passion was different from that we are used to. Despite and because of the formal legal situation, I have shown, it appears not to have attracted very much attention; it was partly

compatible with marriage, and was partly supported by legitimate institutions of friendship, patronage and service. It is not
that Shakespeare was a sexual radical, therefore. Rather, the
early modern organization of sex and gender boundaries was
different from ours, and the ordinary currency of that culture
is replete with erotic interactions that strike strange chords
today. Shakespeare may speak with distinct force to gay men
and lesbians, simply because he didn't think he had to sort out
sexuality in modern terms. For approximately the same reasons,
these plays may stimulate radical ideas about race, nation,
gender and class.

As for using *The Merchant* as a way of addressing problems in
gay subculture, the bonds of class, age, gender and race
exhibited in the play have distinct resonances for us. The traffic
in boys may help us to think about power structures in our class
and generational interactions. And while an obvious perspective
on the play is resentment at Portia's manipulation of Antonio
and Bassanio, we may bear in mind that Portia too is oppressed
in hetero-patriarchy, and try to work towards a sex–gender
regime in which women and men would not be bound to
compete.[9] Above all, plainly, Antonio is the character most
hostile to Shylock. It is he who has spat on him, spurned him
and called him dog, and he means to do it again (I. iii. 121–6).
At the trial it is he who imposes the most offensive requirement –
that Shylock convert to Christianity (V. i. 382–3). Seymour
Kleinberg connects Antonio's racism to his sexuality:

> Antonio hates Shylock not because he is a more fervent
> Christian than others, but because he recognizes his own
> alter ego in this despised Jew who, because he is a heretic,
> can never belong to the state. . . . He hates himself in
> Shylock: the homosexual self that Antonio has come to
> identify symbolically as the Jew.
>
> (Kleinberg 1985: 120)[10]

Gay people today are no more immune to racism than other
people, and transferring our stigma onto others is one of the
modes of self-oppression that tempts any subordinated group.
And what if one were Jewish, and/or Black, as well as gay? One
text through which these issues circulate in our culture is *The
Merchant of Venice*, and it is one place where we may address them.

7

'In what chapter of his bosom?':
reading Shakespeare's bodies
KEIR ELAM

I What a fall

'. . . and put a tongue
In every wound of Caesar'

Whatever happened to whassisname? Perhaps the reason why
this question haunts the contemporary media, as well as our
more trivial domestic pursuits, is that it is the postmodern
equivalent to the old Fortune's Wheel trope, a comforting or
disquieting testimony to the indifference of History as it levels
and devours its own progeny. Whatever happened to: ageing
rock star A; retired tennis ace B; disgraced political whiz-kid
C . . .? All restored to consoling ordinariness. And then there
is the rather more rarefied academic version of the same
discursive genre, marking the rise and fall of intellectual van-
ities: Whatever became of Discipline D? Whatever became, for
example, of the once sovereign Germanic Philology? Of the
once swashbuckling Generative Grammar? Of the once all-
conquering Semiotics? Levelled all, albeit stubbornly unextinct.

Well, whatever *did* become of semiotics? Back in the distant
1970s and early 1980s the semiotic enterprise promised to
provide a key able to unlock the Bluebeard's Castle of Culture,
disclosing therein a hidden labyrinth of Systems and Codes and
a secret web of Discourses and Texts. And the beauty of the

promise lay in the fact that a single key would suffice, a single 'unified approach', in the words of Umberto Eco, 'to every phenomenon of signification and/or communication . . . able to explain every case of sign-function in terms of underlying systems of elements mutually correlated by one or more codes' (1976: 3). Explain *every* case of sign-function: one of the nobler qualities of the semiotic project was its very ambitiousness. If culture is one giant System of (sign) systems, one great overarching or underlying Code, then it has to be taken on whole. Semiotics intended to decipher the world, in Roland Barthes's phrase, as a vast Empire of Signs.

A sub-question in the whatever-became game: whatever became of the semiotics of drama, and more specifically of the semiotics of Shakespearean drama? Drama and theatre represented, in the words of the Russian semiotician Yuri Lotman, 'an encyclopaedia of semiotics', given that 'on stage there is so varied and complex an array of elements at work' (Lotman 1981; my translation). The appeal to 'unification' in the case of the drama was particularly powerful, given the evidently multi-medial or trans-semiotic nature of performance. Hence the ambitiousness of the imperial project at large was reflected in the microcosmic design of theatrical semiotics to address all forms of signification, the verbal and non-verbal, the dramatic and the performative, within a single discursive space. And Shakespearean drama – as text and as performance – was the true test of semiological prowess.

Such ambition was a necessary ideological condition for dramatic semiotics and also the main source of its energy. But as we know from the old Fortune's Wheel narratives, or indeed from Shakespearean drama, ambition is both the making and downfall of emperors and imperial schemes. Brutus says Caesar was ambitious, and we all know what happened to *him*, with his eloquently signifying wounds: 'poor poor dumb mouths'. One of the reasons for the levelling of the semiotic enterprise was precisely its Caesarean imperialism, its totalizing *hubris* as self-elected guide to universal discourse, or more modestly, in our case, to dramatic and theatrical discourse.

And yet it would be a mistake to equate the decline of the empire with the demise of semiotic enquiry as such. Indeed, the primary cause of the passing of semiotics as 'unified' science is that its lesson was absorbed and its methods appropriated by other academic discourses. Certain former semiological buzz words, such as Kristeva's 'intertextuality' or Eco's 'code', became part of the general critical currency, while the overall proposal to 'read' culture as discourse has been taken over, for example, by cultural studies, which probably would not have assumed its current form and force without the example of semiotics. Rather than a collapse, what we have witnessed is a diaspora or dissemination, putting an end to the dream of unification.

In the field of Shakespearean and Renaissance drama, analogously, some of the more powerful and original recent critical discourses – especially feminist, new historicist and cultural materialist discourses – adopt semiotic concepts with varying degrees of awareness and to quite different ends. If the old imperial faith has been replaced by a probably healthier scepticism – if, as Claudio puts it in *Much Ado About Nothing*, 'There is no believing in old signs' – semiotic analysis none the less survives, however much disguised or transformed. In this essay I propose to examine certain 'crypto-semiotic' aspects of contemporary Shakespeare criticism before proceeding to propose a 'post(humous)-semiotics' of Shakespearean drama that might take us beyond the old imperialism but also beyond mere critical appropriation.

II Body boom: the Shakespeare Corp

The site of this discussion will be the human body. One of the more striking events in recent critical discourse, especially in the field of Renaissance drama, has been the shift from a primary concern with 'language' to a primary concern with the body. In imagining culture as a language or system of signs, semiotics was one product – together with structural and transformational linguistics, speech-act philosophy and the rest – of the 'linguistic turn' that marked post-war culture. As a result of this dominance of the linguistic model, the body became for semiotics both its principal object of 'scientific' enquiry or desire – as the overdetermined agency of all signifying modes – and its most embarrassing problem. Embarrassing, since the body stubbornly resists reduction to language or signification, not only because the number of heterogeneous discourses that intersect it cause any 'unified approach' to implode, but also and especially because the semiotization of the body fails to come to terms with its sheer untidy, asyntactic, pre-semantic *bodiliness*. The Last Emperor Umberto Eco's rationalistic conception of the body as a 'multi-channel' communicating machine at once reifies and idealizes it, if not as a Cartesian *res cogitans* then as a cybernetic *res significans*, leaving out of the picture its irreducible and unrationalizable materiality.

The hegemony of the linguistic model was equally visible within the semiotics of drama in its restless search for a specific dramatic language, or in its worries over the bona fide status of performance as 'discourse' or 'text'.[1] The actor's body, again the main object of analytic desire, became a stage 'sign vehicle' or multiple theatrical signifier. The result was a mode of sanitization that tended to delete the unrepentant physicality of the performer's being and doing on stage, just as it tended to evade the crucial corporeality of the dramatic role and its 'embodiment' in performance. Falstaff's heaving, carousing, fornicating fleshy mass will not be squeezed either into a buff jerkin (see below, p. 155) or into a sign vehicle. Shakespeare's bodies remain, to quote Edgar in *King Lear*, obstinately 'unaccommodated'.

The reaction against the linguistic turn and its prophylactic sterilizing of the body has been what we might term the *corporeal* turn, which has shifted attention from the word to the flesh, from the semantic to the somatic; or rather has insisted on the *priority* of the somatic over the semantic. This shift was in some ways pre-announced 'within' semiotics in Julia Kristeva's notion of the pre-verbal and pre-semantic semiotic *chora*, the battleground of the subject's competing bodily drives which 'makes the semioticized body a place of permanent scission' (1974 [1990]: 95).

Not by chance, the privileged point of reference for the corporeal turn has been the early modern body, precisely because the late sixteenth and early seventeenth centuries saw the codification of modern subjectivity and the consequent attempt to contain (or perhaps semioticize) bodily drives. As Dympna Callaghan observes, 'Once a marginalized object in traditional literary scholarship, the body has emerged as a crucial category of critical inquiry. In Renaissance studies, it has become the focus of attention as site of emergent notions of the modern subject' (1993: 428). The past decade or so has thus seen a boom of 'corporeal' criticism in the field of Renaissance and especially Shakespearean drama, giving rise to a veritable ghost army of early modern organisms to anatomize. The Shakespearean critical industry has become the Shakespeare Corp.

Not that the corporeal turn has been limited to Renaissance studies. Indeed, the early modern body boom has run parallel with the analogous foregrounding of bodily discourse not only in other critical domains such as cultural studies and post-modernist theory, but also in 'popular' culture, with its increasingly dominant Arnold Schwarzenegger workout ethic and Cindy Crawford corporeal self-cultivation imperative. The critical flexing of discursive triceps might be seen as the 'high' cultural other of this ever more invasive physical culture. But while contemporary iron-pumping gym ideology is obsessed with the icon of the hypervitaminized whole or wholesome physique, contemporary critical discourse has instead elected as privileged object the split, suffering, diseased, tortured and transgressive body (Kristeva's 'place of permanent scission').

If Renaissance critics have put together an army, therefore, it resembles not a squadron of rippling-muscled Schwarzenegger marines but Falstaff's muster of afflicted conscripts in *1Henry IV,* 'as ragged as Lazarus in the painted cloth'. The assembled critical corps has been made up of bodies tremulous (Barker 1984); bodies single-sexed (Greenblatt 1988; Laqueur 1990); bodies double-natured (Paster 1993); bodies enclosed (Stallybrass 1986); bodies intestinal (Whigham 1988); bodies consumed (Stallybrass 1986); bodies carnivalized (Stallybrass and White 1986); bodies effeminized (Levine 1994); bodies embarrassed (Paster 1993); bodies sodomized (Goldberg 1992); bodies emblazoned or dissected (Sawday 1995); bodies castrated (Elam 1996); bodies disease-ridden (Fabricius 1994; Barroll 1991), etc.

One reason for this emphasis on stricken flesh and *disjecta membra* in recent Renaissance drama studies – sweet Caesar's wounds again – is that the crucially influential model has been not Cindy Crawford but Michel Foucault. In particular, Foucault's project, in *The History of Sexuality,* for a 'politics of sex' whereby 'the mechanisms of power are addressed to the body, to life, to what causes it to proliferate' (1979: 147), has been taken up in the simultaneous eroticization and politicization of the early modern subject. At the same time, Foucault's enquiries into the 'body politic' in *Discipline and Punish*, with their thesis that 'in our societies, the systems of punishment are to be situated in a certain "political" economy of the body' (1977: 172), have led to the election of the body as the primary object of the 'microphysics of power' in Renaissance society. And if there is a general semiotic principle that has guided recent readings of the body, it is the principle of similitude or resemblance, elected by Foucault in *The Order of Things* as the governing paradigm of the sixteenth-century 'episteme': 'It was resemblance that largely guided exegesis and the interpretation of texts; it was resemblance that organized the play of symbols, made possible knowledge of things visible and invisible, and controlled the art of representing them' (1971: 17).

Foucault's similitudinous, split, eroticized and politicized body has its own Shakespearean pedigree. In *The History of Sexuality*, Foucault reworks Ernst Kantorowicz's classic 1957 essay on the duality of the King's body, in a constant state of tension between his 'body natural' and his 'immortal body politic': a distinction that Kantorowicz himself applies to Shakespeare's *Richard II*.[2] There is thus a kind of aesthetic circularity in the return of the Shakespearean body politic: not the King's alone, but anybody, or any body, elected as a suitable case for critical anatomy. But what kinds of anatomy is it subjected to?

III 'Where lies your text?': The Shakespearean *corpus*

To see what is going on in the Shakespeare Corp, let us take an exemplary and indeed aristocratic early modern body: Duke Orsino's in *Twelfth Night*. Orsino's body is both subject and object of the comedy's opening speech, in which the Duke appears to be musing on his unrequited desire for Olivia, but is in fact thinking about himself: 'If music be the food of love, play on, / Give me excess of it, that, surfeiting, / The appetite may sicken, and so die' (I. i. 2–3). Orsino is caught up in a narcissistic preoccupation with his own sexual and physiological processes: his call for an excess of 'it' – music, but also the 'food' of love – evokes a vision in which his 'appetite', alimentary and sexual, will be overfed to the point of nausea and death: death of appetite itself, death of desire in the form of orgasm ('die' in its Elizabethan erotic sense) and perhaps even death of the body in an intestinal/seminal explosion. The narcissism of Orsino's sexual drives is confirmed in his later fantasy of being turned into a hart/heart: 'And my desires, like fell and cruell hounds, / E'er since pursue me' (22–3). His desires pursue not Olivia but himself. Olivia's reprimand to Malvolio might well be directed towards Orsino: 'O you are sick of self-love' (I. v. 89).

Orsino's auto-erotic food-and-sex fantasy corresponds to various recent discourses on the early modern body, and most immediately to Frank Whigham's endoscopic probing of the alimentary tract within Renaissance drama. According to Whigham, 'the combination of the alimentary focus with deep-seated improper hungers' in Elizabethan and Jacobean drama produces an emphasis 'on obscure interiorities, often involving sex, violence, humiliation, abjection and death – in short, perhaps, some portmanteau of fundamental desires' (Whigham 1988: 341). Orsino's concern with his own obscure interiorities and (self-directed) fundamental desires – his 'improper hungers' being a form of *amour propre* or rather *impropre* – may be seen as part of what Whigham terms the discourse of 'the body politic in privacy', a discourse of 'ingestion, retention, and evacuation' enacting the social coding of the intestine (1988: 333). What we might call the semiotics of bowel movements, translated into polite privatized discourse, or vowel movements.

Orsino returns later to the alimentary tract and other obscure interiorities in his misogynistic discourse on female desire, addressed to the disguised Viola–Cesario:

> they lack retention,
> Alas, their love may be call'd appetite,
> No motion of the liver, but the palate,
> That suffers cloyment, and revolt;
> But mine is all as hungry as the sea,
> And can digest as much.

(II. iv. 99–102)

In contrasting his own passion with mere female 'appetite', Orsino conducts a comparative physiological anatomy of the organs of love (the liver) and of sexual desire (the palate), and finds women to be in possession only of the latter. There are various ironies in this discourse, all at Orsino's own expense. First, he is reducing the idolatrized object of his own noble passion, Olivia, to animal-like libidinous flesh, incapable of love. Second, he rightly supposes his interlocutor Cesario to be capable of 'male' love, but is blind to the fact that 'he' is a woman and he, Orsino, 'his' beloved object. And third, his talk of female 'appetite' and 'cloyment' recalls his earlier self-description, and his own rapidly surfeited desire ('Enough, no more; / 'Tis not so sweet now as it was before', I. i. 7–8) suggesting an implicit confession of effeminacy that undermines his present claims to masculine passion.

But there may be still darker organic things going on in Orsino's unpleasant speech. His claim that women 'lack retention' has as its immediate meaning their incapacity for love. But the accusation also raises the spectre of female incontinence: the sexual incontinence already implicit in the 'appetite' charge – and which was an essential ingredient of early modern misogyny and of the privatizing discourses regarding the (female) body[3] – but also, perhaps, menstrual and urinary incontinence. Gail Kern Paster has suggested, in her important study of early modern 'disciplines of shame' ('influenced', as she admits, 'by Michel Foucault' [1993: 1]), that Shakespearean and Renaissance drama frequently represents women as 'leaky vessels', incapable of bladder control (1993: 23–63), and that such bladder incontinence is a source of embarrassment and, consequently, of comicity. For Orsino and others, women – in this case Olivia – wet themselves. This may in part explain the liquid terminology – what Thomas Laqueur (1990: 43) and Alphonso Lingis (1994: 133) term the 'fluid economy' – of Orsino's discourse: 'hungry as the sea' (compare his earlier 'Receiveth as the sea', [I. i. 11]). Although this again implicates Orsino in the accusation, since the 'sea' in question is his own.

The 'joke about the spectacle of women urinating', as Paster puts it (1993: 30), recurs in Malvolio's letter scene, and the micturating lady is once again Olivia. On finding 'Olivia's' billet doux, Malvolio thinks he recognizes her handwriting: 'By my life, this is my lady's hand these be her very C's, her U's, and her T's, and thus makes she her great P's.' (II. iv. 87–90). The obscene pun in Malvolio's CUT is evident enough, as is Malvolio's 'unconscious' reference to urination in 'her great

P's', although how one interprets Olivia's CUT. and P's is another matter. For Jonathan Goldberg, for example, they are castrating letters that point to 'a desire unattainable on a stage that can only impersonate sexual difference', due to the use of boy-actors in the Elizabethan theatre (1986: 217). The cut is not so much Olivia's as Malvolio's and the actor's. For Dympna Callaghan, somewhat similarly, Malvolio has been 'feminized, ridiculed, castrated' and his body has been 'reduced to the most denigrated bodily part – a "cut"' (1993: 436). Paster, instead, sees a trajectory in Malvolio's voyeuristic desire 'from the genital to the excretory', which simultaneously degrades Olivia's body, reduced to 'the lowly status of generic female by that specifically shameful female signifier – the "cut"' (1993: 33).

From bowel movements to bladder evacuation: in any case 'what is at stake here', asserts Paster, 'is a semiology of excretion' (1993: 34). What may really be at stake here is a semiology of social aspiration. The joke is not so much on Olivia's body as on Malvolio's secret hope to reach Olivia's social level. Watching Olivia pee is a sign not so much of sexual pleasure as of social equality: only her husband (C[o]unt Malvolio?) has the right to do so. Like Orsino, Malvolio, sick of self-love, does not desire Olivia but, in his case, his own social advancement.

Malvolio's deciphering of Olivia's false epistle posits her body as a set of graphic signifiers, and thus as a corpus, a text, but at the same time it puts us on guard about over-hasty readings of the body-text. This brings us back to Orsino and his own self-admired body. In another of the play's ironies at his expense, Olivia sarcastically imagines her suitor's body as a book:

> OLIVIA   Where lies your text?
> VIOLA   In Orsino's bosom.
> OLIVIA   In his bosom? In what chapter of his bosom?
>
> (I. v. 226–8).

Olivia's caustic interrogation of the go-between Cesario justifiably questions Orsino's sincerity, suggesting that the Duke's 'bosom' is an empty text, not only performed but composed by another. Olivia claims to be able to 'read' Orsino without hearing the speech, because the enamoured discourse of his languishing body and delegated heart is *déjà lu*, a poor imitation chapter-and-verse Scripture. And Viola herself, willing her own mission to fail, contributes to the satirical deconstructing of the Orsino-book in her able pastiche of Petrarchan court-ship, figuring her master's bosom not just as a text but as the most hackneyed of intertexts ("Tis beauty truly blent, whose red and white / Nature's own sweet and cunning hand laid on . . .', [I. v. 242ff.]). And yet the real joke this time is on Olivia, who, confident in her own ability to read the male bosom, misreads Viola as Cesario, and falls in love with 'him'. The sexual irony is underlined by the supposed location of Orsino's text, since Viola is hiding, among other things, her own 'bosom' as part of her Cesario performance.

Not by chance, *Twelfth Night* has itself been elected as a key text in recent anatomies of the early modern body, which have frequently borrowed the book of Viola's ambiguous body as their reading matter, under the general aegis of Foucault's 'sixteenth-century episteme'. The play's conceit of the body as book reworks the Neoplatonic idea of the *liber naturae*, the Book of Nature in which all bodies – human and animal, worldly and celestial are potentially readable to the trained eye. This is the idea at the core of Foucault's episteme of similitudes and signatures: 'There are no resemblances without signatures. . . . This is why the face of the world is covered with blazons, with characters, with ciphers and obscure words – with "hiero-glyphics". . . . And the space inhabited by immediate resemb-lances becomes like a vast open book; it bristles with strange figures that intertwine and in some places repeat themselves' (1971: 26–7). The interpretation of the world and the body is thus a matter of close reading, a search for textual resemblances: 'The sixteenth century', asserts Foucault, 'superimposed her-meneutics and semiology in the form of similitude' (1971: 29).

Like Malvolio, Olivia superimposes hermeneutics and semi-ology, trying to uncover signs and similitudes, although her irreverent tone suggests a degree of scepticism towards the status of Orsino's body as hieroglyph: his eager bosom is not so much a Platonic shadow or signature as a fake, a bad copy of the ideal lover. She prefers his stand-in Cesario, copy of a copy, resemblance of a resemblance, and yet closer to the supposed original. It is in her misreading of Viola that Olivia more earnestly and explicitly discerns Foucauldian cyphers and

blazons: 'Thy tongue, thy face, thy limbs, actions, and spirit /
Do give thee five-fold blazon' she exclaims ecstatically at the
end of her encounter with Cesario (I. v. 296–7). And even if
her reading is mistaken on the gender plane it is accurate on
the social plane, since Olivia correctly interprets Viola's bodily
behaviour as a 'blazon' – armorial bearing or sign – of her high-
class origins, despite her servant role.

Olivia's blazon may itself be a 'secret' cipher pointing to a
world of unsuspected resemblances and unimagined bodily
practices. Jonathan Sawday, in his cultural history of the 'body
emblazoned', locates the literary convention of the blazon
within what he terms the 'culture of dissection'. The literary
blazon – the poetic anatomizing or detailed enumeration of the
beloved's body: her eyes, eyebrows, bosom, etc. – is, according
to Sawday, closely linked to the new science of anatomy and
thus to the literal dissecting of corpses: 'The "vogue" for the
blazon was a part of the scientific urge which was displayed in
Renaissance anatomy theatres' (1995: 192). Here we encounter
again split and abused flesh, poor poor dumb mouths: 'the
blazon of the tortured body' (Lingis 1994: 55).

The anatomical blazon is one of the literary/corporeal
games that Viola and Olivia play. As she launches into her
conventional homage to Olivia's charms – ''Tis beauty truly
blent, whose red and white . . .' (I. v. 242ff.) – Viola is again
interrupted by her audience, who produces a parody of the
blazonic anatomy: 'As, item, two lips indifferent red; item, two
grey eyes, with lids to them; item, one neck, one chin, and so
forth' (I. v. 250–2). Olivia transforms the enumeration genre
into a catalogue or shopping list. In playing the anatomical
game, as Sawday observes, the women appropriate a male
literary genre 'in which the female body was the currency . . .
here, on the contrary, two women (who are not women) have
commandeered both the form and the competitive nature of
the contest' (1995: 202). Olivia not only misreads Viola's body
as male blazon, she mistreats her own as assembled or dissected
female parts, travestying the poetical/surgical male gaze. And
given the male (Orsino's) attitude to the female body in the
comedy, the anatomical game takes on sinister overtones.

It is precisely in this region of gender relationships that
Viola's body has been subjected to 'surgical' critical anatomies
within the framework of a semiology of resemblance. Any

number of critics have been fascinated by Cesario's doubly
seductive (for Olivia and Orsino) androgyny, attempting to
accommodate it within Renaissance corporeal culture.[4]
The most influential of these readings has undoubtedly been
Stephen Greenblatt's celebrated essay 'Fiction and Friction'
(1988), a perfect emblem of the Shakespeare Corp, since
Greenblatt's 'cultural poetics' is an outstanding example of
crypto-semiotics in the Foucauldian mode.

Drawing heavily on Thomas Laqueur's 'one-sex/flesh'
theory, according to which early modern anatomy viewed the
female sex organs as similitudes or homologues of male organs,
but turned inside out – 'Women . . . are inverted, and hence
less perfect, men. They have exactly the same organs but in
exactly the wrong places' (Laqueur 1990: 26) – Greenblatt sets
off in search of resemblances not only between sex organs but
between text organs, and in particular between dramatic and
medical texts: 'we must historicize Shakespearean sexual
nature,' he affirms, 'restoring to it its relation of negotiation
and exchange with other social discourses of the body' (1988:
72). This allows Greenblatt to find homologies between Renaissance medical studies of hermaphrodites, or of girls with secret
penises which unexpectedly spring forth under the pressure of
heat, and Viola's game of hide and seek with her own sexuality
or still more with the boy-actor's secreted member. The
relationship between medical and theatrical discourses is an
Eco-like 'shared code' or (the same thing?) Foucault's 'set of
interlocking tropes and similitudes' (Greenblatt 1988: 86).

The precise point of contact between the comedy and the
doctors is 'sexual heat', the friction or 'sexual chafing' that in
the medical anecdotes turns apparently female organs magically into penises (Greenblatt 1988: 89). This heat is translated
in *Twelfth Night* into erotic discursive energy, 'a system of
foreplay', a 'dallying with words', which presumably turns
Viola back into the male actor she is to begin with, and which
in any case chafes or arouses the (early modern? postmodern?)
audience: 'a powerful sexual commotion, a collective ex-
citation' (1988: 89).

For all the energy or discursive heat of Greenblatt's own
virtuoso performance, his contribution to the Shakespeare
Corp raises various questions. The play of sexual resemblances
makes two large and somewhat arguable assumptions. First, it

takes the 'one-sex' theory as chapter-and-verse gospel, earnestly literalizing what Sawday persuasively describes as 'the fluid metaphoric language with which men and women in early modern culture described their own bodies' (1995: 214). The play of resemblance is a rhetorical, as well as pseudo-scientific, principle, and surely Viola's 'as if' games have more to do with the conventions and ironies of comic disguise than with any homogenizing homology with medical tracts.

Second, like other Foucauldian resemblance-seekers, Greenblatt takes the 'episteme' as the monolithic or monologic Word, superimposing, like sixteenth-century Man, hermeneutics and semiology in the form of similitude.[5] But as with any other grand historical generalization – Great Chains of Being and the rest – the Renaissance 'resemblance' cannot be taken as absolute, being one (Platonic) discourse in a play of competing discourses (including anti-Platonic scepticism).[6] Foucault himself states that this episteme was on its way out at the end of the sixteenth century, and in any case recognizes, in Jean Howard's words, 'that the discursive practices of an age, while producing or enabling certain behaviours, never coincide with them exactly' (1986: 19).

As for the actual similitudes and signatures discovered by Greenblatt's historical hermeneutics, if the face of the world is covered with blazons and ciphers, they all turn out to be phalluses. The clitoris turns into the 'feminine penis'. The medical phallus turns into the discursive stage phallus. The stage phallus excites the collective audience phallus. This is not so much phallocentrism as absolute phallocracy. And all these homologized members are hectically chafed or dallied with until, to use Orsino's term, they die. In the end the similitudinous glue that holds together the various text organs is a suitably sticky fluid, 'not thin and watery like a woman's but, like a man's, thick and white' (Greenblatt 1988: 74). The Duke of Illyria would doubtless have approved.

IV Pestilential poetics: the body as symptom

What happens, then, to bodies in the Shakespeare Corp is that they become part of a great chain of beings, linked through textual relations in the *corpus*, the 'vast open book' of the world. The early modern body turns out to be more bookish than corporeal, its readability guaranteed by the fact that it is already constituted by the play of discourses and intertexts. And the primary intertexts of Shakespeare's bodies are found to be medical treatises.

This points to a crucial feature of contemporary critical discourse. In its surgical reduction of the body to obscure interiorities or ambiguous exteriorities, body criticism adopts as its own universe of discourse the realms of early modern gastroenterology (the alimentary tract), uroscopy (great P's), gynaecology (the cut) and comparative reproductive physiology (one-sex/flesh). What this implies is that Shakespeare's bodies are no longer signifiers but symptoms, and the study of their place in the drama not a semiotics but a 'symptomatology' (Paster 1993: 52) or semeiotics, 'the branch of medical science relating to the interpretation of symptoms'.[7] At the same time, this semeiotic reading of the drama tends to collapse the distinction between the 'two bodies', the represented body of the dramatis persona and the 'body natural' of the actor – especially the cross-dressed boy-actor hiding both his actual phallus and his fictional 'bosom' – since it is the stage body that is necessarily the material bearer of the symptom.

The ideological implications of this medicalizing of the dramatic body are far-reaching. What is at work here, in my view, is a return to a Puritan aesthetic, or anti-aesthetic, of the drama as pathology. The enemies of the theatre in early modern England also saw the actor's body as moral and medical symptom (see Mullaney 1988: 48–51). And, like some contemporary critics, they eliminated any distinction between the body represented and the (performer's) body representational. The actor's mind and body are directly infected by the pathology of his dramatic role, through mimesis, 'Seeing that diseases of the mind', as John Rainolds puts it, 'are gotten far sooner by counterfaiting, then are diseases of the body: and diseases of the body may be gotten so' (1599: 20). Rainolds and his fellow anti-theatricalists set up a symptomatological chain that leads from the represented role (especially female: the cross-dressed actor being himself a symptom of 'unclean affections' [1599: 11]) to the actor's 'defiled' body; from the actor's body to the spectator's 'entised' mind; from the spectator's mind to the spectator's 'diseased' body; and from the spectator's body to the community at large, since playgoers, as

William Prynne puts it, '[are] contagious in quality, more apt to poyson, to infect all those who dare approach them, than one who is full of plague-sores' (1633: 152): a veritable mimetic epidemic.

What is interesting to note in this passing on of diseases and symptoms along the theatrical body-chain is that the agents of contagion are precisely the Greenblattian forces of 'heat' and 'dalliance': 'They engrave [writings of base and filthy qualitie] by heat in the remembrance,' proclaims Rainolds, 'they meditate how they may enflame a tender youth with loue; entise him to daliance, to hoordom, to incest' (1599: 127). In all fairness to Greenblatt, he happily acknowledges this closeness to the Puritan charge of contamination: quoting Philip Stubbes's definition of the playhouse as 'Venus palace', he affirms that 'For all its insistence upon the solemn ceremony of marriage, Shakespearean comedy curiously confirms the charge . . . by the staging of its own theatrical pleasures' (Greenblatt 1988: 88). Similarly Dympna Callaghan, from a quite different critical standpoint, admits candidly of the attack on cross-dressing: 'From the perspective of my analysis, the Puritans had a point' (1993: 445).

It is doubtless an elegant paradox for drama critics to ally with drama-haters. But if the Puritans had a 'point', what point were they making? The sanitary discourse of the anti-theatricalists has an obsessively recurrent point or theme word: the plague. Prynne defines the playhouses as 'the very sinckes of all uncleanenesse . . . The Chaires of Pestilence, and corruption' (1633: 67). Stubbes warns theatregoers that 'God his Plagues are prepared, if we repent not' (1583[1887]). The threat of bubonic infection through the drama is both moral and medical. Elizabethan moralists anathematized theatre-going not only as a form of ethical contagion but as a mode of social, sexual, tactile and respiratory contact causing the rapid diffusion of the disease. Dramatic representation was a multi-channel system of deadly communication. And a system that justly brought about its own destruction, since the pestilence was more effective and more precocious than the moralists themselves in getting the playhouses closed (during the epidemic 'visitations' of 1593–4 and 1603). This is the pathological semeiotics of theatre. This is the Puritans' 'point'.

And it is a point that takes us back, perhaps surprisingly, to

Twelfth Night. At the end of her encounter with Cesario, Olivia soliloquizes on the effects of his charms:

> OLIVIA   How now?
>   Even so quickly may one catch the plague?
>   Methinks I feel this youth's perfections
>   With an invisible and subtle stealth
>   To creep in at mine eyes. Well, let it be.
>
>   (I. v. 298–302)

Olivia's 'catch the plague' is of course metaphorical, since she has been struck by an infection of the amorous kind that the moralists warned audiences about (and from a doubly cross-dressed boy-girl-boy to boot). But the 'plague' recurs other times in the play's opening scenes, forming what Shake-spearean critics used to call an 'image group'.[8] Earlier in the same scene Olivia's kinsman Sir Toby presents his corporeal credentials:

> SIR TOBY [*Belches.*] A plague o' these pickle-herring!
>
>   (I. v. 121–2)

Sir Toby – like his drinking companion Sir Andrew, an Ague-cheeked or thin-buttocked sign of fever and cowardice – is himself a humoral symptom, a Belch, of the 'sharp belchings, fulsome crudities, wind and rumbling in the guts' class that Robert Burton attributed to 'windy hypochondriacal melan-choly',[9] but which in his case indicates, on the contrary, windy, sanguine and dyspeptic *joie de vivre.* And the redundantly belch-ing Belch's 'A plague . . .' appears to be simply an imprecation against his own troubled intestine. Just as his opening lines in the play –

> SIR TOBY   What a plague means my niece to take the death
>   of her brother thus? I am sure care's an enemy to
>   life.
>
>   (I. iii. 1–3)

– are an imprecation against windy or tearful melancholy itself: still more, against melancholy death.[10]

Against death: here is the 'point' of Belch's pestilential image group, of his recurring 'plagues': they are part of his steadfast stand against the mortality of his abundant flesh. Like Falstaff, with his 'What a plague have I to do with a buff jerkin? (*1 King Henry IV* I. ii. 44), Belch opposes his eructating sub-Rabelaisian carnivalesque body (see Bakhtin 1984; Bristol 1985) to the world and its reality principle, which is to say to its death principle. Like Falstaff, he refuses to dress up or thin down, since thinness is a symptom of the Ague, perhaps of the Plague, and so of death: 'Confine? I'll confine myself no finer than I am', he shouts, when Maria enjoins him on behalf of her mourning mistress to confine or contain his body within decorous limits (I. iii. 8–10). Confinement is the privilege of the grave.

Belch's corporeal campaign against the mortal reality principle is no mere 'comic' detail in a play which begins with two male deaths – the 'real' death of Olivia's brother and the 'false' death of Viola's brother – and ends with belated news of a third male death, that of Viola's and Sebastian's father (V. i. 242–6). What if we were to take Belch's talismanic 'plagues' literally? What if the unnamed cause of death of Olivia's unnamed brother were indeed the pestilence?

Belch's swearing is not the only trace or shadow of the plague in *Twelfth Night*. And it is not the only link between Olivia and the disease. In the play's opening scene, Orsino's one memorable compliment to Olivia explicitly opposes her to the epidemic:

> ORSINO O, when mine eyes did see Olivia first,
> Methought she purg'd the air of pestilence;
>
> (I. i. 20)

Orsino's encomium may be a conceit ('Methought'), but it is rooted in early modern medical lore. The pestilence was believed – not only by the Puritans – to be transmitted through the air by infected breath, for example from spectator to spectator. Apostrophizing London three years after the devastating epidemic of 1603, Thomas Dekker tells the city that 'Sicknes was sent to breathe her unholsome ayres into thy nostrils' (1884–6: 10). And Jehan Goeruot warns in his *Regiment of Life* (1546) that 'the venomous air itself is not half so vehement to infect as is the conversation or breath of them that are infected already' (quoted in Barroll 1991: 94). 'Conversation', or social intercourse: the plague is a communicative disease. Olivia instead – like the air sweeteners used by Shakespeare's contemporaries to disperse the noxiousness of the atmosphere (see Barroll 1991: 94) – purges the unwholesome air for Orsino, even if she has lost her own brother.

What may well be at stake in this dialectic of plague and purgation is a claim concerning the comedy itself and theatrical representation in general. *Twelfth Night*, like Olivia – and indeed 'through' Olivia and the women, given the mortality rate among the males – does not transmit unwholesome airs into the nostrils of London but on the contrary 'purges' the air of pathology by taking on and exorcizing death. This is no Aristotelian catharsis but an anti-epidemiological act of resistance, pitching the life of the comedy, of the playhouse, of the actor and his performance against the mortal enemies of the theatre, whether they be virological or ideological. Rather than confirm the moralists' charge of contagious dalliance, *Twelfth Night* refuses the deadly culture of the symptom: not by chance the play's own 'Puritan', Malvolio, is subjected to a ritual purging, even if he does promise post-dramatic revenge (the epidemic of 1603? the closing of the theatres in 1642?).

Representation against visitation: this is a large claim to make on behalf of the drama. It is a claim that opposes to the lethal poetics of the symptom a vital poetics of signification. But if such a claim may be staked by and for *Twelfth Night*, what of later and more directly pestilential dramas – *Troilus and Cressida* with its lustful and pus-exuding syphilitic bodies ('the figure of desire's excess', Belsey 1992: 92); or the violently vituperative and disease-fixated *Timon of Athens*?

If there is a play that corresponds literally to the Puritans' nightmare of the drama as pestilence, it is *Timon of Athens*, which presents a veritable outbreak of 'plagues' (fourteen occurrences) and whose 'Misanthropos' protagonist repeatedly wills the disease on his fellows, and so on the audience: 'More man? Plague, plague!' (IV. iii. 199). The play, probably written not long after the 1603 visitation in London, offers the most virulent, and at the same time most chillingly analytic, semeiotic discourse in Shakespeare, as the self-exiled Timon catalogues, in a sort of sadistic anti-blazon, the devastating effects he hopes the disease will wreak on the community:

> TIMON   Consumptions sow
> In hollow bones of man; strike their sharp shins,
> And mar men's spurring. Crack the lawyer's voice,
> That he may never more false title plead,
> Nor sound his quillets shrilly. Hoar the flamen
> That scolds against the quality of flesh,

> And not believes himself. Down with the nose,
> Down with it flat; take the bridge quite away
> Of him that, his particular to foresee,
> Smells from the general weal. Make curled-pate
>   ruffians bald,
> And let the unscarred braggarts of the war
> Derive some pain from you. Plague all . . .
>
> (IV. iii. 153–64)

Like many of his contemporaries, including the Puritans, Shakespeare uses 'plague' here as a synonym for another deadly contagious disease, the pox. Addressing the whore Timandra, Timon encourages her to transmit infection ('Give them diseases, leaving with thee their lust'), and gives what Johannes Fabricius has justly described as 'one of the most vivid clinical pictures of the secondary and tertiary symptoms of syphilis written at the time' (1994: 240): syphilitic osteitis ('consumptions sow'); tabes with leg ulcers ('strike their sharp shins'); laryngeal syphilis ('crack the . . . voice'); crusted lesions ('Hoar the flamen . . .'); flattened 'saddle nose' from *gumma* or gummy tumours ('Down with the nose'); and syphilitic alopecia ('Make . . . bald'). Here we have an eloquent realization of the Puritans' theatrical apocalypse, with its disease-spreading playgoing whores and lechers ('our Play-haunters [are] . . . whoremasters, whores, bawdes . . . the Drones and Cankerwormes of the Commonweale', Prynne 1633: 145) bringing the 'weal' or commonwealth to an end.

Later events in *Timon* throw a dubious light on the pretensions of the Poet in the play's opening scene. In his dialogue with the Painter on the representational modes of their respective arts, the Poet figures his own art as a form of natural secretion:

> POET   Our poesy is as a gum which oozes
>   From whence 'tis nourish'd;
>
> (I. i. 21–2)[11]

The Poet is claiming that his inspiration issues from him spontaneously like resin from a tree. But his 'gum' is suspiciously close to the syphilitic *gumma* or gummy nose-destroying tumours of Timon's tirade. Perhaps dramatic poesy itself is a bubonic or venereal disease, or at least a symptom thereof, a gummy, oozing, encrusted, ulcerous sore. In *Timon* there is no clearing the air of pestilence, least of all through theatrical representation. Or is there?

V The body performative: towards a post(humous)-semiotics of Shakespearean drama

'Above all we must agree stage acting is a delirium like the plague, and is communicable.' This is not Philip Stubbes or William Prynne speaking, but Antonin Artaud. In his classic 1938 essay 'Theatre and the Plague', the visionary poet of modern theatre professes his dream of a pestilential drama able to provoke 'a complete social disaster' by the intensity of its verbal and stage language: 'The plague takes dormant images, latent disorders and suddenly carries them to the point of the most extreme gestures' (1970: 18). Artaud's own paradigm of a theatre of pestilence is an (imaginary) performance of John Ford's *'Tis Pity She's a Whore*, with its 'extreme' incestuous and homicidal passions. But it might have been an (imaginary) performance of the fearsome plague-invoking *Timon*.

Artaud's pestilential theatre, unlike the Puritans', is virulently contagious but at the same time homeopathically curative in its effects, a 'redeeming epidemic' causing 'either death or drastic purification' (1970: 22). Only in performance can such a provocative-purgative force be achieved, since it is the actor's stage embodiment of extreme gestures that effects the drama's political influence over the community. And in exerting its powers over the *polis*, drama in performance leaves the realm of symptomatology in order to occupy the domain of signification: 'It restores all our dormant conflicts and their powers,' says Artaud, 'giving these powers names we acknowledge as signs' (1970: 18).

Now it is more than conceivable that *Timon* was designed to exert, in performance, an analogously virulent but purgative oppositional power, recovering – thanks in part to Thomas Middleton's probable collaboration on the text – the critical social function of the satirical tradition from which it derives. In particular, the language of epidemic was directed at a Jacobean society that was at once literally plague- and syphilis-ridden and politically and socially ulcerous, increasingly dedicated to the substance that Timon first loses and then digs up again while looking for roots: gold. The play figures the nascent capitalism of early modern London, via Timon's Athens, by representing the cash nexus as plague: not by chance Marx quotes Timon's 'Gold? Yellow, glittering precious gold?' speech (IV. iii. 26ff.) in support of his critique of the accumulation of capital, whereby 'everything, commodity or not . . . becomes saleable and buyable'.[12] The force of such a social critique, however, can only be realized in the performer–audience transaction: 'theatre is collectively made to drain abcesses' (Artaud 1970: 22).

Artaud's bubonic performers and their political powers of signification raise the problem of how to 'read' the other body in question, the body of the actor on stage. Perhaps the most serious limit of recent body criticism is its lack of reference to performance. Paradoxically, historicist semeiotics tends – like 'linguistic' semiotics – to idealize the body by collapsing actor and role into a single, if 'split', historical trope within the similitudinous chain of early modern discourses. Little reference is made to the conditions and conventions constraining the performer's body on the Elizabethan stage. And still less to the practice of modern or contemporary performance. Most Shakespearean corporeal criticism is altogether removed from our own theatrical culture, and thus, in a sense, from our own historical moment. The history of Shakespeare's bodies is also and above all the history of their embodiment on stage. As, for example, in the case of the pestilential bodies of *Timon*. What becomes of Timon's epidemic in performance?

In practice *Timon*, being a 'corrupt' and 'contaminated' textual body, an apparently unfinished collaborative effort, was almost certainly never performed in Shakespeare's lifetime. And indeed it has remained largely unperformed ever since, being usually considered unrepresentable: actors and directors have avoided it like the plague it constantly invokes. There is a particular irony in this fate, since one of the causes of Timon's misanthropy is precisely his disappointment at man's failure to 'perform', that is to carry out his verbal undertakings or promises (which should by their nature be 'performative'). 'Promise me friendship but perform none', he berates Alcibiades; 'If thou wilt promise, the gods plague thee, for thou art a man!' (IV. iii. 74–7).

The play, in fact, had to wait more than two hundred years for its first significant performance, Edmund Kean's 1816 production whose 'extreme gestures' would have won Artaud's approval: 'Kean started, listened, leaned in a fixed and angry manner on his spade,' reported Leigh Hunt, 'with frowning eyes and lips full of the truest feeling.'[13] And it waited a further 150 years for its one memorable modern performance, namely Peter Brook's 1974 French-language production at the Théâtre des Bouffes du Nord in Paris. Brook's staging of the play was an enactment precisely of the drama's capacity in performance to transform the symptomatic into the signifying, the somatic into the semantic (not by chance Brook had earlier experimented an Artaudian 'pestilential poetics' in the London Theatre of Cruelty season to which his work in Paris was in part heir).

First, Brook and his translator Jean-Claude Carrière undertook an assault on the body of the text, further 'contaminating' it in the use of a stripped-down colloquial French version. The resulting linguistic and cultural hybrid was materialized in performance by the use of non-French actors, like Bruce Myers (Alcibiades), with palpably 'bad' accents, thereby undermining the seductive musicality of the verse and leaving intact only the play's naked and unsettling rhetorical force. The result was harsh discursive attrition, a 'corps à corps explosif', in Georges Banu's words (1991: 37). Working with a multi-ethnic group of actors, Brook similarly used their bodies to disrupt automatic cultural categories, their (in)different skin colours suspending racial identities (a 'plague' of our own society). The costumes confirmed this process of bodily hybridization: underneath their largely symbolic stage apparel (Timon's initial designer suit and gold lamé shirt, for example, later become rags), the actors' 'ordinary' clothes were visible. Thus the production emphasized the separation – more Brechtian than Artaudian – of the two bodies: the dramatic body performed and the actor's body performative.

As for the political signifying force of the body performative, the production defined both dramatic power relations and actor–audience relations through a shifting proxemics, or spatial semiotics, of vicinity and distance. The initial stage configuration was the most conventional of geometrical symbols, the circle, with François Marthouret's Timon at its centre like an absolute centripetal monarch, a James I or a Louis XIV, *Timon-soleil* (Banu 1991: 100). With Timon's fall from wealth and thus from power, the circle broke up in a centrifugal social diaspora, only to reform again around Timon's discovered gold. Performer–spectator transactions likewise shifted along the vicinity axis, the audience now distant, now contaminated by direct contact as they moved into the acting area or as the actors moved towards them.

Such interplay between the corporeal and the symbolic made this one of Brook's most politically incisive productions, allowing Timon's Athens to evoke partly the Generals' totalitarian Athens of the 1970s, partly the First World staggering under the monetary shock of the 1973 oil crisis (see Williams 1988: 247). *Timon* finally fulfilled its vocation as a purgative assault on the epidemic of capitalistic 'consumption', to abuse its protagonist's medical term.

It is performance that permits us to read Shakespeare's bodies both in their non-idealized or em-bodied corporeality and in their signifying power. And that permits us to historicize those bodies within our own cultural moment, our own episteme. But what of the em-bodying of Sir Toby's unconfined flesh and its stand against the pestilence? The staging of *Twelfth Night* that has come closest to an irreverently and vitally Belchian celebration of the body and its pleasure principle was perhaps Declan Donnellan's 'colonial' Cheek by Jowl production in 1986, with its riotous carnival atmosphere, and with Keith Bartlett's Belch at its centre as an MCC-tie-sporting, *Sporting-Life*-reading, guitar-playing British Empire knight whose aggressively unconfinable behaviour gets him into a bottle fight. Other roles were given analogously powerful and transgressively physical life, notably Clare Hackett's (trumpet-playing) Viola, who obliged Timothy Walker's Royal Navy Commander Orsino to feel her 'bosom', violently shifting the gender terms of her disguise with regard to the Elizabethan stage (in this production it was Feste who was the cross-dressed male; see Reade 1991: 91–4).

Cheek by Jowl's *Twelfth Night* was a celebratory End of Empire play. I began this essay by discussing the end of the Semiotic Empire, which – like the lost Illyrian-British Empire – calls for no effusions of nostalgia. If there is something to be recovered from the 'lost' semiotics of drama, it is perhaps the proposal to create a discursive space within which social, dramatic and theatrical perspectives intersect in the analysis of the production of meaning. As Alessandro Serpieri put it in his chapter on the semiotics of Shakespearean drama in *Alternative Shakespeares 1*, 'A semiotic reading of the dramatic text must be aware not only of the cultural pragmatics of its historical context, but also of the potential pragmatics of the stage relationships that are inscribed in the strictly verbal make-up of the text itself' (1985: 122).

A revised – which is to say historicized and materialized – post-semiotics of Shakespearean drama might offer an analogous space where social history, dramatic history and stage history interrogate each other. But in order to be both fully historicized and fully materialized, such an enterprise can only set out from the one historical and material dramatic body we have, the actor's. Where lies your text? In the performer's bosom.

8
Shakespeare and cultural difference
ANIA LOOMBA

I

Empire, race, colonialism and cultural difference are rather belatedly becoming central to Shakespeare criticism. In 1985, when the first volume of *Alternative Shakespeares* was published, it was necessary to establish that colonial expansion was a crucial Shakespearean theme, rather than just a backdrop (Barker and Hulme 1985). In 1987 an important review essay of 'political criticism' of Shakespeare remarked on the significant absence of a full-length account of Shakespeare and race (Cohen 1987), but some years later 'race' as an analytic category was still conspicuous by its absence, even when questions of 'difference' in Shakespeare were being addressed (Wayne 1991).[1] That several authors of a 1994 feminist anthology take that absence as their starting point and seek to redress it is some indication that 'race' is being lifted out of the category of 'a special topic' and woven more widely into the critical vocabulary of early modern studies (Hendricks and Parker 1994). The academic encounter between a variety of post-structuralist critical methods and the political concerns of historically marginalized groups has fostered studies of all kinds of 'difference' – including cultural and racial difference. Still, those who write about these issues today do not necessarily share political or intellectual assumptions. For some, the question of 'difference' in early modern drama is at a remove from contemporary affairs, while for others, it is a means of discussing the world we live in. For others still, 'race' and 'cultural difference' are distinct from questions of empire and colonialism. Whether a critic lives in (or comes from) Britain, North America or the 'third world' also has a strong impact on both the meanings and the broader pedagogical and political significance she finds in 'race' and Shakespeare.[2]

Despite these disparities, however, considerations of 'cultural difference' have been crucial in producing several 'alternative Shakespeares' – a Shakespeare who displayed 'otherness' to sixteenth- and seventeenth-century English audiences; a Shakespeare who, beginning with performances on board ships of the East India Company, took 'English culture' abroad; a Shakespeare recast by a host of readers and performers in all parts of the globe. This seems like progress. Yet even such alternative Shakespeares, to the extent that they maintain the myth of an endlessly pliable Bard who has said it all, and through whom we can say everything, ironically undercut the effort to seriously re-think the place of Shakespeare in early modern English theatrical culture. A recent MLA bibliographical search showed up nearly 400 essays on *Othello* produced in the last five years, most of them including some discussion of 'race', but only one study related to Heywood's *Fair Maid of the West* – a saga of mercantilism, interracial sexual relations, cross-dressing and the production of emblematic English femininity.[3] Shakespeare continues to be generally regarded, somewhat contradictorily, as both unique and more emblematic of attitudes (dominant or contestory) in 'his' period than any other playwright. He also continues to be considered in isolation from, or in a privileged relation to, other writers. While the centrality of Shakespeare to school and college curriculi often determines the agenda of even alternative criticisms, only the insistent placing of Shakespeare alongside other texts can help us to think seriously about 'cultural difference', even 'in' Shakespeare.

It has not been easy for recent criticism to address the intersection of various categories of social 'difference'. The two books which seek to offer exhaustive accounts of race in Renaissance drama – those by Elliot H. Tokson (1982) and Anthony Barthelemy (1987) – extend the gender blindness of the pioneering studies of Samuel Chew (1937), Eldred Jones

(1965 and 1971) and G. K. Hunter (1978). Feminist critics, on the other hand, have only recently begun to theorize the question of cultural difference: some of them have been explicitly nervous that including 'race' on their agenda will pose a threat to the consideration of gender issues, although the majority tend to regard gender and 'race' as overlapping and intensifying a variety of cultural and social effects.[4] Such an incremental approach fits in with earlier work on colonization and empire which had remarked on the spectacular use of the female body in colonial discourses as a metaphor for the colonized land, and identified gender difference as the language in which colonial relations were first articulated.[5] And while feminists have produced some excellent accounts of individual texts, or cultural moments, we still don't have an extended study of the early modern connections between the formation of the 'modern' family, the consolidation of the imperial state and Europe's global domination.

New historicist writing on early modern travel and colonization and its gendered inflections has paid sustained attention to themes of overseas domination, violence and the gendered and sexualized nature of these operations, while offering exciting readings of individual plays and of emerging colonial discourses. But new historicists show preference for the study of exceptional or powerful individuals, especially monarchs, and 'high cultural' texts, especially Shakespeare. Combined with their preferred analytic method of unravelling larger sociocultural effects outward from particularly telling historical or textual moments, this means that these exceptional individuals or texts are, often brilliantly, cast as emblems of culture at large.[6] Thus the eroticized relationship of courtiers to Elizabeth, and courtly gender relations, especially as refracted through a small cluster of literary texts, become disproportionately important to the understanding of Renaissance sexualities and gender relations. Analyses of colonialism too centre on individual colonists (especially Raleigh) and their relationship to either Elizabeth or James and their courts.[7] Although new historicist work on colonialism and the work of contemporary anthropology have been mutually interactive, the former has stood somewhat aloof from the imperatives that characterize attention to race, empire and cultural difference in postcolonial historiography and criticism; despite insights into gender, it is also far removed from the political concerns of feminist criticism. One result of this is its lack of interest in the reproduction of the Shakespearean text in contemporary classrooms or other institutions.

John Gillies's recent book *Shakespeare and the Geography of Difference* (1994) takes this isolation even further because it lacks the sustained attention that new historicists pay to early modern history. Gillies suggests that Shakespeare's 'world view' was shaped by the legacy of classical literature rather than the 'new geography', not because Shakespeare was less intimate with cartographic advances than his contemporaries, but because 'in the Shakespearean moment, the old geography had the advantage of what Greenblatt has called "the power of forms", of historically entrenched mythological and rhetorical forms' (1994: 36). While this is an interesting suggestion, Gillies does not examine how the older forms might now have cradled the restive child of the newer history of contact.[8] Further, he wants to locate 'a conceptual purchase on the construction of otherness in Shakespeare that is completely independent of the anachronistic terminology of "race", "colour" and 'prejudice"' (1994: 25). These moves result in his suggesting a drastic difference between Shakespeare's *Othello* and Aphra Behn's *Oroonoko*. *Othello*, he argues, is conceived within 'the Elizabethan norm' of difference, which 'is governed by the full repertoire of the ancient discourse of barbarism' and which posits irreducible differences between Europeans and others. On the other hand, 'Behn's idea of "otherness" . . . can be grasped in terms of post-Renaissance forms of the discourses of race, slavery, "the noble savage"'. This is a 'softer' notion of the exotic, 'suggesting rather the fashionably strange or merely piquant' because it admits of an exotic and Europeanized otherness. However, we are also told that 'Oroonoko's tragedy is accidental in the sense of being unnecessary: in the sense that slavery has no necessary relationship to his imaginative being (his colour, his primitivism, his Restoration "exoticism")' (1994: 27–8).

This reading isolates both texts from the social dynamics of their times, and from each other. In *Othello*, the bridge suggested between a single 'Elizabethan norm' and an 'ancient discourse' of barbarism omits contemporary history and excludes the intervening ('medieval') history between 'ancient' and 'Elizabethan', including North African inroads into Europe, the

Crusades, as well as Turkish intervention into Europe. Even before the newer voyages to the Levant or Africa or India or the Americas, the European sense of those 'others' was markedly different from that which emerges in the classical texts which Gillies privileges as models for Shakespeare – and in any case we cannot assume that Pliny and Herodotus were read in one way over the ages. Of course *Othello* and *Oroonoko* register a very different sense of 'otherness'. But certain conceptual similarities between the two texts help locate those differences in history. Exoticism marks Behn's novella but is also germane to *Othello*: Othello's conflicted presence in Venice includes, crucially, the glamour that attaches to the exotic, as it does the horror attendant upon the 'turban'd Turk'. Both versions of black men are placed within the discourse of European civility, and both are unyoked from that by violence. Slavery has everything to do with Oroonoko's tragedy, and it is also central to the exoticism that Behn attributes to him. He is a royal slave, as was Othello, and as was the first batch of African slaves brought to Portugal in 1440 (Scobie 1985: 191). Moreover, he himself is a slave owner, a fact that offers a sort a sort of structural alibi for European slave ownership in the Caribbean. To suggest that Restoration cultural identities were 'soft' compared to those of the Renaissance is to forget that although Behn's discourse derives from anti-slavery sentiments that were beginning to take root, slave traffic and violence against black people only increased during the intervening period.[9] One only need turn to Southerne's revision of Behn's novella (1695), which blanches Oronooko's wife Imoinda and thus reverts to the disturbance at the heart of *Othello*, to realize that *Oroonoko* alone cannot function as a register of 'Restoration attitudes' (Kaul 1994: 80–96). Similarly, to take *Antony and Cleopatra* back to a Herodotean discourse of difference is useful to the extent that it indicates the mobility over centuries of a certain European vocabulary of cultural difference. But it also folds the play away from a newer English urgency in mapping and staging the East, to which I shall return shortly.

This brings me to a rather knotty issue for critics of colonialism. The curious absence of women from a certain body of new historicist work has been remarked on earlier; analogously, the colonized native is missing from many illuminating studies of the imperial fantasies and operations of Renaissance culture.

For example, Louis Montrose's insightful 1986 essay on *A Midsummer's Night's Dream* (to pick on a critic who has done much to open up the imperial theme) glosses over the Indianness of the boy over whom Oberon and Titiana quarrel. Of course, the play itself never shows us the Indian boy whose acquisition and loss nevertheless engender the dreamwork of the play. In a revisionist account, Shankar Raman (1994) connects the patriarchal fantasies of the play with the colonial dream. He suggests it is no accident that psychoanalysis has provided the dominant framework for some of the most provocative *Dream* criticism because 'Freud's dream . . . doubles and extends Shakespeare's' by repressing the presence of the non-Western subject. Raman revises the relations between text, critic and analytical method by inserting colonialism as the 'boy' repressed by all three.

Raman takes as his starting point the fact that existing Renaissance scholarship concentrates almost exclusively on the colonization of the Americas. But the pattern of slavery, genocide and European settlement that emerged here was not the *modus operandi* in the East, where mercantilism and trade were the motor of colonialism. Peter Hulme refers to the gap between them as a 'central division', exemplified by America and India, and manifested as 'a discursive divide between those native peoples perceived as being in some sense "civilized" and those not' (1986: 2–3). These differences have not sufficiently inflected our understanding of how early modern colonial discourse or ideologies of difference were constituted. Despite the monumental work of Samuel Chew and Boies Penrose, despite the extensive documentation of journeys to the East Indies by the Hakluyt Society, and despite the influence of Said's *Orientalism* on the understanding of 'difference', English contact with the East – India, the Spice Islands, Turkey, Persia, China and Japan – has not become part of the working vocabulary of Renaissance scholarship.[10] As Peter Erickson, following Alan Sinfield, remarks, the stories we need to retell are the ones that trouble us, and the legacy of the New World encounters is what legitimately haunts and concerns many Western critics (1993: 504). But the result has been that some stories have obscured others, and have thus distorted our view of the genesis of colonial relations.

It is true that Columbus's 'mistake' about the location of

India swelled to become a metaphor for a division between Europe and its others: in Samuel Purchas's well-known words, the 'name of India is now applied to all farre-distant Countries, not in the extreeme limits of Asia alone; but even to whole America, through the error ... in the Western world' (1614: 451; see also Hahn 1978). It is also the case that even as Renaissance travel writings marked the movement from fictional narratives to precise lists of commodities found in particular parts of the world, and from romances to early ethnographies and geographies, the details of each encounter recorded by Eden and Ramusio, Hakluyt and Purchas contributed to the consolidation of various European national cultures and a pan-European 'Western' culture as well (Eden 1577; Ramussio 1550; Hakluyt 1904; Purchas 1905). The seemingly universal tropes of colonial domination seem to function without too much regard to regional differences. Ambiguity is generally pressed into the service of profit – as Falstaff says about his desire for other men's wives: 'I will be cheater to them both, and they shall be exchequers to me; they shall be my East and West Indies and I will trade to them both' (*Merry Wives of Windsor* I. iii. 71–2).[11] But anthropology owes much to the ethnographic detail and the organization and narration of such detail in early modern records, both in India and in the New World (Campbell 1992). Travel collections like *Principall Navigations* or *Hakluytus Posthumus* begin to shape particular groups of 'Indians' – Americans as opposed to 'Turks' or Africans as opposed to the people of 'Indoostan'. While these are rather confused categories ('Moors' for example being a term that applies vaguely to all non-American 'Indians') each nevertheless bears the weight of particular histories. The real difficulty, then, lies in walking the tightrope between highlighting the specificity of various journeys and recognizing the flexibility of colonial discourses.

Renaissance theatricals, including Shakespeare's, repeatedly confuse 'Indians' of various sorts and 'Moors' of different kinds: we have 'negroes in Indian clothes', or black kings of Mexico, or the mixing up of Inca and Zoroastrian religious practices. One fairly common critical response to such mix-ups is to treat various outsiders through a single critical lens. Elliot H. Tokson suggests that, given the early modern blurring of distinctions between 'Indians and Negroes', 'what may be of the greatest significance is the possibility that Shakespeare's treatment of Caliban may apply to the black man as well as to New World "savage"' (1982: 3). For a previous stage in Shakespearean 'race' criticism, such a move was often strategic, since the significance of race, even in a play like *Othello*, was often blurred by debates about the precise shade of Othello's skin (Loomba 1989: 50). But now, as race and colonialism become a legitimate (and even fashionable) part of Renaissance criticism, it is time to unravel the strands, and then see how they are woven together.

It is hard to establish the markers of a difficult concept like 'racial difference', especially as they operated four hundred years ago. The overlap and differences between racial and cultural discourses have provoked recent considerations of various kinds of 'difference' in the early modern period such as Jewishness, or Irishness, and have forced us to think about alignments and antagonisms among those excluded from dominant culture (see Erickson 1993; Boose 1994; Jones 1991). But the *theoretical parameters* within which cultural domination and resistance are understood in Renaissance studies are still overwhelmingly informed by ideas of difference that have emerged from New World materials. In his fine chapter on *The Tempest*, Peter Hulme suggests that the complexity of that play can only be gauged via an understanding of '*the relationship* between the Mediterranean and the Atlantic frames of reference within the play, a task made more difficult by the way in which that Atlantic discourse is itself often articulated through a re-inscription of Mediterranean terms' (1986: 106; my italics). So if Caliban evokes aspects of African as well as Native American identities, is not because these two were represented as identical, but because the play participates in and mediates between several different discourses of travel and otherness.[12] Because at this time several distinct vocabularies of difference emerged from the various itineraries of European travel and then merged, sometimes uneasily, on the stage, such discursive interplay lies at the heart of Renaissance theatre.

II

The linguistic exchange between the learned Prospero and the unlettered Caliban has now become an allegory of colonial relations. It is an allegory which suggests that the cultural

difference between Europe and its others fundamentally revolves around an imbalance of 'speech'. In medieval Europe,
the myth of the 'Wild Man' centered on his inability to speak;
incoherence or muteness, or linguistic confusion, remained
essential attributes of those on the fringes of civilization (White
1978: 162–5). They also linger in contemporary analyses of
colonial encounters. While for many intellectuals and political
activists of once colonized cultures the 'silent native' is a symbol
of the decimation of indigenous cultures by colonial violence,
others locate this imbalance in the early meetings of native and
colonial cultures, thus suggesting that it pre-dates colonial
violence. For example, Stephen Greenblatt points out that even
a scholar like Tzvetan Todorov (1984) 'drastically minimizes
Mayan and Aztec writing' in order to claim that 'the crucial
cultural difference between European and American peoples
was the presence or absence of writing' (1991: 11). Greenblatt
himself contrasts 'the flood of textual representation' produced
by European adventurers to the New World: 'journals, letters,
memoranda, essays, questionaires, eyewitness accounts, narrative histories, inventories, legal depositions, theological debates,
royal proclamations, official reports, papal bulls, charters,
chronicles, notarial records, broadsheets, utopian fantasies,
pastoral eclogues, dramatic romances, epic poems . . .' to
the silences of the indigenous peoples of America:

> The responses of the natives to the fatal advent of the
> Europeans survive only in the most fragmentary and prob-
> lematical form; much of what I would like to learn is forever
> lost, and much of what is not lost exists only through the
> mediation of those Europeans who for one reason or another
> . . . saw fit to register the voices of the other. The natives
> themselves often seem most silent at those rare moments in
> which they are made to speak.
>
> (1991: 145–6)

The 'speech' or the 'voice' of the subaltern subject has
become a shorthand for her consciousness, her ability to
express herself, her cultural tools, her capacity for opposition,
as well as the state of the colonial archives through which these
can be recovered, all of which are in some danger of being read
as interchangeable. The question of orality, for example, is
minimized by an emphasis on writing and records. Caliban's

poetry has long been read as evidence of an oral culture, sensibility and intelligence that undermines and challenges Prospero's view of him as a brute. And if *The Tempest* became a parable it was also because, for a variety of anti-colonial activists, it encoded, or could be altered to indicate, the possibility of subaltern resistance. Caliban's curse became an evocative symbol of native articulation, but it was a symbol that suggested a specific model of that articulation as, to borrow Partha Chatterji's term for nationalist ideologies in India, a 'derivative discourse' (1986). It is Prospero's gift of language that initiates the resistance of his slave. This model has been extremely influential within current theories of colonial discourse. Thus, while it is customary for any criticism dealing with 'colonialism', 'cultural difference' and 'race' to gesture towards the native presence, to the threat she poses to dominant culture, and to the violence she evokes from the latter, we often find that her rebelliousness turns out to be a matter of the 'slipperiness', the 'ambivalence', the 'ambiguity', the 'contradictions' of colonial discourse itself. Theorizing subaltern agency remains a genuine problem, for early modern and postcolonial critics, largely because indigenous cultures are understood as unrecoverable after the colonial holocaust.

Some recent work suggests how we may listen for these 'lost voices'. Mary Louise Pratt's readings of indigenous responses to the Spanish invasion of the Americas are salutary in this respect. She calls these responses 'autoethnographic texts' or texts 'in which people undertake to describe themselves in ways that engage with representations others have made of them' (Pratt 1994: 28). Pratt reads these writings to show how a precolonial consciousness comes together with colonial influences and anti-colonial impulses to produce a certain native 'voice'. She thus amplifies the native element in a hybrid discourse which can no longer be understood as resulting from the slipperiness of dominant discourse. The 'unhappy alienation' of the colonized can thus be seen to emerge from a *clash* of cultures. Of course we cannot describe this clash without working through archival difficulties and assuming the existence of, even before we can locate evidence for, native speech and pre-colonial or indigenous cultures.[13]

A brilliant essay by Irene Silverblatt, 'Andean Witches and Virgins: Seventeenth-century Nativism and Subversive Gender

Ideologies', similarly reveals that the challenges of Andean women to Spanish patriarchal colonialism were composed of a tense amalgam of pre-colonial Inca beliefs, colonial Christianity and gender relations. Like their European counterparts, Andean women were subjected to accusations of witchcraft, and some of them, like one Juana Icha, confessed to a pact with a 'devil' (Silverblatt 1994: 251–71). But unlike the supposed liaison between the devil and witches in Europe, the relations between Juana Icha and her 'devil', Apo Paroto, were not sexual. Apo Paroto nightly appeared in the guise of a hungry Indian man, demanding to be fed. Native Peruvians, Silverblatt tells us, expressed their devotion, their relations with the divine world, through the metaphor of 'feeding'. And ever since the Spanish conquest introduced Christian gods to the Andes, native gods were 'hungry'. But Apo Paroto, 'unlike his European counterpart', was 'poor, stingy, without the means to provide for his acolytes'. Colonial Christianity had left him debilitated. But most significantly, he disapproved of Indians mixing with their enemies, and directed Juana Icha to take various positions against the Spanish authorities (265–6). In a related vein, Natalie Zemon Davis (1994) attempts to discuss the lives of 'Amerindian women of the eastern woodlands in terms of historical change – and not just change generated by contact with Europeans, but by processes central to their own societies'. By not telescoping colonialism back into a European frame of reference such studies remind us that the political study of colonialism must include more than an account of domination and the intricacies of European power.

We have seen how Caliban's speech is more than just his master's voice. Othello and Cleopatra indicate quite another sort of linguistic excess on the part of the non-European subject. Othello claims verbal unsophistication – he is 'rude' of speech, 'little blest with the soft phrase of peace', and 'has not those soft parts of conversation / That chamberers have' (I. iii. 81–2; III. iii. 267–8). Yet his language is laced with hyperbole and ornament; and though he says his 'services' or his royal past will 'out-tongue' his detractors, his success depends substantially on his ability to mingle socially in Venetian society, and on his gift for telling stories. His tales buy him access to Brabantio's home, they fascinate Desdemona and their barest outlines charm the Senate. It has been suggested that Othello's hyperbole betrays an anxiously excessive appropriation of the 'codes of the adoptive civilization' (Serpieri 1985: 142). But his linguistic abilities are also part of his particular foreign-ness, of the seductive charm of another kind of non European-ness than Caliban's. Othello's non-Christian half is the 'malignant and turban'd Turk', whose spectre had long haunted Europe, and whom numerous contemporary commentators regarded as 'the present terror of the world', or 'the common enemie of Christiandome'.[14] I am not interested in identifying Othello literally 'as a Turk', or in divorcing his representation from ideas about Africa. Here I simply want to place his verbosity within the discourse of the 'magic', the 'sorcery' and the seductiveness of Eastern cultures, in order to suggest that the Caliban–Prospero model of cultural and linguistic difference was not the only one operating either within Shakespearean and Renaissance theatre or in early modern English culture at large.

Like Othello, Shakespeare's Cleopatra too is framed by a discourse of non-European devilry and libidinousness. She is an 'enchanting queen' (I. ii. 125) and in her person 'witchcraft' can 'join with beauty, lust with both' (II. i. 22). Though not Turkish, her representation is indebted to contemporary writings about Turks, who occupied Egypt at the time. Cleopatra can also be placed within a theatrical tradition of representing Eastern royalty, and within a set of plays preoccupied with the fragility of a European identity as well as with Christians 'turning Turk'.[15] She is excess itself: she charms and confounds her audiences, exceeding their expectations and even their imaginations – she is 'cunning past men's thought' (I. ii. 143), her love demands spaces the earth cannot provide (I. i. 17) and to describe her smallest gestures is to require an expanded vocabulary: 'we cannot call her winds and waters sighs and tears; they are greater storms and tempests than almanacs can report' (I. ii. 145–7). Speech is an important part of this excess – Cleopatra not only speaks more than any other woman in Shakespeare, she also controls the speech of others. Even Antony is often unable to break into her speech and get a word in (I. iii. 23–32; IV. xv. 42–5). At the same time, their rhetorical splendour betrays Othello's and Cleopatra's vulnerability to their adversaries' words. Voices from Rome repeatedly seek to disrupt Cleopatra's court and to reconstruct her – Antony asks the Messenger from Rome to 'mince not the general tongue: / Name Cleopatra as she is call'd in Rome; / Rail thou in Fulvia's phrase' (I. ii. 102–4). And Othello's wordiness clashes with a competing vocabulary of difference in which his 'thick lips' become a marker of his distance from European civility, and through which he is reduced to one incapable of speech – 'an old black ram', 'a Barbary horse'.

Othello and Cleopatra's verbosity is thus a sign of a specific kind of cultural difference – not simply their difference from Venice or Rome, but their difference from Caliban. If Caliban is a means of discussing the contours of the colonization of the Americas, the other two characters allow us to open up the question of Europe's interaction with the 'old world'. The cultural difference between it and Europe could not be expressed as one between unlettered and lettered cultures. The East was not, at least not then, Europe's silent 'other'. Colonial discourses may have subsequently muffled the 'voice' of the colonized people around the world, but the processes of silencing differed. Eastern scripts had long been objects of display much in the same way as gems or artifacts, and they were also subjects for serious study; both display and inquiry stemmed from the status of these languages as the necessary currency for trade in the largest markets of the world. The idea of a shared linguistic ancestry between Indian and European languages developed much later but, during the early modern period, the renewed and expanded contact with the East resulted in what Donald Lach has called the 'rebabelization' of European languages whose vocabularies literally renewed themselves with words from Malay, or Tamil, or Malayalam or what Purchas calls 'the bannian tongue'. Antonio Pigafetta, a companion of Magellan, compiled a list of Asian words that were reproduced in French, Venetian and English; Richard Eden, Samuel Purchas and Richard Hakluyt all issued similar lists.[16]

The linguistic difference between Caliban and Othello/ Cleopatra reminds us that if New World natives were placed within a discourse of primitivism, the peoples of the East – Turkey, Egypt, India and Persia – were embedded within a discourse of cultural excess.[17] Both discourses fed into the notion of barbarism, and both played with the idea of alien monstrosity. Hayden White indicates a distinction between the

Wild Man and the Barbarian in Greek and medieval European discourses – the former was generally mute, outside civil society, and thus potentially a noble savage, whereas the latter was marked by linguistic chaos, lived under an alien law, and was therefore knowingly evil (1978: 165). While these are not discrete prototypes, they are useful in thinking through the different images of otherness in Renaissance travel narratives and literature. New World peoples were extensions of the Wild Man idea – cannibals, unlettered, child-like, innocent, natural, unworldly, while those from the East were caught up in difference as decadence and barbarism – luxurious, opulent and depraved. Both were seen as violent or promiscuous, and in practice any rigid demarcation of categories is qualified by their various permutations and combinations: 'Moors' for example, embody anyone from Africa to India and range between primitivism and excess. Still, Othello and Caliban can be seen as roughly indicating this division.

Perhaps the most crucial distinction between these discourses is that the aggressive metaphoric use of the female body, which is so blatant in representations of the New World, is missing in the Eastern materials. If the famous picture by Stradanus of a naked America half rising from her hammock, literally dis-covered by and looking back at a clothed Vespucci, set the tone for all future Renaissance representations of that continent (le Corbeiller 1961: 210), iconographic representations of Asia such as the influential ones by Cesare Ripa show her sumptuously clothed, riding on a camel and carrying an incense burner, wearing either a wreath of flowers and fruit or a turban. In Cesare Vecellio's well-known costume book (1598), for example, women from India, Turkey and Persia are heavily draped in comparison to their naked African or American sisters. If the African or American woman stands in for Woman as Nature, ripe for ravishing, her Eastern counterpart becomes the embodiment of Woman as Artifice – ever ready to ensnare.

Fairly typical in its pictures of Turkish women is George Sandys's travelogue *Relation of a Journey Begun Anno Domini 1610*. Sandys spends much energy in describing their elaborate toilette – the application of henna and kohl, the parting and combing of hair, the details of the many garments. The account flounders when it dwells on the long moments when women are cloistered with each other and engaged in pampering their bodies: 'Much unnaturall and filthie lust is said to be committed daily in the remote closets of these darksome *Bannias* [bathhouses]: yea, women with women; a thing incredible, if former times had not given thereunto both detection, and punishment' (Sandys 1627: 69). The sensuality of Eastern women repeatedly becomes the basis for predicting the downfall of Eastern empires. Greville's biography of Sir Philip Sidney evokes 'the Grand Signior asleep in his Seraglio; as having turned the ambition of that growing monarchy into idle lust; corrupted his martiall discipline' (Greville 1987: 86). These lines are echoed by the commentaries of various Romans on Antony's downfall: 'he fishes, drinks, and wastes / The lamps of the night in revel' (I. iv. 4–5); he is the 'ne'er-lust-wearied Antony' who cannot be plucked from 'the lap of Egypt's widow' (II. i. 37–8) and transforms his men 'to women' (IV. ii. 36).

It has been suggested that, in Shakespearean plays, and in Shakespeare's day, intense liaisons with all women, not just non-European women, lead to the effeminization of men (Rackin 1994: 69). The 'Orient' magnified such threats to European masculinity – Turkey, Persia, India and the Spice islands were associated with both excessive effeminacy and excessive libidinousness. Men from these regions were thereby placed in an especially contradictory position: the supposed effeminacy of their cultures rendered them less than masculine, while their lust (seen as sanctioned by their culture and religion) made them exceed the norms of civilized masculinity. Both excess and lack in these terms connote bestiality. African men occupy a similar position because of a shared Muslim (Moorish) culture's supposed hedonism. Renaissance writings on Islam emphasize three things – that it is 'cruel and bloody'; that it is 'false' because its prophet Mohammed was an imposter; and that it is sensual and decadent in promising 'marvelous beautiful women, with their Breastes wantonly swelling' as well as 'fair Boyes' in Paradise, thus encouraging their pursuit in this life also (Warmistry 1658: 145). Phyllis Rackin argues that homosexuality between European men was not regarded as threatening male virility but in the case of African and Eastern men, it (along with heterosexual love) became indicative of their effeminacy and extended the notion of the degenerate harem. Othello is caught between imputations of bestiality and decadence. Iago repeatedly suggests to him that his vulnerability to Desdemona renders his masculinity, and humanity, suspect (III. iii. 378; IV. i. 61, 65, 88–9). He appeals to the commonplace that uxoriousness undercuts masculinity, but of course the simultaneous suggestion is that Othello is not quite the European man he has fashioned himself to be. Desdemona's power over him thus threatens to return him to a luxurious, undisciplined creature, the 'circumcised dog' that lurks beneath his European martial self.

The distinctions between gender coding in discourses about the New World and the Old does not mean that Eastern women and lands were not conceived of as interchangeable terrain on which colonial power could be deployed. But European traders in Asia could hardly encode themselves as the male deflowerers of a feminized land. Alternative discursive strategies thus came into play: the Oriental male was rendered effeminate, or depicted as a lusty villain from whom the virile but courteous European could rescue the native (or the European) woman. As we might expect, 'the turban'd turk', the harem, the palanquin, the eunuch, the veiled female body and the secrecy, mystery and enclosed spaces signified by these become recurrent symbols of this world. The seclusion of both Hindu and Muslim women from the public, and particularly the foreign gaze, only fuelled the recurrent fantasy of their possession. For William Lithgow, to take one example, the fact that Turkish women are 'modestly masked' merely indicates that they are 'fearful and shame-fast abroad, but lascivious within doors, and pleasing in matters of incontinency'. Such duplicity on the part of its women becomes emblematic of the East itself – Constantinople is 'A Painted whore, the maske of deadly sin, / Sweet faire without, and stinking foul within' (Lithgow 1632: 101, 84–5).[18] The two different kinds of representations of women thus come to signify both their availability, and the sanction for Europeans to possess them.

I have outlined how clothing and speech function as signifiers of two different kinds of non-European-ness, evoking both the cultural nakedness of a Caliban, and the decadence and 'magic' of an Othello and a Cleopatra.[19] Both clusters of ideas are the site of a process of historical layering whereby older notions of the noble savage, the Wild Man, or barbarism are reworked through each subsequent cross-cultural encounter. The alterity between Europe and 'the East' (especially in its Christian versus Turk variant) often tends to be regarded as a static inheritance from medieval or even older encounters. While the 'facts' of early contact between 'black people' and England form the staple opening of any discussion of 'race' in Renaissance drama, these facts are generally confined to the development of the slave trade. Othello continues to invoke the history of slavery, which is of course the most obvious route by which the pre-colonial subject can be seen as diminished into a colonial position. But this renders Othello and Caliban comfortably similar, and deflects attention from another, perhaps more problematic because less obvious, 'pre-history' of empire – the trade with the East. Sixteenth-century drama registers these differential beginnings. It repeatedly engages with and re-constructs the relationship between European, Christian or English society and an 'other' who is neither silent nor outside civil society.

III

Shakespeare's 'others' are remarkably few in number – Othello, Caliban, Shylock, Jessica, Cleopatra and her train, Aaron, Tamora if we wish, and Morocco. Of course Shakespeare's views on 'race' and difference are not contained by them; the Moor made pregnant by Launcelot is merely mentioned by other actors in *The Merchant of Venice* and yet she can indicate much about 'race' in the plays and in Renaissance studies (Hall 1993). Even plays without any hint of 'foreigners', like *Love's Labours Lost*, are eloquent in this respect; others, such as *Troilus and Cressida*, frame the Greco-Trojan conflict in terms inflected by contemporary ideas of racial and cultural difference. But there were the hundreds of dark-skinned characters on the Elizabethan and Jacobean popular stages, as well as in court theatre, city pageants, masques and public as well as private entertainments, and even though there are several studies of these figures, Shakespearean drama still tends to be read as isolated from them, or simply as more liberal, or more complex in its representations of otherness.

For centuries, folk entertainments as well as upper-class pleasures rehearsed the encounter of Europe and its others and insistently reproduced cultural difference on its stages. It is well

known that 'blacked up' figures, 'wild men' or 'village grot-
esques' appeared in the morisco (the word itself meant 'Moorish'); that the dance arrived from North Africa via Spain, and
even that it represented 'a mock fight between Moors and
Christians' (Welsford 1926: 26–8; Withington 1918). 'Blacking
up' appears to have been a persistent feature of court entertainments, even involving royalty. There is the rather spectacular instance of Charles VI of France who, with five lords,
entertained some guests at a wedding on 29 January 1393:
masking and covering themselves with pitch and frayed linen
'they appeared as *hommes sauvages* covered with hair from head
to foot, and in this guise they rushed into the hall holding
hands, making queer gestures, uttering wolfish cries and performing a mad dance'. This performance ended in a fiery death
for four of the maskers, accidentally torched by the Duke of
Orleans, who was anxious to discover their identity (Welsford
1926: 43). In Scottish tournaments in 1505, James IV scandal-
ized society by setting up a black woman as the Queen of
Beauty and himself as the 'wild knight' who defended her. Four
black men danced naked in the snow (and later died) at the
wedding of James I and Anne (Williams 1970: 21), and Queen
Anne and her ladies blacked up in Inigo Jones's *The Masque of
Blackness* (1605). But the most common form of representation
of outsiders was to show them paying homage to European
royalty. During the entertainments for Elizabeth at Kenilworth
Castle in 1575, for example, it was arranged that a *Hombre
Salvagio* or wild man should testify to the queen's 'glorie'
(Bergeron 1971: 30–2). Such figures rather nebulously evoked
a whole range of people and ideas that indicated the margins
of European civil society, but they created a theatrical lineage
for future representations of cross-cultural encounters.

The spectacle of the homage-paying stranger also reworked
the story of the black Magus, which, prior to the sixteenth and
seventeenth centuries, had 'provided a principal convention for
the visual representation of blacks', as well as the legend of the
Queen of Sheba's spice and gem-laden arrival at Solomon's
court (Erickson 1993: 504).[20] Sheba, the story goes, laid the
riches of her Arabian kingdom (Saba) at the feet of the wise
king, and Solomon 'gave unto the Queen of Sheba all her
desire' (1 Kings 10: 1). The child of their union is supposed to
have begotten the ruling dynasty of Ethiopia. Such was the

attraction of the story that it was somewhat incongruously included in Caxton's translation of *The Lives of the Saints*, painted by (among others) Piero della Francesca, Raphael and Rubens, and evoked by numerous Renaissance theatricals. As English interests in the East grew, the central image of the tale of Sheba – an Eastern Queen who *willingly* gives her wealth *in exchange* for sexual satisfaction and Western 'wisdom' (be that the Christian religion or European civility) – was continuously retold, shaped by multiple encounters, especially those that resulted from the newly set up East Indian spice trade. Of course, the theme of an 'enamoured Moslem princess' who helps her Christian lover escape from her father's captivity, and either runs away with him or makes him ruler of her own country, is a staple feature of medieval romance. It has even been suggested that such a tale worked its way into French literature from *The Arabian Nights* (Warren 1914). But now the tale was to be shaped further by developments that I can only briefly indicate.

During the last years of the sixteenth century, the image of the East was recharged by gathering excitement about its new potential: the English translation of the Dutchman Jan van Linschoten's work *Itenario* in 1598 made a great impact on English merchants, as did Theodor de Bry's lavish travel collection, *Collectiones peregrannationum in Indian Orientalem et Occidentalum*, which was issued from Frankfurt between 1590 and 1634. Richard Hakluyt had hardly touched on Asian materials in the first edition of *Principall Navigations*, but after 1590 he became one of the most assiduous collectors of information on Asia, acquiring travellers' logs and price records, reproducing travel narratives with the object of providing the first fleets bound for India with as much authoritative data as possible. Similar publications increased over the next two decades (Birdwood and Foster 1893: xviii). Hakluyt persuaded the traveller Ralph Fitch, who had returned from India in 1599, to write his 'wonderful travailes', which became the first English account of India. The final edition of *Principall Navigations* (which was issued between 1598 and 1600) also carried a translation of the Venetian merchant Cesare Federici's book on India, along with John Newberry's letters from that country and many other related documents. The other pioneering English collector of travel accounts, Richard

Eden, was similarly interested in stimulating interest in Eastern expansion.[21]

Then there were the actual voyages which literally re-opened 'the Orient' to the English gaze. Trading stations sprung up all over the Ottoman Empire following the Anglo–Turkish treaty and these generated first-hand accounts of the East. In March 1588, the *Hercules* returned from Tripoli in Syria, 'the richest ship of English merchant goods that ever was known to come into this realme', as described by John Eldred (Hakluyt 1904: III, 328). Its cargo included 'silk from Persia, indigo and cotton from India, cinnamon from Ceylon, pepper from Sumatra and nutmegs, cloves and mace from the Moluccas', convincing sceptics about the viability of trade in the East Indies. The huge profits made by the Dutch East India Company, the defeat of the Armada and the continual and steep rise in pepper prices between 1592 and 1599 all contributed to the initiation of direct English trade with India. The East India Company, set up on the last day of 1600, averaged enormous profits of 101 per cent over the first five voyages. Contemporary tales of Eastern pleasures were woven from these golden threads.

Because the Eastern enterprises were conceived of as 'trade' (as opposed to colonization or settlement), in the dramatic literature the motif of exchange is often repeated, and the willingness of the other to enter into a transaction with the West is emphasized.[22] Because older legends of Eastern wealth were transformed by newer reports of Eastern courts and monarchs, with whom European factors had to negotiate at length, the figures of non-Europeans are often royal; because of the iconographic tradition that represented continents and countries as female, and because gender relations often encode colonial fantasies, these Eastern royals are often women. We can see why the homage-paying stranger of the court entertainments becomes the 'Indian' king or queen of London civic pageants, which were sponsored by specific companies such as the Company of Grocers who had an obvious interest in the Eastern trade. In Middleton's *The Triumphs of Honour and Virtue* (1622), for example, 'a black personage representing India, called, for her odours and riches, the Queen of Merchandise' is 'attended by Indians in antique habits: Commerce, Adventure and Traffic'. Like the Moorish king in Middleton's earlier pageant *The Triumphs of Truth*, India offers her own conversion to Christianity as a justification for English trading practices overseas. She asks the viewer to observe her 'with an intellectual eye', to see beyond her native blackness, which was commonly associated with the devil, with depravity, sin and filth, and to perceive her inner goodness, which, she suggests, is made possible by her new faith. 'Blest commerce' is literally a crusader for Christianity and 'settles such happiness' on the Indian queen that the English merchants' cargo of 'gums and fragrant spices', indeed all 'the riches and the sweetness of the east', are only fair exchange for the 'celestial knowledge' that is now hers.

Predictably, such appearances were common in the Jacobean mayoral shows through several decades: to cite just a few instances, in Anthony Munday's *The Triumphs of Re-united Brytannia* (1605), for example, an Indian king and queen come to England, bringing with them 'no meane quantity of Indian Gold'; in *Chruso-thrambos, the Triumphs of Golde* (1611), a 'King of Moores' appears 'gallantly mounted on a golden leopard, he hurling gold and silver every way about him'. The pageants sponsored by the Company of Grocers, whose members were instrumental in setting up the East India Company, were especially fond of this theme throughout the century: Middleton's *The Triumphs of Honour and Industry* (1617) contains a personification of India, 'the seat of merchandise'; John Squire's *The Triyumphs of Peace* (1620) shows the figures of America, Asia and Africa crowning Europe as empress of the earth; John Tatham's *London's Triumph* (1659) depicts 'several of the places or countries, in which the commodities belonging to the Grocers Trade doe grow'; Thomas Jordan's *London Triumphant* (1672), includes an Indian emperor, 'negroes in Indian habits' and the figure of America; and his *The Triumphs of London* (1678) has an 'East Indian' deity 'called Opulenta, a representative of all the intrinsic treasure in the Oriental Indies'. The Grocers' shows routinely began with black boys, mounted on griffins or camels, strewing the streets with the 'delicious traffic of the Grocers Company': company records show payments for '50 sugar loaves, 36 pounds of nuttmegs, 24 pounds of dates and 114 pounds of ginger' which were used in this manner in the 1617 show (Heath 1869: 430).

In the theatre too the figure of an Eastern queen repeats the pattern of assimilation and homage. For example, Fletcher's

Shakespeare and cultural difference 185

The Island Princess, performed in 1621, enacts the story of a love affair between Quisara, princess of Tidore, and Armusia, a Portuguese voyager. Tidore was one of the Moluccan islands which were the heart of the spice trade, and the seat of long drawn colonial competition between the Portuguese, the Spanish, the Dutch and the English. Fletcher's play, based on a history of the Spanish conquest of the islands – *Conquista de las island Moluccas* (1609) by Bartolemé Leonardo de Argensola – begins with Quisara demanding of her first Portuguese suitor, the captain Ruy Dias, that he convert to her religion in order to marry her. It ends with her own conversion to Christianity as the wife of Armusia. This drama enacts and refigures the politics of the spice trade, and of English voyaging to the East in general (Loomba 1996; Raman 1994). The pattern is repeated in Philip Massinger's play *The Renegado* (1621). Donusa, a niece of the Turkish sultan Amurath, falls in love with Vitelli, a Venetian, and tries to convert him to Islam. At the same time Vitelli's sister Paulina has been captured by the Turks, and is at the mercy of their lust. Both siblings resist 'turning Turk', but while Paulina remains chaste, Vitelli becomes sexually and emotionally involved with Donusa. The play ends with Donusa's conversion to Christianity and escape to Europe as Vitelli's wife. Of course, the motif of a native queen marrying the white colonizer is familiar to most students of the Renaissance through the story of Pocahontas. But it is a measure of the relative neglect of non-New World materials that Pocahontas's tale has hitherto functioned to eclipse its 'Eastern' variations.[23] I have tried to indicate some examples of its 'relocation', which is really a parallel story arising from specific historical developments. If there is a similarity in the Pocahontas narrative and the stories of the Eastern queens it is because of a shared dream of empire in both places.

It is within this literary pattern that we can place *Antony and Cleopatra*. The play participates in recurrent contemporary debates on disorderly women, and it reveals the intersection of such debates with colonial ideologies by showing a feminized Egypt in a sexualized struggle for power against a masculine imperial Rome (Loomba 1989: 75–9). But Cleopatra cannot stand in for a homogenized female 'other' – she derives quite specifically from Eastern colonial discourses which, as we have seen, implicate women somewhat differently than do New

World writings. Critics have remarked that Cleopatra carries no trace of the Greek lineage of her historical or Plutarchan counterpart – she is 'with Phoebus' amorous pinches black' (I. v. 28), she embodies Egyptian sorcery and magic, she is described in terms of Egyptian snakes and crocodiles, she *is* Egypt itself. The sexual tension between her and Antony is mapped onto the political, gendered tension between Orient and Occident, Egypt and imperial Rome. One expression of the threat Cleopatra presents to Rome is the reversal of gender roles: Antony dons her robes and she his sword; Antony's comrades think he is emasculated by her; and whereas women's personalities are normatively understood as rewritten by their relationships with men, here Antony's identity is remoulded and in crisis. After Antony's death, Cleopatra continues to resist being incorporated into Rome, but she allows herself the indulgence of representing her relationship with Antony as one between husband and wife – terms that she had denied throughout his life. Her suicide is also symbolically double-edged: it outwits her would-be captors, but it also marks her adoption of 'the high Roman fashion' (IV. xv. 87) – a trademark of Antony's culture (Loomba 1989: 128–30).

Each text plays with and on the vocabulary it inherits. Like Quisara in *The Island Princess* and Donusia in *The Renegado* Cleopatra is in love with a white man, but unlike them, she does not surrender her sovereignty to imperial culture. Unlike the figures of Eastern royalty paraded on London streets (and unlike the real-life Pocahontas), she does not leave the shores of her native land. Rather than the image of a kneeling queen, *Antony and Cleopatra* ends with the picture of the 'old serpent of the Nile' outwitting her adversaries by holding a snake to her breast, desperately trying to mask her defeat 'in this vile world' by invoking 'immortal longings' and a language of the sublime (V. ii. 313, 280). Instead of a European traveller who brings away a converted black queen, in this play it is that queen who tempts the visitor to 'flee himself' (III. xi. 7) and 'turn Turk'.

In the context of the precariousness of the English toe-hold in Eastern lands, we can appreciate the meaning of the recurrent image of a converted and compliant queen for audiences at home. The triumphal arches and pedestals erected in Lisbon when Philip of Spain made his formal entry there in 1581 depicted personifications of various territories in the East which had been conquered by Portugal, all offering their products to the new king. Goa, Portugal's main outpost in India, was represented as 'Queen of the East' and occupied a central position in the show (Lach 1968–94: II. i. 13). The English representations had no such territorial backing. The English had only recently staked their claim to the wealth of the Indies and had to contend with moody monarchs and hostile bureaucracies in places like Turkey and India, Portuguese, Spanish and Dutch rivalry all over the East Indies, and some scepticism at home.

Given the elusiveness of the fabled Oriental wealth, a slippery Cleopatra, 'cunning beyond man's thought' (I. ii. 143), takes on a special resonance, if only in retrospect. The plays as well as the other entertainments repeatedly picture the conversions of 'others' to Christianity, or their fraught attempts to appropriate European civility and culture. But, as Peter Hulme reminds us,

> the boundaries of civility proved extraordinarily permeable in the *other* direction. Just as Othello was a single, fictional counterexample to the thousands of Christians who 'turned Turk' in the ports of Southern Europe and North Africa in the sixteenth and seventeenth centuries, so Pocahontas was a unique convert, uniquely remembered.
>
> (Hulme 1985: 26)

Cleopatra's 'cunning' evokes the unmanageability of the East. Akbar and Jahangir constantly flirted with Christianity, and the letters of Jesuit priests publicized their embassy in Indian courts. But the East yielded hardly any stories of royal conversions, and in fact Church history 'records only one baptism of an Indian into the Church of England in the whole of the seventeenth century' (Neill 1966: 75).

Narratives such as that of Othello, or 'real life' stories describing the conversions of Muslims or 'infidels' to Christianity 'manage' a pervasive cultural anxiety at the heart of European expansion, an anxiety about a reverse movement whereby Europeans are swallowed up by foreignness (see Warmistry 1658). Islam's proximity to Christianity and their mutual animosity together made the slide from one to the other a constant nightmare which is revisited by plays, sermons and travelogues. Robert Daborne's play *A Christian Turn'd Turke*

(1612) staged a bizarre conversion ritual – Ward, an English pirate who becomes a Turk in order to marry a Turkish seductress, has to swear on 'Mahomet's head', reject a 'cuppe of wine' offered by a Christian and take off his sword, put on rich clothes including a turban with a half-moon in it, and mount a richly clad ass. We do not see the circumcision, but it is mentioned as having taken place. The play is based on the life of John Ward, who absconded from England and joined forces with the Turkish operator Kara Osman, and later with a Dutch pirate Simon Dansiker who also appears in Daborne's play.[24] Stories featuring an 'Escape from Barbary' and escape from Turkish pirates were staple parts of both fiction and travel collections (Purchas 1905: VI, 146–71; see also Starr 1965 and Chew 1937: 373–86). Real or imagined castration is repeatedly evoked in the narratives of 'turning Turk' – Heywood's *Fair Maid of the West*, Part I, for example, hints at the castration of the foolish Gazet, who is dazzled by the promise of Moorish lucre, and Donusia's companion in *The Renegado* is an English-born eunuch, Carazie. The Janizzaries who were the strongmen of the Turkish court were reportedly not Turkish at all, but castrated European men.

Read against these narratives, stories such as those of Jessica's conversion to Christianity, Othello's Europeanization, or Caliban's education are rendered 'incomplete' in themselves. Every Shakespearean representation of otherness is thus not only in dialogue with other plays and other contemporary accounts about foreigners, but also, implicitly, with what these outsiders were saying to Europeans.

IV

The extent and meaning of English Renaissance drama's fascination with the Orient still needs to be established. Louis Wann (1914) estimates that forty-seven plays produced between 1579 and 1642 deal with 'the Orient' alone; between 1587 and 1607 at least twenty-five of these dealt with Turks.[25] Thematically and ideologically, the East Indies may have inflected the drama to a much greater extent. Certainly drama participated in reorienting the Orient for Europe. Various critics have remarked on the theatricality of the formal Orientalism of a later period – Edward Said calls the Orient 'the stage on which the whole East is confined' (1978: 63); in *Writing Culture*, James Clifford says it functions 'as a theater, a stage on which a performance is repeated, to be seen from a privileged standpoint' (quoted in Case 1991: 111). George Sandys indicates another sort of Oriental theatricality which is exploited by English travelogues and plays: describing the Turkish sultan's passage from his seraglio to Aya Sofia, he writes, 'there is not in the world to be seene a greater spectacle of humane glory'.[26] Not only were the fabled riches and the glamour of the East Indies fodder for spectacles, but the essence of the East was seen to lie in public situations which were obviously theatrical – courts, processions, pageants or festivals. Travel accounts as well as all the plays I have mentioned exploit this sense of Eastern theatricality – Enobarbus's description of Cleopatra on her silver and gold barge, the Moorish court scenes of *Fair Maid of the West*, or the Turkish court scenes of *The Renegado*, the conversion ritual of *A Christian Turn'd Turk*, or even the sumptuous displays of 'Indian' royalty in the civic pageants. This sense of the East as inherently dramatic could also have contributed to the oft-noted histrionic quality of figures such as Cleopatra and Othello.

Earlier I discussed the ideological tension between narratives of conversions to the religious, civil and sexual order of Europe and reports of Christians 'turning Turk'. If the theatre dominantly enacted the former scenario, it quite literally involved a version of the latter – while black entertainers were common in English courts, black characters on the public stage were exclusively played by white men who had to acquire 'sooty bosoms', 'fleeces of woolly hair', 'mores garments' by putting on 'black vellet', 'maskes' or 'corled hed sculles of blacke laune' to turn Turk, Persian, African or American (Jones 1962). Studies of this aspect of theatrical representation of cultural difference remain surprisingly thin. We know that masks gave way to black paint – Isabel in *Lust's Dominion* calls it 'the oil of hell' – which was used at least as early as in Ben Jonson's *Masque of Blackness* (1605). We even have the process of 'blacking up' depicted on stage, as in Brome's *The English Moor* in which Millicent is disguised as a Moor. But were there any particular kinds of actors who played the non-white parts? How did the physical representation of 'Oriental' people differ from that of Africans? Were any of the black people living in Britain ever employed in the public theatre? Answers to such questions would be very useful for locating the historically shifting meanings of racial/cultural difference as well as the ways in which they might have been questioned.

The ideological/critical ramifications of white actors playing non-white persons remain even less explored. The neglect can most easily be illustrated by pointing to the comparatively dense studies that have been undertaken with respect to gender. Boys playing female parts has been the crux of critical re-evaluations of gender, sexuality, sexual difference and eroticism in the period. We have debated whether theatrical cross-dressing destabilized gender roles or in fact reinforced them, and asked how it intersected with the representation of masculinity and femininity in the plays themselves, with cross-dressing off the stage, and with social mobility in general.[27] No similar studies have been undertaken with respect to race – why is it, for example, that while men dressing as women can be regarded as potentially 'unsettling' gender categories, no such radical meaning attaches to 'blacking up'?[28] Can this be one point of entry into considering the tensions between 'race' and other categories of social difference? It is also worth considering the double-play that produced non-European women on stage. What processes of fantasy and disguise on the part of both actor and audience, for example, were involved in the transformation of a certain Edward Rogers who played the Turkish beauty Donusia in Massinger's *The Renegado*? What intersections of homoeroticism and cross-cultural disguise are visible in these performances?

This essay cannot explore these issues in greater detail. It has tried to suggest that critical studies of 'race' or 'culture' in Shakespeare should reconsider the existing paradigms of colonial relations and look at an expanded historical and theatrical archive. Although such a reorientation derives in part from the urgencies of post-colonial criticism's attention to subaltern agency, I have not touched upon what is arguably the most important and most neglected dimension of any such inquiry – pedagogy. Teaching Shakespeare in a non-Western classroom is a daily reminder that it is impossible to divorce what cultural difference means 'in' the plays from what it means in our lives; others may be reminded of this overlap by different urgencies in their own teaching and writing lives. To the extent that work on appropriations and contemporary performances of Shakespeare has multiplied over the last decade, Shakespearean criticism has extended its reach into cultural politics. But to the extent that in recent years very few analyses of 'race' or cultural difference in Shakespeare address themselves to pedagogy or institutional politics, 'alternative' criticism seems to be operating within a shrunken sphere where the 'world', not the classroom, is its oyster.[29]

9

'Othello was a white man': properties of race on Shakespeare's stage

DYMPNA CALLAGHAN

At James VI's marriage to Anne of Denmark in 1589, four young black men danced naked in the snow in front of the royal carriage (Hall 1991: 4). In 1554 five black men from Guinea were brought to London by traders, and one of the men fathered a child who became the object of intense scrutiny because, even though his mother was English, he was 'in all respects as black as his father' (Tokson 1982: 1; Jordan 1968: 6). In 1577 an 'Eskimo' couple captured by Martin Frobisher's expedition to Meta Incognita were brought to London where they could be found on the banks of the Thames with their English-born child, fishing and hunting swans and ducks by royal licence (Mullaney 1988: 65). In 1596 Elizabeth (unsuccessfully) issued a warrant ordering that all 'blackamoors', black servants, exotic signs of their masters' wealth, be rounded up so that Casper Van Senden, a merchant of Lubeck, could trade them for English prisoners held captive on the Iberian peninsula (Cowhig 1985: 6; Hill 1984: 8). Between 1585 and 1692, numerous civic pageants, *tableaux vivants* devoid of action and dialogue, specify the inclusion of 'Negroe boys' or 'beautiful Raven-black negroes' (not just English people in blackface), sitting astride effigies of lions, camels, griffins and unicorns (Barthelemy 1987: 50, 47). These are not representations of racial otherness performed by the English (or, in the first instance, the Norwegians, since the royal couple were married in Oslo), but the display of people from Africa and the New World motivated by curiosity and profit.

If, as James Walvin claims, Africans, who were by far the most numerous and conspicuous racial others in early modern England, were an everyday sight in London (Walvin 1971: 61–3; Drake 1990: 274; Shyllon 1977: 3) and participated in the forms of cultural exhibition outlined above, why is it that an African never trod the boards of a Renaissance stage? Given that Africans and representations of them were so popular in exhibitions, and such a potential box-office attraction, one might expect some venturesome theatre owner or playwright to have included an actual African in his group of players, problems of training and apprenticing a foreign actor not withstanding. Shakespeare was in fact more enterprising in this regard than most of his contemporaries, incorporating a role for the Prince of Morocco in a plot that did not originally require one and, in the case of Othello and Aaron, elaborating extensively on the nameless prototypes in his sources (Gillies 1994: 102). Despite the intensive use of 'exotic' characters in the plays, however, they were always depicted by white actors. Yet, as the above instances of an African presence in England indicate, there was no paucity of Africans in England, a fact which bespeaks complexities of racial impersonation unaccounted for in our habitual assumptions that there were no Blacks in Shakespeare's England. This essay will investigate the obvious but none the less curious fact that in Shakespeare's plays there are histrionic depictions of negritude, but there are, to use Coleridge's infamous phrase, no 'veritable negroes'. There are, indeed, no authentic 'others' – raced or gendered – of any kind, only their representations.

The first part of the essay will address the histrionic mechanisms of racial impersonation and their attendant social dynamics, while the latter part will attempt to grasp the striking but ineluctable discrepancy between the cultural performance of alterity on the one hand and its lived condition on the other, as a function of the representational systems required by emergent capitalism.[1] I will insist throughout, though not in the sense meant by the critic I quote, that 'Othello *was* a *white* man' (see the Arden edition of *Othello*, p. li).[2] This proposition was put forward by one Miss Preston, writing in the notoriously racist pre-Civil Rights South. Preston, doubtless, would be less enthusiastic about endorsing the notion, equally true, that if Othello was a white man, so was Desdemona.

While all representation is predicated upon the absence of the thing represented, in the instances of race and gender on the public stage, there is a perfect coincidence between social exclusion and exclusion at the level of dramatic representation. Neither Africans nor women[3] performed on the public stage in Elizabethan and Jacobean England although both were present in other forms of cultural display: Africans were involved in civic presentations and women in non-mimetic performances of the court masque. While neither court nor public theatres employed racial others, in civic pageants racial impersonation seems to have persisted alongside the actual exhibition of alien peoples (Barthelemy 1987: 50). However, the representation of Africans is far from being neatly analogous to the question of female impersonation. In fact, it troubles the paradigm of gender representation most clearly when we consider that white women are never exhibited as such, and we do not find them dancing naked before the royal coach.

In what follows, I will describe the operations of two distinct, though connected, systems of representation crucially at work in the culture's preoccupation with racial others and singularly constitutive of its articulation of racial difference: the display of black people themselves (exhibition), on the one hand, and the simulation of negritude (mimesis), on the other. These are the poles of the representational spectrum of early modern England, and their respective mechanisms can be defined as follows: in exhibition, people are set forth for display as objects, passive and inert before the active scrutiny of the spectator, without any control over, or even necessarily consent to, the representational apparatus in which they are placed. Mimesis, on the other hand, entails an imitation of otherness, and its dynamism is a result of the absence of the actual bodies of those it depicts, whose access to the scene of representation, therefore, needs no further restriction or containment. Theatrical mimesis, however, involves the active manipulation of the body of the actor in the process of representation, and regardless of the power of the theatre owner, the director, the patron or the playwright, acting finally involves an embodied performance, in the actor's interpretation of the role (Gurr 1992: 99). By contrast, in the forms of attention which constellate the representational mechanisms of exhibition, power resides almost entirely with the spectator. The actor, then, at least in the context of early modern society, has more power than the exhibit. For all that, the actor cannot control the meanings ascribed to his performance, as we will see, in the historically subsequent instances of African-American and female actors. Here, mimesis and exhibition tend to overlap because the actor is always already construed as an exhibit in a representational context that severely curtails the actor's creative control.

Traversing intricate structural continuities and discontinuities between exhibition and mimesis in the complex representational economy of Renaissance England, femininity (rather than actual women) is itself used to trope racial difference – whiteness – and plays a pivotal if problematic role in the relation of race and sexuality (Doanne 1991: 243, 245). For race, crucially *both* black *and* white, is articulated as an opposition on stage principally by means of cosmetics: burnt cork negritude projects racial difference against white Pan-Cake. The elaboration of cosmetic practices will, I hope, bring into sharper focus the relation between race and gender in drama, showing how whiteness becomes visible in an exaggerated white and, crucially, feminine identity.[4]

I

Racial difference on its most visible theatrical surface requires make-up, and the representation of race on the Renaissance stage is fundamentally a matter of stage properties (see Bristol 1990: 7). Because it is closer to the body of the actor, blackface is a less superficial theatrical integument than the black mask and gloves sometimes used in popular festivities (Jones 1965: 30). Blackface consisted of soot at the level of village theatricals while performances at court and theatre used charred cork mixed with a little oil, 'the oil of hell' as it is referred to in *Lust's Dominion* (1599) (see Jones 1965: 60–8). To complete the representation of negritude, 'Cappes made with Cowrse budge', that is, stiff lambskin fur, 'Corled hed sculles of blacke laune' (Jones 1965: 30, 123) served for African hair. More striking than all other features and accoutrements of alterity, such as nakedness or sartorial splendour, the definitive characteristic of the racial other both on stage and in the culture remained skin colour. Black skin persisted as the most conspicuous marker of racial difference despite burgeoning distinctions between peoples of other races, such as 'white Moors', 'black-amoors', 'tawny Moors', and 'savage m[e]n of Inde'.[5] As the primary histrionic signification of racial otherness in Renaissance court and public theatre, blackface concealed under the sign of negritude a host of ethnicities from Eskimo to Guinean.[6] Indeed, in regimes of cultural representation, negritude became the *sine qua non* of Renaissance alterity. The capacity of blackness simultaneously to intensify, subsume and absorb all aspects of otherness is a specifically Renaissance configuration of othering. Later, with the tawny Restoration heroes such as those of Behn and Dryden, the exotic would part company with blackness (Gillies 1994: 33). But on Shakespeare's stage, blackness marked sheer difference. As the polar opposite of absolute coincidence in the period's antithetical episteme, the culture's construction of its own 'unmarked' (male) identity, black skin was pre-eminent as an integer of a starkly demarcated racial difference.

Blackness, whether natural or cosmetic, was defined by an anterior whiteness just as the exotic in Renaissance systems of representation functioned as accident rather than essence. That is, the not yet systematic distinction between white and black finds itself expressed as ornament, as an overlay of whiteness, not, in Winthrop Jordan's famous phrase, 'White over Black', but precisely its opposite, black over white. This understanding of negritude as an augment to whiteness stresses blackness *as representation*, that is, as an (anti) aesthetic as opposed to an essence, and was corroborated in the period by a climate theory of racial difference, which proposed that blackness was an extreme form of sunburn. In *The Merchant of Venice*, for example, the Prince of Morocco uses the theory in order to forestall objections to what the Venetians regard as a monstrous bid to secure a union with a wealthy white woman:

> Mislike me not for my complexion,
> The shadow'd livery of the burnish'd sun,
> To whom I am a neighbour and near bred.

> (II. i. 1–3)

Rehearsing the latitudinal aetiology of race does not, of course, bring the Prince his hoped for success, and Portia, relieved of him, says 'A gentle riddance . . . / Let all of his complexion choose me so' (II. vii. 78–9). Climate theory both coexisted with and contradicted competing theological and empirically based understandings of race (black skin did not fade when Africans were shipped to England), none of which was entirely discrete or coherent. In crediting the make-up artist for *The Gypsies Metamorphosed* (1621), Ben Jonson ironizes a range of Renaissance theories of racial origin from the mark of Ham to Phaeton's chariot flying too close to the sun:

> Knowe, that what dide our faces was an oyntmen[t]
> Made and laid on by Mr Woolf's appointment.
> (Herford and Simpson 1941: vol. VII, 615, lines 1481–5)

The nature of dark skin as an indelible tincture is conveyed in the Renaissance commonplace that one cannot wash an Ethiop white (see Newman 1987). Black skin becomes at once immutable *and* superficial, analogous to blackface that cannot be washed off.[7] Skin colour thus bears an arbitrary rather than necessary relation to the essential racial identity negritude is assigned to express. It is precisely this inessential status that made negritude vulnerable to the obsessive economy of the visual.[8] For example, when, in *Titus Andronicus*, Aaron asserts the indelibility of blackness, he focuses the audience's attention not only onto the conceptual priority of whiteness, but also onto the fact that he is a white actor whose black veneer is stage make-up:

> Ye white-lim'd walls! ye alehous painted signs!
> Coal black is better than another hue,
> In that it scorns to bear another hue;
> For all the water in the ocean
> Can never turn the swan's black legs to white,
> Although she lave them hourly in the flood.
> (IV. ii. 100–5)

Elsewhere in the play, Aaron rehearses cultural commonplaces about the demonic quintessence of negritude, but here he posits a monstrous inversion of racial identity: whiteness is merely a temporary emulsion ('white-lim'd' suggests that whiteness is not intrinsic but consists only of paint) in contrast a fast and permanent black identity. Black, says Aaron, is better than white because white is characteristically subject to black inscription: it can be defaced. Black, in contrast, can neither be written on, nor can it be returned to white. In arguing for the positive specificity of negritude, Aaron counters the dominant idea of an originary whiteness.

Whiteness, especially when complemented by red, was 'the color of perfect human beauty, especially *female* beauty' (Jordan 1968: 8).[9] That is, in its chromic opposition to blackness, what allows whiteness to be represented at all is 'a certain conceptualization of sexual difference' (Doanne 1991: 224). Race – black *and* white – thus becomes cosmeticized, but in the case of whiteness, also feminized.

Both negritude and whiteness are, for the Renaissance stage, the cosmetic though far from superficial surfaces of difference (see Copjec 1994: 13). In practical terms, 'fair' femininity consisted of a wash for blanching the complexion and rouge for cheeks and lips. Whiteface was a lethal concoction of ceruse or white lead, sometimes mixed with sublimate of mercury and ground orris; occasionally it included slightly less noxious ingredients such as ground hogs' bones, powdered borax, beaten egg whites and lemon juice. Rouge consisted of red ochre and mercuric sulphide, vermilion or cochineal (see Garner 1989: 132; Drew-Bear 1981: 75). Rather less deadly preparations made of powdered brick, cuttle bone, coral and egg shell were available as tooth whiteners. Blackface thus found its practical equivalent in cosmeticized femininity, 'white and red'. Both were referred to as 'face-painting', a derogated species of art. Stage directions for Richard Brome's *The English Moor* (1637), for example, specify that 'A Box of black painting' is required (Jones 1965: 122). William Carleton who witnessed a performance of Jonson's *The Masque of Blackness* also provides evidence that racial difference was conceptualized as a species of comparative cosmetology: the ladies,

> as a part of greatness, are privileged by custom to deface their carcasses. Instead of Vizzards, their Faces, and Arms up to the Elbows, were painted black, which was disguise sufficient, for they were hard to be known; but it became them nothing so well as their red and white, and you cannot imagine a more ugly Sight, than a Troop of lean-cheek'd Moors.
>
> (Orgel 1969: 4)

While blackface was traditionally an aspect of the grotesque in popular entertainments (Jones 1965: 28), one senses that Queen Anne and her ladies intended an erotic presentation of themselves, which Carleton reads, contrary to their intention, as defilement of the pure aristocratic body. For Carleton, the ladies' impersonation is a failure; implausible (they are lean-cheeked) and inappropriate because their dress is 'too light and Curtizan-like for such great ones'. There is a tension here between diaphanous raiment and the impenetrable cosmetic, the opacity of the latter perhaps licensing the transparency of the former. Dense black painting (which, because of the practical difficulty of washing it off, meant that the transformation from black to white promised at the end had to wait until the *Masque of Beauty*) thus becomes congruent with the unveiling of the aristocratic female body and produces the exotic as sexually charged.

Jonson wrote the masque at the request of Queen Anne, who specifically wanted to perform in blackface.[10] That she chose to exercise this degree of creative control is significant in a culture which did not permit women to act on the public stage or even to speak in court entertainments. By engaging with the fascinations of alien femininity the ladies of the court do not involve themselves in the mimetic performance of the type found on the public stage because they are always, to some degree, representing themselves. None the less, such representation is, as Carleton is quick to point out, a form of privilege. Yet, in refusing 'their white and red', which in the context of the masque at least would be entirely conventional, the Queen and her ladies resist an orthodox model of female beauty. Contrary to cultural propriety, they, the mute referents of culture, endeavoured, 'as a part of greatness', to possess their own representation (see Rogin 1987: 224). Seen from this perspective, Carleton's disapproval of blackface and costume is less the product of a racist repulsion than it is part of the general censure of women's power over cultural representation.

The printed text informs us that *Blackness* was '*Personated* at the court at Whitehall on the Twelfth Night, 1605'. While this term was sometimes used synonymously with 'acting', 'personate' has more the force of 'bearing the character of' (*OED*). One might imagine the court lady almost ritualistically bringing to the stage, as a precious and perhaps fragile object, her own character, in its most highly stylized and emblematic form. This requires a more passive enactment than the active character-ization we associate with mimesis, where a character, not the actor's own, has to be 'brought to life' on stage. 'Personate', which, as Andrew Gurr argues, indicates a relatively new theatrical development, (1992: 99), is perhaps closer to our modern word 'impersonate', a simulation whose contours are fully visible, rather than hidden and naturalized in the manner of a theatrical *trompe l'oeil* (see Parry 1990: 103). Blackface, then, by far the most popular way women represented themselves in masques (see Barthelemy 1987: 41), takes the place of acting in *Blackness*, standing in not only for what is not there – black women – but also for the limits of female cultural production. Interestingly, these limits remain visible after the Restoration when actresses were not permitted to use blackface.[11]

That cosmetic adornment registered as an act of cultural representation, a species of theatricality, is apparent in the 'highly artificial, mask-like appearance' produced by cosmetics of the Elizabethan and Jacobean era (Garner 1989: 133). Elizabeth I, of course, not only concealed her smallpox scars but also exercised her power behind a mask of whiteness. Sovereignty became the art both of occlusion and display. Little wonder, then, that an impetus to restrict women's cultural self-representation informs the period's misogynist invective against *women's* use of cosmetics.[12] (Men, like Benedick in *Much Ado About Nothing*, also used cosmetics and while they are subjected to a certain amount of ridicule, they are spared the fierce invective unleashed upon women.) Ostensibly, it was because of their power to beautify that the white and red were assumed to be a form of hypocrisy, misleading men by feigning a beauty that women did not really possess. Cosmetics were associated with prostitutes, as for example in Hamlet's reference to 'The harlot's cheek, beautied with plast'ring art' (III. i. 51). Women's use of cosmetics was roundly condemned, often by the same people who fulminated against theatre and associated all manner of artifice with femininity. In his *Treatise Against Painting and Tincturing of Men and Women*, Thomas Tuke condemns 'painting' as an interference with nature (Garner 1989: 124) while Philip Stubbes argues that the use of cosmetics impugns God, 'for if he could not have made them faire, then hee is not almightie' (quoted in Garner 1989: 133; see also Dolan 1993).

This condemnation of cosmetics as a barbaric practice is also to be found in relation to exotic peoples. Celts, of course, ornamented their bodies with blue woad, and New World peoples engaged in body painting as well as more permanent forms of cosmetic mutilation (such as piercing). John Nicholl records the Olive Branch expedition encountering the inhabitants of Santa Lucia in 1605:

> These Carrebyes at their first coming in our sight, did seem most strange and ugly, by reason they are all naked, with long black hair hanging down their shoulders, their bodies all painted with red, and from their ears to their eyes, they do make three strokes with red, which makes them look like devils or Anticke faces, wherein they take a great pride.
>
> (quoted in Hulme 1986: 129)

The natives' childish pride seems to align them with the vanity of English women. The objection to painting here presents itself merely as an aesthetic objection, while the objection to women's conventional white and red painting is more often a moral one. That the problem is not merely one of cosmetics as an extension of costume but with cosmeticizing as a low-level mimetic practice becomes apparent when we consider male appropriations of female beauty. Shirley Nelson Garner remarks:

> In the picture of beauty drawn in poetry from the Middle Ages through the Renaissance and after – and even still imprinted in the Western imagination – women were admired for their golden hair, high foreheads, blue eyes, lily-white skin, rosy cheeks, cherry lips, and teeth of pearl. The marked white and red of the makeup available allowed them to imitate literally if they wished, the beauty praised in the sonnets.
>
> (Garner 1989: 132–3)

It is striking that precisely the qualities admired in verse, the rhetorical devices which constitute femininity in poetry – ruby lips, rosy cheeks, white flesh – are condemned when women employ cosmetic artifice to enhance their own appearance. The male-controlled discursive display of women in the blazon tradition is culturally valourized, while women's hold on even the lowest reaches of the representational apparatus, cosmetics, is condemned.[13] Women's use of cosmetics might be seen as a sort of writing on the body but, even though it is a practice enacted in conformity with male definitions and fantasies of female beauty, because it is performed by women, as Frances Dolan has argued, it takes on the features of transgressive femininity. What is art in the hands of a poet and presumes a superiority of imitation over nature becomes vanity and artifice in the hands of a woman (Dolan 1993).

White and red, like blackface, is both racial and mimetic (see Hall 1994: 179). That is, anxiety over the use of cosmetics by women betrays itself as an endeavour to exclude women from even the most lowly and personal representational practice and thus discloses their marginal relation to, or more accurately, exclusion from, mimesis. The theatrical depiction of women through cosmetics, on the other hand, uncovers the pivotal role of white femininity in the cultural production of race.

On stage, whiteface was probably the primary way of signifying femininity. It was an impersonation, just like blackface.[14] Not only does female characters' use of cosmetics become a recurrent issue in plays of the period (see Garner 1989 and Dolan 1993), but also, as Annette Drew-Bear has shown in her splendid study of the moral significance of face-painting on the stage, there is a wealth of specific evidence for players' whitening their faces, for example in the account books for Coventry, Cambridge and Chester. The boy playing Ganymede in Ben Jonson's *Poetaster* is admonished that he 'should have rub'd [his] face, with whites of egges ... till [his] browes had shone like our sooty brothers here [i.e. Vulcan, whose face is 'collied' or blackened] as sleeke as a hornbooke' (Drew-Bear 1994: 32–3, 34). Although race is not directly at issue here, the now reflective surfaces and textures of difference, 'sleeke' and 'shone', refer to emergent, if displaced, concepts of race, which they help frame, coordinate and unify.[15] The sensous difference between black and white here is reminiscent of Olivier's blackened body, silk-buffed to a sheen for his performance of Othello. Olivier played opposite Billie Whitelaw, as Desdemona, who was covered from head to toe with white Pan-Cake.

> Olivier was blacked up to the nines, of course. Only the part covered by his jockstrap wasn't. It took him about four hours to get himself buffed up. Jack, his dresser, put rich

browny-black pancake onto his body and buffed him up with silk so that he really shone. Olivier was a master of make-up and he really looked magnificent. . . .

To make my own skin look 'as white as alabaster' as the bard says, I had alabaster make-up all over my body. Once, as I knelt down at his feet, I put my hand on his knee. He glared down at me: there was a white mark on his black knee! Some of my white alabaster had come off on his beautiful shiny black make-up.

(Whitelaw 1995: 13)

In contrast to *Poetaster*, where we see, in the endeavour to make whiteface aesthetically superior to blackface, spectacles of difference becoming racialized for the first time, Olivier and Whitelaw cosmetically enhance already instantiated racial and gender aesthetics.

In the process of early modern theatrical impersonation the dominant group, white men, take on the characteristics of subordinate groups, namely Africans and women. Because women cannot impersonate a femininity they already embody, offstage, women's use of make-up is not impersonation, but an attempt both to 'normalize', to blend in, and a transgression of the boundary that marks subordination. Women's use of cosmetics was at once an attempt to meet an ideal standard of beauty (sometimes, for instance, in an attempt to hide smallpox scars) and a breach of the restrictions on women's representation.

The obverse of impersonation is 'passing', a twentieth-century term, one of whose principal connotations is the imitation of whites by blacks in an attempt to gain access to social privilege from which blacks are excluded (see Robinson 1994). The representational *mechanisms* inherent in women's cosmetic practices (though not their social significance) bear a resemblance to the subordinate's imitation of the dominant we find in twentieth-century 'passing'. They do so in that both passing and impersonation raise hermeneutic problems of knowledge, identity and concealment (see Doanne 1991: 234; Robinson 1994). These are issues central to *Othello* and are articulated with reference to female beauty by Iago, who manipulates Petrarchan tropes about dark and fair female beauty as the play's *blazoner manqué*: 'What an eye she has, / A parley to provocation.' By way of entertaining the ladies, he rhymes his praise of women at the dockside, surveys and evaluates their parts:

IAGO	If she be fair and wise, fairness and wit;
	The one's for use, the other using it.
DESDEMONA	Well prais'd! How if she be black and witty?
IAGO	If she be black, and thereto have a wit,
	She'll find a white, that shall her blackness hit
	(II. i. 129–33)

Possible glosses on Iago's puns are that the dark lady will find a partner like herself, that she will conceal her lack of virtue, or become sexually 'covered' by a man of a lighter complexion, or, alternatively, transform her darkness with white cosmetics. That this is not merely a primordial opposition between fair and dark supremely apposite for Shakespeare's purposes may be glimpsed from Kim Hall's compelling argument that the use of 'fair' to connote light complexion dates back only to the mid-sixteenth century (Hall 1994: 179). In using cosmetics, women attempt, then, by morally dubious means, to assume an ethnically and aesthetically unreproachable raced identity.

In the Renaissance, the spectacle of absolute racial otherness – too disturbing for subsequent audiences – is staged via the trope of gender difference. That is, by virtue of stage cosmetics, the marriage of Othello and Desdemona presents itself as the union of absolute antitheses, black and white. While racial intermarriage in *Othello* symbolically overturns racial hierarchy in terms of the mimetic process itself, there is not an inversion but an exact replication of the performance of negritude. Miscegenation in the play consists precisely of 'black over white' (Jordan 1968: 38) and has its parallel in the techniques of Renaissance theatricality – white skin *under* black make-up. Further, the coincidences between miscegenation and the practice of blackface could never be entirely expunged in performance because black always evoked its underlying antithesis, whiteness: 'One of the marveylous thynges that god useth in the composition of man, is colour: whiche doubtlesse can not bee consydered withowte great admiration in beholding one to be white and an other blacke, beinge coloures utterlye contrary' (Peter Martyr, quoted in Jordan 1968: 7). No other colours were so frequently used to denote polarization.

By the time of Edmund Kean's tawny Moor, there is literally a toning down, using make-up, of what is constructed all along as an irreducible disproportion between Othello's 'begrim'd' countenance and 'sooty bosom' and Desdemona's 'whiter skin of hers than snow'.

The double impersonation of Othello – the white actor playing a Moor who is trying to assimilate in Venice – focuses the structural ambivalence on which impersonation is founded (see Neill 1984: 115). Othello's appearance at the Senate is a defensive simulation of dominant racial and sexual mores. He duplicates the tropes of civilization – deference and decorum: 'Most potent grave, and reverend signiors. My very noble and approv'd good masters' (I. iii. 76–7). Having probably (depending on the time sequence) just committed gross miscegenation with Desdemona, he attempts to play white and straight, against the aberration signified both by his blackface and by his sexual transgression (See Silverman 1992a: 148–50; Neill 1989: 391–2). What Othello self-deprecatingly describes as his '*Rude* . . . speech' and '*round unvarnish'd*' story turns out to be not so much the plain tale he promises, but a compelling and flagrant rendition of the exotic, replete with proper names, marvels and geographical specificity (Gillies 1994: 31). That his tale would win the Duke's daughter too is indicative not of assimilation but of the sexual potency of racial alterity. Othello's appearance at the Senate articulates difference at the level of the visual, and then his narrative obsessively refers us, even in its most compellingly aural aspects (the famous 'Othello music' caricatured by Iago as grotesque 'bombast', and 'horribly stuff'd'), to the *spectacle of tactility* Jonson urged in *Poetaster*; to the 'rude' (i.e. stark), 'round' surfaces of a difference we might touch.

Michael Bristol has argued that, for Shakespeare's playgoers, Othello in the blackface familiar from carnival 'would confront the audience with a comic spectacle of abjection rather than with the grand opera of misdirected passion' (Bristol 1990: 10). There is, he claims, a burlesque element to *Othello* which critics have been reluctant to notice because of their desire to recuperate Othello as tragic hero. As a result, Bristol powerfully contends, critics have ignored the fact that *Othello* is 'a text of racial and sexual persecution' doing the cultural work of *charivari*, and employing many of its methods – impersonation, ridicule and social control, a ritual unmarrying of the couple whose marriage represents the erotic grotesque – beauty and the beast, so to speak. Bristol does not, however, attempt to reduce *Othello* to *charivari*, but to show the elements of punitive exhibition inherent in it.

Building on Bristol's recognition of these critically suppressed dimensions of the play, it is also important to consider how the dramatic form of theatre *does more than* 'make an exhibition' of the culprits who have violated social norms, which is the object of popular rituals such as *charivari*. Theatre is able to negotiate the entire representational register from exhibition to mimesis, and the racial register from deficiency (Moors as subhuman) to excess (libidinous, 'extravagant and wheeling stranger[s]'). Theatre thus allows for more nuanced depictions – that is, more finely calibrated productions of difference – even while working with thoroughly emblematic depictions of Moors and a polarized conception of woman.

Desdemona, probably in whiteface, is, after all, as potentially comic as Othello. Although she would have been the principal object of ritual punishment in *charivari*, she is not the carnivalesque feminine of the play. Rather, the alabaster Desdemona is a plausible impersonation of transgressive femininity, certain formations of which are both punished and valourized in tragedy (Callaghan 1989: 34–73). Indeed, Desdemona, 'smooth, as monumental alabaster' (V. ii. 5) is aligned with the acceptable representational practices of the sepulchre. Bianca, by contrast, who as her name indicates is the play's other rendition of ultra-white womanhood, is associated with the derogated cosmetic arts. As a Cypriot, her histrionic femininity may also entail an element of racial impersonation in that she is 'passing' as a white Venetian beauty.[16] Bianca is probably heavily made up, grotesque, depicting the hyper-femininity that registers the proximity between transvestism and prostitution:

> She was here even now, she haunts me in every place. I was t'other day talking on the sea-bank with certain Venetians; thither comes this bauble; by this hand, she falls me thus about my neck . . . So hangs, and lolls, and weeps upon me; so hales, and pulls me: ha, ha, ha!
>
> (IV. i. 132ff)

Bianca, the 'bauble' who has made her chastity a gaudy plaything, constitutes a commentary on the construction of Desdemona's absolute virtue, that is on the production of difference among women and the elision of polarized categories of femininity. Bianca thus displaces Desdemona who, because she has made an improper marriage, would be the proper object of ritual subjection. As an 'impersonation' both of Desdemona in particular and of women in general, Bianca acts out the difference between the resemblance to and correspondence with 'the thing itself', and thus marks out the space of referentiality inherent in dramatic representation. In this play, of course, 'the thing itself' is figured, not as the real women who are not on stage, but as female chastity, a reified and essentialized femininity, whose fundamental characteristic is an inherent vulnerability to gross dissimulation, such as that practised by Iago.

If, in subsequent historical moments, darkness is always visible and whiteness invisible, so that white women have been able to claim the dominant group's privilege of denying their racial identity, this is not so on the Renaissance stage. This subsequent development is what Mary Ann Doanne calls 'the exercise of whiteness *rather than its representation*' (1991: 245, my italics). In Shakespeare's theatre, however, in the figure of woman – in alabaster Desdemona and the racially not-quite-white, but cosmetically ultra-white, Cypriot Bianca – we have precisely the representation of the dominant race.

II

In the theatre, the exotic, as John Gillies has argued, is a relation of exclusion from the commonwealth (Gillies 1994: 99–100), a condition whose spectacular liminality might be identified with femininity. There is perhaps more of a continuity between the different representational registers of the culture and between economics and the stage than is suggested by Anthony Barthelemy's none the less acute perception that: 'If the politics of otherness and exclusion are the primary forces in determining the portrayal of blacks in the masque, the economics of colonialism play an essential role in creating the black stereotypes found in Lord Mayor's Pageants' (1987: 12). In a burgeoning market economy, liminality inheres in the alienated status of the commodity. Exotics in civic pageants, for instance, literally celebrate the opulence of an alterity accessible through trade. At the London Drapers' pageant in 1522, as well as the obligatory integumentary blackness, the Moor was costumed in a 'turban of white feathers and black satin, sylver paper for his shoes, &c.', while at a Henrican court festivity torchbearers were appareled in 'Crymosyn satyne and grene, lyke Moreskoes, their faces blacke' and six ladies had their 'heads rouled in plesauntes and typpers lyke the Egipcians, embroudered with gold. Their faces, neckes, armes and handes, covered with fyne plesaunce blacke . . . so that the same ladies seemed to be nigrost or blacke Mores' (Jones 1965: 29, 28).[17] In civic and stage simulations, then, 'exotics' could be identified by an almost grotesque 'spectacle of strangeness' (as Jonson refers to the anti-masque in *Queens*) – feathers, gaudy satins, gold embroidery, silver shoes. Such splendid accoutrements reflect the fact that in non-dramatic presentations the function of African characters was primarily (rather than merely) 'decorative'. Indeed, as another of the surfaces of racial difference reproduced on the stage, its superficiality belies its complexity. More than simply a representation of the exploitation of foreign resources and labour, the exotic (which might even be said to be the originary commodity) instantiates the representational apparatus necessary for the advent of the commodity proper. The dehumanization of Africans required to rationalize slavery and the alienation intrinsic to commodification (which makes the products of human labour seem to exist independently of it) have their origins at the same historical moment and in the same representational nexus. The 'appetite for the wonderful' that has been seen as a natural facet of Western culture (Jordan 1968: 25) was fuelled, if not itself produced by, the mechanisms of alienation that are, crucially, at once representational and economic.

Commodities now appeared to have an objective, 'real' existence, independent of the relations of production from which they were made. This fuller development of the mechanisms of alienation constitutive of the commodity, most crucially enabled by the slave trade, made possible as never before an elision between the representational and the real (see Appleby 1978: 243–79). So, when the American Ira Aldridge played Othello in London in April 1833, one critic opined:

In the name of propriety and decency, we protest against an interesting actress and lady-like girl, like Miss Ellen Tree, being subjected by the manager of the theatre to the indignity of being pawed about by Mr. Henry Wallack's black servant; and finally, in the name of consistency, if this exhibition is to be continued, we protest against acting being any longer dignified by the name of art.

(Cowhig 1985: 20)

Importantly, neither Ellen Tree nor Ira Aldridge is here understood to be acting: they are seen to be merely playing themselves.[18] The critic objects to seeing the figure of pure womanhood 'literally' in the 'gross clasps of a lascivious Moor'. For this critic, when the distance between Shakespeare's Othello and Ira Aldridge is diminished by being performed by an African-American, his performance becomes an exhibition as opposed to 'art'; it ceases to be acting, becoming not the *representation* of the-thing-itself, but instead *the-thing-in-itself*. Comparison with Shakespeare's stage is instructive: unlike Aldridge, Burbage could not have been understood as a barbarian *prior* to the fact of mimesis, whatever his interpretation of Othello. That is, the physical presence of a black man is always already an exhibition of monstrosity, whereas his absence on Shakespeare's stage allowed the sign of negritude, that emblem of barbaric alterity beyond the parameters of civilization, to represent tragic humanity.

But before determining whether representations of racial otherness in the Renaissance were relatively benign when compared to the regimes of racial representation that succeeded them, it is worth considering the ideological work of subsequent instances of racial impersonation such as D. W. Griffith's negrophobic film *Birth of a Nation* (1915). In Griffith's 'classic' members of the Ku Klux Klan revivify a post-Civil War South, where freed slaves allegedly pose a threat to civilization. No African-American actors were given major parts and the hundreds used as extras throughout the film did not appear in the list of credits (Rogin 1987: 224). There was a great deal of doubling too, with white bit-part actors playing 'renegade colored people' one moment and the whites pursuing them in Klan robes the next. Gus, the black rapist in *Birth of a Nation*, is played by a white actor since 'no black could be allowed to manhandle Lillian Gish' (Rogin 1987: 225). Griffith claimed that blackface enabled whites to 'impersonate' both sides. However, as Michael Rogin has argued, white control over the cultural production of racial difference also propelled white America's economic hegemony, by making readily available for foreign and domestic policy an image of the demonized other which, in its paradigmatic form, bears a black face (see Rogin 1987: ch. 1).

The progenitor of Griffith's movie is of course the minstrel show. In antebellum America, people of African ancestry were condemned to a system of hereditary slavery in order to provide free labour for Southern plantations. Despite the fact that they existed in sufficient numbers to represent themselves, white men donned blackface to imitate them. Ridicule can only have been part of the motivation; such derision seems superfluous in the light of the daily humiliation and degradation of black labour. Writing in the *North Star* on 27 October 1848, Frederick Douglass denounced blackface imitators as 'the filthy scum of white society, who have stolen from us a complexion denied to them by nature, in which to make money, and pander to the corrupt taste of their white fellow citizens' (quoted in Lott 1993). For Douglass, such travesties of negritude marked the expropriation of both black labour and culture, a phenomenon already incipient, as we have seen, in early modern instances of racial impersonation.[19]

It would be anachronistic to suggest direct parallels between the early modern use of blackface and subsequent constructions of white supremacy not fully instantiated in early modern England. But that the practice of blackface went on when there was no practical necessity for it serves to demonstrate that the ideological and cultural motor of black impersonation has no alliance with the practical necessity we habitually assume in relation to Renaissance theatre.[20] Shakespeare's audience would have witnessed in Othello and Desdemona the spectacle of two men, one young with his face whitened and one older with his face blackened. While, culturally, blackness and femininity become identified with one another, literally, as I have argued above, it is not blackness and femininity that are the same, but the extra-diegetic white masculinity that underlies them both. While the history of *Othello* criticism from Coleridge onwards occludes, rationalizes and temporizes about race, the theatrical necessity of Shakespeare's stage was to *produce* racial difference *and to control it nevertheless.*

III

Both Africans and white women present the peculiar practical and conceptual obstacles inherent in the dramatic depiction of those categories of persons whose cultural alterity, for different reasons, requires their exclusion.[21] Despite significant differences between both the representation and the exclusion of women and Africans from the stage, members of neither group are understood to be capable of mimesis even though Moors were thought to be suitable objects of exhibition. In discursive exhibitions of femininity, as for example when women's 'private parts' are displayed in graphic detail in medical treatises of the period, the oversized labia and clitorises of alien races excite the most interest and curiosity (see Parker 1994: 84–91). White women themselves, however, were not thought of as exhibits until the Restoration. The privilege of becoming an actress was somewhat tainted by the fact that women were understood not to be exercising the thespian arts but engaging in a species of natural, feminine self-display (see Howe 1992).[22]

The difference in the representation of Africans and women, is, I believe, a result of their different roles in emergent capitalism, which uniquely expropriates the labour of both groups. Africans and women supply 'free' labour – women in the domestic sphere and black men and women as slaves.[23] As the *ideolo*gy of gendered division of labour intensified, women, newly relegated to the domestic sphere, became the objects of intense scrutiny at close quarters, which cultural representation reflected accordingly. Increasingly seen to embody the qualities of the private, English and other European women were, for example, uniquely probed by the new scopic practices of anatomy (see Parker 1994; Traub 1995: 85–6).

In the gendered division of labour, there was already in place a naturalized rationale for the expropriation of female labour. In contrast, there was no such rationale for the expropriation of black labour: one had to be invented. Slavery, practised on the unprecedented scale required by burgeoning capitalism, had comparatively weak ideological foundations, relying on fairly inchoate connections between black skin and the Prince of darkness and on a hazy history of the marvellous as the benchmark of alterity.[24] On the representational register, the rationalization of slavery had to extrapolate a discourse of the marvellous. Negritude demanded, then, not the close, furtive disclosures appropriate to white femininity, but the 'full scale' exposure of discovery, marked so vividly in the public display of naked Africans at James's wedding.[25] In that instance, representation became quite literally *exposure*, a condition of which the Africans died within days of the event (see Hall 1991: 4).

In the public theatre, where blackness and femininity were both performed rather than simply exhibited, the stage properties ('props') used to represent them secured the etymological and material connection between 'property' (possession) and 'expropriation' (dispossession). Theatrical integuments of black and white thus marked the production of a difference that could not possess itself.

IV

Margo Hendricks has recently argued that, in the Renaissance, people did not equate race with colour as we do in the United States and Western Europe, and that feminist and cultural scholars cannot limit their readings to seeing the 'whiteness' of Renaissance Studies because:

> Such a move will only make more precise the ideological binarism produced by racial categories, not undo it. Rather than marking 'whiteness,' the imperative that faces cultural and feminist scholarship is theoretically and historically to map the discursive and social practices that prompted seventeenth-century Englishmen and women to define themselves not only in terms of nationalism but also increasingly, in terms of color.

> (Hendricks 1994: 226)

Because *Othello* is a paradigmatic instance of race/gender representation, topics which come into focus most sharply on the issue of miscegenation, the play has become the locus of feminist attempts to deal with the issues elucidated by Hendricks. Karen Newman's seminal essay, '"And Wash the

Ethiop White": femininity and the monstrous in *Othello*', argues
that in the Renaissance it is not the dissimilarity but the
equivalent monstrosity of Africans and women that makes
miscegenation doubly fearful. By these means, Newman inter-
rogates the cultural tendency to assume a natural antithesis
between race and gender.

Taking issue with Newman's position, which she sees as
symptomatic of the way Western feminism collapses categories
of difference and assumes a common history of marginalization, Jyotsna Singh contends that while there are certain
parallels in Renaissance attitudes towards racial and sexual
difference, we cannot elide the condition of black masculinity
with that of white femininity:

> Historically we know the taboo of miscegenation was not so
> much based on fear of the femininity of the white woman as
> it was on the potential phallic threat of black men, who,
> incidentally, bore the brunt of the punishment for violating
> this taboo.
>
> (Singh 1994: 290–1)

Seen in the context of feminist politics, however, these essays
reflect urgent debates and are perhaps less incompatible than
at first they might seem: Newman emphasizes the shared
investment white women and people of colour have in over-
turning patriarchal precepts, while Singh shows how cultural
constructions of white women as the victims of black men
buttress patriarchy.

Virginia Mason Vaughan's wonderfully comprehensive con-
textualization of *Othello* similarly insists that 'race was (and is)
integrally tied to the concept of gender and sexuality' (1994: 5)
and in particular details this connection in the performance
history of the play.[26] When William Charles Macready toured
America, playing Othello in blackface and native costume, he
recorded his horror at the treatment of the slave population in
his diaries, though he makes no connection between slavery
and his own performance. In this respect, Vaughan observes,
he is just like his white slave-owning audiences, who con-
veniently severed art from life, and who 'could accept a black
Othello on stage where they would not welcome a genuine
Negro' (1994: 155). Although, of course, in Britain there was
never a regulation prohibiting black performance, black actors,

most notably Ira Aldridge, were not permitted to perform at the prime professional London theatres in Drury Lane and Covent Garden. This uncodified colour bar persisted until Paul Robeson broke it in 1930 in the face of a barrage of racism from the play's producers as well as audiences. Even those who liked the first performances understood Robeson to be more naturally suited for the part because they thought he possessed primitive black emotions (Vaughan 1994: 188).

The uphill struggle for black representation in elite culture and, perhaps more crucially, for recognition of the capacity of people of African ancestry to engage in mimetic performance, should not be underestimated. Recently, racially mixed casting has become more common in British and American theatre. African-American director Hal Scott used African-American actors to play both Othello and Iago because he does not believe in casting 'solely on the basis of someone's skin color' (Vaughan 1994: 198). Vaughan is critical of this manoeuvre because, she argues, this helps to explain why Othello is so willing to believe Iago, but obscures Iago's racism as his motivation for ruining Othello. Whatever the merits and failures of this particular production, however, Scott's comments indicate that the issue turns on understanding the relation between Blacks and their capacity for mimesis. The point is not that society has reached a sufficient point of enlightenment that we can now afford to be colour blind, but that white racism is a quality that an African-American actor can act without regard to skin colour (see also Orkin 1987; Salway 1991).

V

In his powerful examinations of contemporary racism, Immanuel Wallerstein suggests that xenophobia only becomes the ideological formation of racism with the development of capitalism, and only then develops its 'symbiotic relationship' with sexism to produce free and cheap labour (1991: 29). In all prior historical systems, xenophobia meant the ejection of the other from the community, but with the advent of capitalism and its need for constant expansion and cheap labour, ejection becomes counter-productive. Racism is the magic solution to the capitalist objective of minimizing the costs of production and the resistance of the labour force to that process (Waller-stein 1991: 33). The boundaries of race definition within this system need to be fluid enough to meet specific and changing economic needs. Racism is constant in form and in venom, but somewhat fluid in boundary lines (Wallerstein 1991: 34). The theatrical evolution from inhuman Mully Mahomet in George Peele's *The Battle of Alcazar* (*c.* 1588) to Othello, the humanized Moor, indicates precisely the origins of such ideological flexibility. *Othello* dramatizes the possible consequences of not excluding the racial other from the community and so presents the dazzling spectacle of someone who is, like Caliban, both monster and man. Yet, even as it does so the play reenacts the exclusionary privilege on which such representations were founded. Othello was a white man.[27]

10
Watching *Hamlet* watching: Lacan, Shakespeare and the mirror/stage
PHILIP ARMSTRONG

I A strange accident happening at a play

The scene: a town in Norfolk, late sixteenth century. A theatrical company is performing the *History of Friar Francis*, in which a woman, besotted with a younger man, murders her husband. Subsequently, the dead man's ghost continues to appear to her in private. Now, however, as the spectre comes onstage, a certain woman in the audience, a respected local widow, cries out in distress. Distracted from the play, the other spectators turn to stare as she claims to see before her eyes the menacing ghost of her own dead husband. She requires no further prompting to confess that seven years ago, she too had been infatuated with a young gentleman, and had poisoned her husband. To her, the ghost onstage represents his exact likeness. Following this incident, an investigation by the local justices results in this woman's conviction for murder and, presumably, her death.

In his *Apology for Actors* (1612) Thomas Heywood recounts what he calls this 'strange accident happening at a play' as evidence of the power of drama to improve the moral and social responsibility of its audience (Heywood 1978: sig. G1v–G2r). But Heywood's anecdote also suggests an intriguing moment of interaction between audience and stage. Not only does the woman's outbreak cut into the performance, it actually inverts the conventional trajectory of the theatrical gaze. Everybody, actor as well as spectator, turns from staring at the play to focus on this other drama taking place among the audience. Instead of theatre reflecting 'real life', the reverse occurs: a spectator repeats exactly the scene of accusation and guilt she has just witnessed onstage.

Nobody writing in Heywood's time seemed to doubt the capacity of theatrical representation to produce such effects in its beholders. Whether these might be for good or ill, however, remained a vexed question. For the Puritan anti-theatrical pamphleteers, the power of theatre to mould its spectators into copies of the characters seen onstage was altogether pernicious.[1] According to Phillip Stubbes, 'if you will learn falshood' – along with slaughter, robbery, rebellion, greed, idleness, bawdiness, venery and a half-page list of other sins – '. . . you need to goe to no other schoole, for all these good Examples may you see painted before your eyes in enterludes and playes' (1877, 1: 144–5).

Like Heywood, the Puritan pamphleteers ultimately seek to prove their point by turning from the examples shown onstage to the responses of the playgoers. Stubbes fixes his critical gaze obsessively upon the spectators:

> but marke the flocking and running to Theatres & curtens, daylie and hourely, night and daye, tyme and tyde, to see Playes and Enterludes; where such wanton gestures, such bawdie speaches, such laughing and fleering, such kissing and bussing, such clipping and culling, Suche winckinge and glancinge of wanton eyes, and the like, is vsed, as is wonderfull to behold. Then, these goodly pageants being done, euery mate sorts to his mate, euery one bringes another homeward of their way verye freendly, and in their secret conclaues (couertly) they play the *Sodomits*, or worse.
>
> (1877, 1: 144)

Stubbes urges his readers to 'marke' the spectators, whose acts are 'wonderfull to behold', as they reproduce what the theatre has shown them, taking part in a 'play' of their own. Again and again, contemporary critics of the theatre will turn from their scrutiny of the play to concentrate upon the farcical performance enacted by the audience. Stephen Gosson remarks, not of the players but of the playgoers, 'when the sportes [i.e. the plays] are ended, that it is a right Comedie, to marke behauiour, to watch their conceites' (1974: 92). For these writers, the play – whether a 'Comedie' or any other genre – is not simply something that occurs onstage. It is also constituted by, and it constitutes, what happens among the audience.

II The glass of fashion

> I have heard
> That guilty creatures sitting at a play
> Have, by the very cunning of the scene,
> Been struck so to the soul that presently
> They have proclaim'd their malefactions.
> For murder, though it have no tongue, will speak
> With most miraculous organ. I'll have these players
> Play something like the murder of my father
> Before mine uncle. I'll observe his looks . . .
> (*Hamlet* II. ii. 584–92)

Hamlet seems familiar with the kind of incident documented by Heywood, in which the stage, like the ghost of a murder victim, casts its accusing gaze upon the audience. And like the Puritan pamphleteers quoted above, Hamlet identifies with this reverse gaze returning from the stage upon its spectators: he intends to 'observe' the king's 'looks', to watch the king watching the performance.

In his stage-managing of this play within the play – as he selects the plot, revises the script and coaches the actors – Hamlet offers various insights into the contemporary under-standing of the transaction between audience and stage. He extols above all the concept of *imitatio*, according to which 'the purpose of playing . . . both at the first and now, was and is to hold as 'twere the mirror up to nature; to show virtue her feature, scorn her own image, and the very age and body of the time his form and pressure' (III. ii. 20–4). The metaphor of the stage as a mirror appears ubiquitous in the Renaissance.[2] The writers cited so far, however, suggest that the stage, if it is a 'mirror', must be double-sided, for the trajectory of theatrical imitation proves consistently liable to inversion, so that spec-tators appear to emulate what they see in the playhouse. This provokes anxiety among contemporary writers, for if drama does not passively imitate real life, but actually participates in its formation, the power of theatrical representation becomes frighteningly versatile.

Hamlet's comments imply just such a double view of the theatre. First, the stage displays the reflected image of the culture, showing to 'the very age and body of the time his form and pressure'. Drama works not only like a mirror, but like a mould, keeping the impression or imprint left upon it by contemporary society. But any 're-flection', by definition, implies a movement of return from the mirror. So when Hamlet also describes an audience 'struck' by the 'very cunning of the scene', he imagines the stage turning upon them with a violent reflex action, showing something quite different from the passive or receptive face normally associated with the mirror. Moreover, the word 'strike' connotes the operation of a mould, the inscription of a mark, the minting of a coin or the printing of a text, as well as the impression of a sensation or image in the mind.[3] An audience, then, also offers a receptive surface upon which the scene leaves its mark. Similarly, Stephen Gosson remarks that in the theatrical transaction, 'impressions of mind are secretly conueyed ouer to the gazers, which the players do counterfeit on stage' (1974: 192–3). Stubbes also spells out the visual, even typographical, mechanics of this process: 'For such is our grosse & dull nature, that what thing we see opposite before our eyes, do pearce further and printe deeper in our harts and minds, than that thing which is hard onely with the eares' (1877, 1: x). As in a printing press, the visual images from the stage pierce the heart and mind of the spectator, inscribing or copying themselves there.

Many contemporary references repeat this ambivalence between the mirror as a passive reproduction of the image, and its more active role in constituting the beholder. Hamlet himself, for example, will be described as 'The glass of fashion and the mould of form, / Th'observ'd of all observers' (III. i. 155–6). In *2 Henry IV,* Hotspur is remembered as the 'mark and glass, copy and book, / That fashion'd others' (II. iii. 31–2). Both phrases repeat the ambiguity observed already, according to which the mirror replicates the twofold functions performed by a mould, or a printer's template: that of recording impressions, and that of stamping these upon another receptive medium. The mirror 'speculates' the image of the observer, in the economic as well as the visual sense: it invests the image with a value which returns to the gazer redoubled and augmented.

Theatrical representation appears ambiguous, then, because of its unpredictable and uncontrollable 'reflective' capacity, its tendency to reverse and turn upon the beholder, forming, informing and reforming identity and behaviour. Does the spectator of *Richard II*, for example, identify with Richard or with Bolingbroke, with the inadequate monarch or the energetic usurper? The supporters of the Earl of Essex had a version of this play performed before their abortive rebellion against Elizabeth I, whose famous remark to Lambarde on a later occasion suggested an acute awareness of the potential for revolutionary identifications offered by historical figures: 'I am Richard II,' she said, 'Know ye not that?' (Ure 1956: lix). Essex's attempted insurrection may well lie behind the reference to a 'late innovation' which in *Hamlet* exiles the players from the city and brings them to Elsinore (II. ii. 331; Jenkins 1982: 255). The Prince's stagecraft, and his discussions of audience identification, are therefore most likely provoked by an actual Elizabethan crisis arising from precisely these concerns.

In such a context, questions relating to the transactions taking place between audience and stage assume a certain degree of urgency. A more thorough consideration of the different kinds of identification occurring between spectator and actor is needed to elucidate the issues involved.

III Enter the imaginary and symbolic

Psychoanalyst Jacques Lacan defines 'identification' as 'the transformation that takes place in the subject when he [sic] assumes an image' (1977b: 2). Like the theorists of early modern theatre, moreover, Lacan invokes the mirror as a paradigm for this adoption, appropriation or putting on of the 'image' of the viewer's own body. He describes the formation of the ego as a series of such 'assumptions', and envisages this process in explicitly theatrical terms: 'the ego is like the superimposition of various coats borrowed from what I would call the bric-à-brac of its props department' (Lacan 1988b: 155).

Insisting, however, that 'the word identification, without differentiation, is unusable', he qualifies it by drawing a distinction between 'projection' and 'introjection' (1988a: 125). Projection, for Lacan, describes the spectator's perception of itself according to the apparently complete and masterful image seen in the mirror. An infant, held up to the glass, reaches out towards its reflection, which appears coordinated and erect, unlike its actual body. This illusion of an equivalence between the child and its image, along with the false sense of mastery it excites, provides the defining paradigm for what Lacan calls the 'imaginary'.

The concept of introjection, by contrast, describes subsequent attempts to incorporate the mirrored image, by assimilating it 'within' the archive of identifications that compose the 'self'. However, in its very reliance upon successive recognitions of displaced and alien images, this 'self' remains constitutionally 'other'. The moment of identification threatens always to replace the ego with its own image or representation. Thus introjection, in contrast to projection, engages predominantly with what Lacan designates as the 'symbolic' register – the domain of language – which functions through this unending substitution of signifiers. In exchanging image for image, representation for representation, the symbolic renders the 'original' point of reference – the body or the 'self' – inaccessible.

Lacan's double version of identification recalls the oscillation observed so far in relation to the theatrical stage, between an image left *in* the mirror and an image left *by* the mirror: 'The projection of the image is invariably succeeded by that of desire. Correlatively, there is a reintrojection of the image and a reintrojection of desire. Swing of the see-saw, a play of mirrors' (1988a: 179). In assimilating its image from the mirror, the subject adapts itself to an imagined gaze from outside. The 'imaginary' relation, a fascinated absorption with its own reflection, is interrupted by the spectator's awareness of how it 'looks', its subjection to a perspective directed back upon itself, just as the theatrical gaze might swing round to survey the performance of the spectator. By means of this dialectic of projection and introjection, then, the spectator enters the imaginary and symbolic registers. Alternatively, it might be said that these registers enter the spectator, through the imprinting of both image and language upon the psyche.

This construction of identity according to the impressions left by images can also be compared with the conventional understanding of memory in the Renaissance, where the mind was frequently imagined as a book, canvas or table upon which memories were inscribed. Mnemonic systems were devised whereby data was collected in a so-called 'theatre of memory', within which images could subsequently be prompted to reappear. Robert Fludd's *History of the Two Worlds* (1619) describes how 'all actions of words, of sentences, of parts of speech or subjects, are demonstrated as in a public theatre, where comedies and tragedies are acted'.[4] So Hamlet, in response to his dead father's injunction to 'Remember me', responds 'Ay, thou poor ghost, while memory holds a seat / In this distracted globe' (I. v. 91–7). Hamlet's memory will rehearse its store of images and words within the 'globe' of his head, just as the spectator identifies with the characters onstage in the 'Globe' theatre, in which the performance of this play might well be taking place.

For psychoanalysis, of course, with its constant emphasis on the unpredictability and waywardness of the unconscious, the kind of intellectual and rational mastery which the theatre of memory claims to grant the mind over its images would have to be considered an illusion. While the desire for such masterful consciousness is characteristic of Renaissance humanism, Hamlet's description hints that the actual public theatre of Shakespeare's time still represents something other than a fully 'conscious' mode of thought. His 'distracted globe' implies that the identifications between the image and the (mind's) eye remain radically dialogic and communal, rather than focused on a central and integrated ego: just as the Elizabethan theatre plays to a dispersed semicircle of gazes, rather than to an audience which, ranged along a 'fourth wall', approximates a singular 'point of view'.

Recalling Stubbes's and Gosson's vivid evocations of the dramatic spectacle 'imprinting' or 'impressing' itself upon the spectator, Hamlet's description of both mirror and stage receiving the 'form and pressure' of the contemporary social body can once again be juxtaposed with its reverse, the impression left upon the beholder by the theatrical image:

Yea, from the table of my memory
I'll wipe away all trivial fond records,
All saws of books, all forms, all pressures past
That youth and observation copied there,
And thy commandment all alone shall live
Within the book and volume of my brain
Unmix'd with baser matter.

(I. v. 98–104)

The traces of any former identifications left upon the 'table' of
Hamlet's memory will now be overwritten by the figure of his
father's ghost, and by his words.

IV The stage mirror

Like the apparition confronting Hamlet at this point, the ghost
of patriarchy haunts both the Renaissance stage and modern
psychoanalysis. Along with the woman menaced by the figure
of her dead husband in the anecdote with which this essay
began, Hamlet typifies the theatregoer confronted by the
spectacle of her or his own subjection to an accusing and
masculinist gaze. For Lacan, patriarchal power will be pre-
figured at first by the position of the 'actual' father within the
family unit, but thereafter manifested in what he calls the
symbolic, the operation of language, through which the subject
comes into being as such and upon which she or he remains
dependent. Lacan nicknames this patriarchal linguistic order
the *nom-du-père*, with a pun on *non-du-père*: the name (word),
or 'no' (prohibition), of the father (1977b: 67, 199, 217; 1988b:
259–60). Once it has been assimilated into the psyche, he
applies to this embodiment of the Law the psychoanalytic term
'super-ego' (1988a: 83). The word introjection, then, refers
specifically to this process, 'when something like a reversal takes
place – what was the outside becomes the inside, what was the
father becomes the super-ego' (1988a: 169). Or, in Hamlet's
case, what was the father reappears . . . where?

HAMLET	My father – methinks I see my father –
HORATIO	Where, my lord?
HAMLET	In my mind's eye, Horatio.

(I. ii. 184–5)

All of these models of cognition – the eye of the mind, mirror of the intellect, mind as inner arena – have been identified by Richard Rorty as emerging in the Renaissance and deriving from Greek and particularly Platonic philosophy (1980: 38–69). Moreover, Rorty relates such metaphors to the capacity of the Cartesian subject to 'reflect' and to 'speculate', thereby emphasizing the close affinity, in the Western philosophical tradition, between the process of conceptual thought and the function of vision; even more specifically, between the perception of the self and the function of the mirror.

It would seem that the psychological and perceptual spaces represented by both mirror and stage have been influential not just in early modern theatre, but also in the subsequent development of both philosophy and psychoanalysis. Lacan, in fact, entitles his initial paradigm for the child's entry into relation with its surroundings 'The Mirror Stage', 'Le stade du miroir'. The word 'stade', like its English translation, signifies both a developmental phase and a stadium, an arena for the repeated performance or playing out of identity: 'The mirror stage is a drama' (Lacan 1977b: 4).

Instead of worrying about the problem of anachronism in reading modern theory alongside early modern drama, the critic might more profitably address the extent to which psychoanalytic models of identity construction remain dependent for their development and representation upon drama; more specifically, upon Shakespeare; in fact, upon Hamlet itself. Lacan, for example, uses this play as a primary instance of the imaginary identification between the ego and its ideal image in the mirror.[5]

In the mirror stage, the child constructs its fantasy ego according to the upright and coordinated figure in the glass. This always and only offers what Lacan calls a méconnaissance, a misleading recognition, because the masterful image apprehended in the mirror does not correspond to the actual degree of muscular coordination attained by the infant. The imaginary identification thereby produces a frustrated aggressivity, for the spectator desires to assimilate this image of the body as a totality, but remains at odds with it, experiencing its own body only partially and in fragments. The ego then desires the destruction of the ideal other but, dependent upon it for its own identification, remains locked in a disabling impasse, like the master and slave of Hegel's dialectic (Lacan 1988a: 170). In his seminar 'Desire and the Interpretation of Desire in *Hamlet*', Lacan takes Hamlet's relation to Laertes as a model for this imaginary fascination. He quotes the Prince's description of Laertes to Osric – 'his semblable is his mirror and who else would trace him his umbrage, nothing more' (V. ii. 118–20) – commenting that 'The image of the other . . . is presented here as completely absorbing the beholder' (1977a: 31). In this struggle only one outcome is possible: the destruction of both parties. In eventually fighting his ego ideal, therefore, Hamlet effects his own death.

> The playwright situates the basis of aggressivity in this paroxysm of absorption in the imaginary register, formally expressed as a mirror relationship, a mirrored reaction. The one you fight is the one you admire the most. The ego ideal is also, according to Hegel's formula which says that coexistence is impossible, the one you have to kill.
>
> (Lacan 1977a: 31)

Characters other than Laertes also function as mirror images in this play. Most interestingly, from the point of view of the theatrical transaction between audience and actor, Hamlet identifies himself with the player who delivers the speech about Pyrrhus, especially at the moment where he describes how the avenger's sword, raised over the head of Priam,

> *seem'd i'th' air to stick;*
> *So, as a painted tyrant, Pyrrhus stood,*
> *And like a neutral to his will and matter,*
> *Did nothing.*
>
> (II. ii. 475–8)

Acting out as well as speaking these lines, the player vividly foreshadows the moment at which Hamlet, a few scenes later, will stand with his sword poised above his uncle's head, embodying once again the inert aggressivity produced by an imaginary identification with the 'painted tyrant' before him.

Hamlet makes his identification with this minidrama even clearer:

> Is it not monstrous that this player here,
> But in a fiction, in a dream of passion,
> Could force his soul so to his whole conceit
> That from her working all his visage wann'd,
> Tears in his eyes, distraction in his aspect,
> A broken voice, and his whole function suiting
> With forms to his conceit? And all for nothing!
> . . .
>   Yet I,
> A dull and muddy-mettled rascal, peak
> Like John-a-dreams, unpregnant of my cause,
> And can say nothing . . .
>   (II. ii. 545–64)

Despite the arguments of the contemporary theatrical pamphleteers, the acting out of Pyrrhus's 'dream of passion' before
Hamlet's eyes suggests that an imaginary identification with the
dramatic 'fiction' produces in its spectator only a disabling
fantasy, a speechless fascination. It fails to prompt him to any
kind of imitative action whatsoever.

However, Hamlet does now recognize the formative power
of another type of identificatory dynamic between stage and
audience, which, following Lacan, I would designate as symbolic. He conceives of the play within the play, recalling
instances in which the stage, by its 'very cunning', has provoked
the participation of its guilty beholders, confronting them with
a sight so striking 'that presently / They have proclaim'd their
malefactions' (II. ii. 586–8).

V The consciousness of the king

Within the visual field, the symbolic order materializes as a look
directed at the subject from what Lacan calls the 'Other', a
gaze that disturbs the imaginary correspondence established
between the ego and the mirror image. The story of the woman
at the performance of *Friar Francis* vividly displays the reaction
of a spectator when subjected to this intrusive gaze. Various
characters in Shakespeare's play repeat this response when
confronted with the figure of the dead king: Hamlet, Gertrude
and, most critically, Claudius.

Claudius reveals his unease before the accusing gaze with

which Hamlet associates himself: 'the king becomes unsettled and visibly reveals his own guilt, incapable of viewing the dramatisation of his own crime' (Lacan 1977a: 17). A famous critical struggle over this scene can be said to circle around the type of audience identification involved.[6] Why does Claudius ignore the dumb-show, and react only to the second, spoken representation of his crime? Both his reactions – ignorance and anxiety – involve a disruption of the spectatorial gaze. He displays a blind ignorance in front of the dumb-show – so that more than one critic has even argued that he simply does not see it[7] – and then responds to the second version with a distress also patently characterized by a failure to see: 'Give me some light' (III. ii. 263).

The difference between these two moments can be seen as a movement from the imaginary to the symbolic register. Initially, Claudius makes an imaginary identification with the drama, rendering him paralysed by a fascinated rivalry with his masterful specular image: he projects himself into the dumb-show as the king, not the poisoner. He remains captivated by the resurrected image of Old Hamlet, his elder brother and rival: 'The ego ideal is . . . the one you have to kill' (Lacan 1977a: 31). Such an identification suits the dumb-show, from which speech, the paradigmatic form of the Lacanian symbolic, remains absent. For his exemplary mirror relation, Lacan specifically posits a child not yet capable of speech, 'at the *infans* stage' (1977b: 2). Similarly, transfixed by a disabling inertia, Claudius cannot even protest. The dumb-show leaves him dumb. Hamlet gives his reconstruction of the crime an apt name – 'The Mousetrap' - for it provides, as Lacan has said of the function of perspective painting, 'a trap for the gaze' of its primary spectator (Lacan 1979: 89).

So it is only when the gaze returns upon Claudius from the second, spoken version of the play that he becomes caught up in the action himself, and begins to perform in turn. Moving from projection to introjection, 'The King rises' as soon as – but not until – the player king, queen and murderer have spoken their lines (III. ii. 259). Lacan describes this gaze returning upon the spectator as 'an *x*, the object when faced with which the subject becomes object' (1988a: 220). Becoming aware of himself as the object of an accusing vision, rather than a spectator, Claudius loses his illusory mastery over the visual field. He cannot see any more, and can only stumble from the stage, calling for light.

Interrupting the duality of imaginary identification, awareness of the gaze of the Other radically challenges the identity of the subject and the security of its location within the optical field. Hamlet signals his identification with this other gaze directed at Claudius by interpolating a speech into the play, and by providing a constant tendentious 'chorus' designed to disconcert his audience (III. ii. 240). The imaginary fantasy of the dumb-show gives way to the intrusion of a third gaze, whereby Claudius, as spectator, finds the spectacle looking back at him: 'There is never a simple duplicity of terms. It is not only that I see the other, I see him seeing me, which implicates the third term, namely that he knows that I see him' (Lacan 1988a: 218).

We have met this uncanny look before, in the gaze of Hamlet's father's ghost, fixed upon its beholder 'Most constantly' (I. ii. 233–4).[8] The ghost assumes the 'questionable shape' which excites Hamlet's own fascinated attention; it commands him before anything else to 'Mark me', and ultimately to 'Remember me' (I. v. 2, 91). Its appearance not only draws out and holds the eye of the observer – threatening to 'Make thy two eyes like stars start from their spheres' (I.v.17) – but, as discussed earlier, also imprints or 'marks' itself upon his mind. Hamlet himself then reproduces this uncanny gaze in the accusing stare that he directs at the king during the play within the play: 'I'll observe his looks; / I'll tent him to the quick. If a do blench, / I know my course' (II. ii. 592–4). The Arden editor remarks that 'a *tent* was an instrument for examining or cleansing a wound', and that the word 'blench' here 'is related to *blink*' (Jenkins 1982: 273). This revealing and excessive gaze penetrates its object like a blade, disrupting and blinding the imaginary vision of the observing subject.

Drama would therefore seem to provide an inherently unstable medium, always possessing the potential to invert the hegemonic play of the gaze, so that the audience finds itself, repeatedly, unfounded. The subject positions occupied by the play's spectators are discomfitted, and the complacent relation between the individual and the social undermined. In fact, producing such agitation in the audience seems to be a sufficiently familiar feature of theatrical practice for Hamlet to ask whether the reaction he has provoked in Claudius 'Would not . . . get me a fellowship in a cry of players?' (III. ii. 269–72). The symbolic identification between spectator and spectacle therefore entails certain risks. According to psychoanalysis, the subject's participation in this visual regime inevitably involves repetition. Freud associates the 'compulsion to repeat' with the operation of the unconscious, and Lacan with the subject's domination by the gaze of the Other, the symbolic order (Freud 1986a: 229; Lacan 1972: 39). Reading Poe's 'Purloined Letter', for example, Lacan identifies three positions in the triangular structure of the gaze, which each of the characters will occupy in turn:

> The first is a glance that sees nothing . . . The second, a glance which sees that the first sees nothing and deludes itself as to the secrecy of what it hides . . . The third sees that the first two glances leave what should be hidden exposed to whomever would seize it . . .
>
> (1972: 44)

Lacan makes analysis, and agency, dependent upon occupation of the third position in the symbolic structure, that of the glance which sees what remains hidden from the two others locked in their imaginary embrace. Drama operates as a means whereby these positions are continually negotiated, transgressed and exchanged. For in order to see and act, the spectator must risk – Lacan speaks repeatedly in both seminars of 'stakes' – exposure to another gaze. The spectator cannot avoid entry into the game. *Hamlet* dramatizes this necessity of taking a position, and foregrounds also the risk of failure. At those moments in which the audience (or critic, or analyst) will be forced by the drama to see itself seeing, the gaze of the Other emerges, looking back at the spectators, who are not just observers but participants, caught in the act, taking (a) part in the plot. Theatre thereby perpetually contaminates the position of pure spectatorship, precipitating its audience into (the) action. These are the stakes in the psychoanalysis of drama, the drama of psychoanalysis: there is no pure interpretive exteriority, and participation always carries the risk of blind repetition, of being written into the script being read.

So, in the final scene of the play, Hamlet repeats the fate of his father, assuming the position of blindness in an imaginary rivalry with Laertes which will betray him to his death, once again by means of poisoning. The audience, Laertes and Claudius all see that the tip of the foil and the wine will prove lethal, but Hamlet does not: 'The foils are blunted only in his deluded vision' (Lacan 1977a: 32).

Hamlet's dying words address both the onstage and offstage observers as 'You ... / That are but mutes or audience to this act' (V. ii. 339–40). 'Mutes', as the term for actors with non-speaking parts, suggests 'non-participants' (Jenkins 1982: 414). But the audience, like Claudius during the dumb-show, only remain mute as long as they are caught in an imaginary identification with the drama. However, the remaining moments of the play show the observers finding their voices, playing their parts and beginning to repeat. Fortinbras enters to occupy the spectatorial position: 'Where is this sight?' (V. ii. 367). But then, at Horatio's prompting, he directs the final scenes of the play, in explicitly theatrical terms: 'give order that these bodies / High on a stage be placed to the view' (V. ii. 382–3). With Fortinbras preparing to 'call the noblest to the audience', and to 'embrace my fortune', the spectator enters the game, and the play begins again, ready for another repetition, a new performance (V. ii. 392–3). Horatio, finally, observes this recapitulation without even noticing: 'let this same be presently perform'd ...' (V. ii. 398).

VI A thing . . . of nothing

I have so far omitted any discussion of Lacan's third category, which he calls the 'real'. This is appropriate, for the 'real' functions more than anything else as what must be excluded from the imaginary and the symbolic, and therefore as that which might unsettle the interpretations produced by concentrating on those registers.

Lacan's deployment of the term 'real' becomes increasingly removed from any suggestion of an unmediated point of reference, or an accessible presence. In fact, the 'real' features in direct contrast to the perceptual or social 'reality' inhabited by the subject, which is by definition always constructed within the imaginary and symbolic registers, and therefore phantasmal. Lacan's 'real', on the other hand, stands for what must be excluded in order to found this imaginary and symbolic universe, and yet which persists as the traumatic condition of both. It is manifest only as a symptom, a recalcitrant element within the subject's discourse which analysis tries to identify but cannot grasp, experiencing it only as 'an essential encounter – an appointment to which we are always called with a real that eludes us' (Lacan 1979: 53). Therefore the 'real' may only be located negatively, through reference to the compulsive attempts made to represent it within the signifying network.

Within the optical field of drama, the 'real' enables the identification of yet another type of gaze. An imaginary vision founds and maintains itself according to the exclusive duality and illusory mastery of the mirror relation. The symbolic gaze of the Other disturbs this imaginary sovereignty of the optical field, by introducing that perspective from which the subject is surveyed as an object. Finally, the gaze as 'real' would suggest an impossible vision which the subject desires but can never attain, for it would dissolve the subject/object split, which founds and orders the symbolic and imaginary optical fields. This 'real' gaze indicates the failure of the other two regimes, as it escapes the representational strictures imposed upon visual perception:

> In our relation to things, in so far as this relation is constituted by the way of vision, and ordered in the figures of representation, something slips, passes, is transmitted, from stage to stage, and is always to some degree eluded in it – that is what we call the gaze.
>
> (Lacan 1979: 73)

In *Hamlet*, there are a number of places where this effect may be located. The play repeatedly gestures towards 'nothing', a recurrent lacuna central to the 'round O' of the Elizabethan theatre. Hamlet locates this lack between Ophelia's legs, precisely in the position from which he will observe Claudius's response to the play:

HAMLET (*lying down at Ophelia's feet*) Lady, shall I lie in your lap?

OPHELIA No, my lord.

HAMLET I mean, my head upon your lap?

OPHELIA Ay, my lord.

HAMLET Do you think I meant country matters?

OPHELIA I think nothing, my lord.

HAMLET   That's a fair thought to lie between maids' legs.
OPHELIA   What is, my lord?
HAMLET   Nothing.

(III. ii. 110–19)

To the Elizabethan audience, this exchange involves a series of sexual puns ('lie', 'head', 'country', 'no thing'), according to which, just as in the Freudian psychoanalytic account, gender difference resolves into the absence or presence of the penis. The unease surrounding this component lacking from the visual field displays all the characteristics of the Lacanian 'real'.

Lacan's own text also returns repeatedly to this same 'nothing'. He quotes Hamlet's exchange with Guildenstern –

HAMLET   The body is with the King, but the King is not with the body. A King is a thing –
GUILDENSTERN   A thing, my lord?
HAMLET   Of nothing.

(IV. ii. 26–9)

– and interprets the lines in terms of the phantom appearance and disappearance of the phallus: 'the body is bound up in this matter of the phallus – and how – but the phallus, on the contrary, is bound to nothing: it always slips through your fingers' (1977a: 52). For psychoanalytic purposes, of course – and this is the point of the joke – the phallus should not be equated with the anatomical organ. 'In Freudian doctrine, the phallus is not . . . the organ, penis or clitoris, which it symbolizes.' Rather, 'the phallus is a signifier' (Lacan 1982: 79). For Freud, sexual differentiation provides the prerequisite for the establishment of a 'normal' (that is, a socially recognizable) human identity (Freud 1979: 380, 397). But Lacan raises the stakes even higher: the phallus, as the 'privileged signifier' of sexual difference, provides the basis and paradigm for the entire network of substitutions and differences upon which the symbolic order and the unconscious, language and patriarchal law, are founded (1982: 82).[9] This 'nothing' of sexual difference, therefore, appears in Lacanian psychoanalysis to be everything. Near the end of the seminar on *Hamlet*, Lacan remarks that 'Claudius' real phallus is always somewhere in the picture . . . that fatal, fateful object, here real indeed, around which the play revolves' (1977a: 50).

Psychoanalytic theory returns recurrently to this no/thing,

manifesting a perpetual unease around, and attraction towards, the issue of sexual difference. For Freud, of course, sexual formation inevitably turns upon the primal scene between the male and female child, that moment of visual apprehension in which anatomical difference, the perception of the absence or presence of the penis, remains always 'somewhere in the picture'.[10] In so far as he depends upon Freud, Lacan therefore cannot avoid, at important moments in his argument, relating the phallus as signifier to its visible, anatomical correlative. He obscures the nature of this relation by presenting many of his most critical assertions on gender in the form of provocative jokes: for example his assertion that the phallus achieves its place as the pre-eminent signifier within the symbolic because it is 'what stands out as most easily seized upon in the real of sexual copulation' (1982: 82). In spite of his other claims, it would seem that for Lacan the phallus recurrently appears precisely as that which does not slip 'through your fingers'.[11]

The texts of both psychoanalysis and Shakespearean tragedy will therefore recurrently approach and retreat from this funda-mental representational abyss constituted by the 'real' of the body, and specifically the anatomical asymmetry between male and female. Furthermore, the trauma raised by this question will always be projected onto the supposed 'lack' in the female body, upon which the masculinist visual regime focuses all its anxieties about the visible signifiers of sexual difference.

Identifying the representation of the woman's body as a location for the disruptive real has obvious implications for Elizabethan drama in general. On the Shakespearean stage, where all female roles were played by male actors, the 'female character' becomes symptomatic of the gap in representation surrounding sexual difference, for she cannot appear in the theatre except insofar as her body is replaced by an elaborate masquerade.

Hamlet will take this theatrical disguise of womanliness as the paradigm for femininity itself, which he persistently charac-terizes as false and duplicitous: 'I have heard of your paintings well enough. God hath given you one face and you make yourselves another' (III. i. 144–5). Using cosmetics to make 'another' face, the woman/actor makes her/himself *into* 'an-other': another gender, another identity. The mask threatens to turn the person who uses it into someone else: the actor becomes the role, the man the woman. For the Puritan anti-theatrical pamphleteers, moreover, the masquerade of femininity also exemplifies the hypocrisy of the theatre itself, which thereby undermines gender differentiation as one of the main foundations of social and individual identity (Gosson 1974: 175–6; Stubbes 1877, 1: 64–7).

The 'real' of femininity radically disrupts the play once more in Hamlet's exchange with the young actor who plays the female roles in the company visiting Elsinore. He comments that, as the boy grows up, he hopes his voice will 'be not cracked within the ring' (II. ii. 424–5). Again, bringing together a reference to the female body (the ring and the figure O were both common slang for the female sexual organs) with the evidence of the impossibility of its representation – displaying a male impersonating a female 'within the ring' of the Elizabethan playhouse – this line betrays the wilful blindness on the part of the audience upon which the actors depend for their depiction of Ophelia and Gertrude. Such a moment manifests the traumatic effect occasioned by the real within the symbolic and imaginary registers. As the boy's mock-female voice 'cracks', and masculinity breaks into the feminine, it threatens to split apart the 'wooden O' of theatrical illusion, the necessary fantasy of the 'female part'.

In terms of a wider Elizabethan politics, the same unease attaches to the body of the queen herself. By the time the first performances of *Hamlet* took place, the English queen's barren and ageing body itself featured as a symptom of the anxieties about the succession and the stability of the Tudor state. Increasingly, therefore, the monarchy relied upon a divorce between the iconography of Elizabeth and her actual body, giving rise to the cult of the virgin queen, Astraea, Gloriana. Identification of this recurrent trauma gives a new twist to the words 'Frailty, thy name is woman' (I. ii. 146), so that 'woman' becomes the name of the frailty of both political and theatrical representation in late Tudor England.

The representation of 'woman' also betrays the frailty of modern psychoanalysis, and of gender differentiation itself. Following Joan Riviere (1986), Lacan also conceives of feminine sexuality in terms of masquerade (Lacan 1977b: 291; 1979: 193). But as in *Hamlet*, this concentration upon the visible signifiers of sexual difference (clothing, facial traits, body shape, genitals) plunges psychoanalysis into a profound uncertainty about the 'deeper' marks of gender, both male and female, making it impossible to define with any degree of conviction an essential psychic distinction between masculinity and femininity. In the ever-more provocative assertions of Lacan's late seminars this effect becomes increasingly manifest: 'A woman is a symptom', '*the* woman does not exist', 'there is no sexual relation' (1982: 167, 168, 170). In so far as '*a* woman' here indicates a subject representing herself according to the conventional 'masquerade' of femininity, she provides a symptom of the impossibility of essential gender: '*the* woman does not exist'. So by implication (although Lacan stops short of suggesting this) masculinity also fades into indeterminacy, inasmuch as it defines itself against its opposite through the male/female 'sexual relation', which cannot therefore 'exist' either.

Consequently, for psychoanalysis, ego-identification within the visual regime itself always betrays the anxious imposition of a gender hierarchy. In Lacan's description of the mirror stage, the idealized reflection seen in the glass already appears to bear visual traits conventionally associated with the male body. Erect, masterful and self-contained, the image in the mirror conforms to the privileged term of a binary gender distinction which portrays the other, the female body, as soft, vulnerable and incontinent. Nevertheless the mirror image also constitutes a masquerade, compared by Lacan to 'the armour of an alienating identity' (1977b: 4; 1988b: 155).

In fact, all the mirror images I have considered so far have been masculine: even the female spectator with whom this essay began was prompted to confess by the persecuting ghost of the dead husband. Introjection of this sort always involves the assimilation of a patriarchal figure, as it does in Lacanian theory: 'what was the father becomes the super-ego' (1988a: 169). Similarly, when Hamlet confronts his mother, he claims he will 'set you up a glass / Where you may see the inmost part of you' (III. iv. 18–19). But what he actually shows her are the portraits of her two husbands - 'the counterfeit presentment of two brothers' (III. iv. 54) - demanding her disidentification with the image of Claudius and her re-introjection of the image of Hamlet's father. Once again, the 'glass' gives back to the woman not herself, but the superegoic patriarchal figure, the assimilation of which implies her guilty submission to the gaze:

Thou turn'st mine eyes into my very soul,
And there I see such black and grained spots
As will not leave their tinct.

(III. iv. 89–91)

Woman has no mirror image on the early modern stage, a double alienation which Gertrude expresses by telling Hamlet, 'thou hast cleft my heart in twain!' (III. iv. 158).

Luce Irigaray criticizes the ubiquity of this masculine optical and specular economy within the Western metaphysical tradition. The rational male subject of philosophical 'reflection' or 'speculation' stands always in relation to the mirror, a position of illusory empiricism. 'Does the subject derive his power from the appropriation of this non-place of the mirror? And from speculation?' (Irigaray 1985: 205). It comes as no surprise, then, that Lacan gives as an example of the introjected gaze of the Other 'the satisfaction of a woman who knows that she is being looked at' (Lacan 1979: 75). Here the subject appears as female, 'objectified' by the gaze which she invites – presumably through sexual masquerade – thereby implying a masculine gaze with which both Lacan and the reader identify, as analyst or voyeur. Again, as Irigaray suggests, 'Woman has no gaze, no discourse for her specific specularization that would allow her to identify with herself (as same) – to return into the self – or break free of the natural specular process that now holds her – to get out of the self' (1985: 224). Female identification with the Other always involves an excursion into 'masculine' territory.

What I wish to suggest, then, is that an identification with the traumatic place of the real within early modern theatre and psychoanalysis will provide, if not a 'feminine' gaze then at least a critique of its absence. The non-existent real of the sexual relation indicates the frailty of the optical field, demanding a constant reassessment of the relation between gender and vision involved in every 'stage' of both early modern theatre and psychoanalysis.

Some critical questions

Any consideration of the conflicting identifications taking place in the theatre therefore invites the formulation of a number of questions which, although they cannot be 'applied' flatly to reading a play, nevertheless point towards the articulation of a relationship between Lacanian psychoanalysis and early modern drama.

Attention to the imaginary, as Lacan conceives it, reveals what fantasies of mastery are evoked in the play, and how the spectacle captivates its audience. In what ways does it offer a trap for the gaze? And – in so far as the composition of any scene institutes a certain position from which it should be observed, and constructs a certain audience appropriate to that viewpoint – to whom is the drama giving itself to be seen?

Along with this, an exploration of the symbolic relationships at stake seeks to identify how the stage reciprocates the spectator's gaze, or how it disconcerts her or his location within the visual regime. This involves looking for what Lacan calls the 'gaze behind' (1979: 113), a look 'on the part of' another: for example Claudius, seeing Hamlet's gaze behind the play, and the ghost's accusing glare behind that. On whose behalf is the audience being invited to look? Emphasis on the symbolic register also involves examining what images, concepts, words or effects might be introjected during the play. In what ways, and by which hegemonic or superegoic figures, is the audience being commanded to respond?

Finally, the problem of the real emerges as a recurrent complication at every stage of the analysis. Where are the disturbances that might betray the locus of a trauma around which the symbolic circles? And where does the imaginary identification falter?

These are questions that criticism of early modern drama needs to confront, not least because they envisage drama as a series of superimposed visions, conflicting gazes and multiple identifications between spectator and spectacle. After all, this best approximates the actual situation in the 'distracted globe' of the Shakespearean public theatre, where the drama does not play to a singular eye, but instead offers a whole array of perspectives to an audience surrounding the stage, whose innumerable lines of sight collide and intersect as the drama unfolds.

11

Afterword: the next generation
JOHN DRAKAKIS

Alternative to what? Not Falstaff's 'damnable iteration' (*I Henry IV* I. ii. 88), but a question which takes us back, as Derrida would have it, to those roots in what has become 'the unity of a context' which itself opens onto a recontextualization (Derrida 1992: 63). If, some ten years after the appearance of the first *Alternative Shakespeares*, the question 'Alternative to what?' carries the force of something other than a rhetorical flourish, then it is, in part, a measure of the distance which Shakespeare studies has travelled during that time. Alternatives to alternatives may sound tautological to dedicated anti-intellectual followers of critical fashion striving to keep abreast, let alone get on top of the task of refurbishing a tired critical terminology. But those theoretical modes of critical practice which began to surface in the late 1970s, and which have now become what is referred to disparagingly by some as 'the new orthodoxy', have themselves undergone considerable transformation during the intervening period as a direct consequence of persistent and detailed forms of self-criticism.

Viewed cynically, we might say that what was marginal has now become central, what was central has now been marginalized. And yet, of course, if we are prepared to take the lessons of post-structuralism seriously to heart, not only will this reversal be perceived as an alternation within an extant binary opposition, but also, when we try to locate these new centres we will find there division and fragmentation. That sneering phrase 'the new orthodoxy' itself turns out to be a misrepresentation, an attempt to impose a specious unity upon diverse fields of critical and scholarly endeavour. If a decade ago the title *Alternative Shakespeares* naively celebrated a burgeoning radical pluralism, we now know too much for this position to be sustained uncritically. It is the case that in the original volume there were important and, as it turns out, proleptic, tensions available to the discerning reader, but it is important for us now to resist the folding back of that initially liberating pluralism into the amorphous body of a traditional liberal humanism eager to display its liberalism in performance by assimilating theory in the manner of a consumer activity.

And yet, of course, these are the forces, institutionally and commercially, with which radical Shakespeareans are forced to negotiate; these are the sites of contestation where hegemonies are forged, resistances articulated, oppositions asserted. It is not uncommon these days to encounter the admissions of otherwise conservative editors that particular textual cruces are 'undecidable', or to be embarrassed by the prospect of ostentatious flirtations with cultural history which can, impossibly, sustain the contradictory assertions that subjectivity is a historical construct whilst the Bard is really an autonomous creative consciousness. Or, even worse, insist, despite overwhelming evidence to the contrary, that 'history' itself can assume the status of an object which is wholly recoverable to the disinterested observer. Even those theoretically rigorous analytical positions which owed much to Althusser in the early 1980s are now forced to call in question the scientific certainty of analyis itself, and where the study of history may be thought to be forensic, there is as much preoccupation with the textual laws to which its findings must be submitted.

It is also unfortunate that during the decade which separates *Alternative Shakespeares* from *Alternative Shakespeares 2* academic institutions have become huge bureaucracies, with intellectual endeavour reduced to the level of a commodity, valuable only in so far as it can be packaged and marketed. The preoccupation with institutions and the politics that derive therefrom is thought to distinguish British cultural materialism, with its ardent politics, from the more professionally urbane, politically reticent American new historicism. It is no accident, however, that the systematic commodification of knowledge has proceeded alongside an increasingly radical turn in the humanities and in the study of Shakespeare in particular both in Britain and the United States. The Elizabethan world picture may, over the past decade, have been shattered, exposed as an ideology, or from a critical perspective, perceived as the fantasy of an embattled culture fearing severance from its origins. But despite the loss of confidence in the power of grand narratives to account for the knowledges we possess, the attempts to help Shakespearean texts 'into coherence', to use Alan Sinfield's phrase, appear to be stronger than ever. It is Sinfield's contention that 'coherence is a chimera ... No story can contain all the possibilities it brings into play; coherence is always selection' (1992: 51). It is the responsibility of what, after a decade of feverish intellectual activity in the humanities, we can now, with some confidence, label alternative criticism, to examine the conditions of such coherence, to plot its laws, expose its assumptions, track down its epistemologies, identify its investments, conscious or otherwise, in particular strategies of thought and political practice. And yet, this cannot itself be undertaken from a position of transcendence, or indeed from a position which simply replaces one totality with another. The displacement of history into histories, or the replacement of 'history' with 'History', is fraught with difficulty, as Geoffrey Bennington observes in a discussion of the work of Fredric Jameson:

> History means Hegel, and Hegel means totality and plenitude: the fall from plenitude means narrative and history and hermeneutics, and all of these mean Utopia and the return to plenitude. All of this means guilt, which again means interpretation and narrative and nostalgia.
>
> (1994: 79)

Sinfield's avowedly cultural materialist project, to undertake a review of 'institutions that retell the Shakespeare stories' while at the same time attempting 'a self-consciousness about its own situation within those institutions', with a view to shifting 'the criteria of plausibility' (1992: 51), borrows from deconstruction the notion that there can be no subject of analysis operating upon the literary text from a position *outside* its domain. The decision to review such institutions cannot, therefore, be purely voluntarist, although we should take care here to distinguish, as Steven Mullaney does in his essay in this volume, between autonomy and agency. If we are to accept the full force of Sinfield's imperative to shift the criteria of plausibility then we must recognize that such an activity can only ever take place in locations that are always already overdetermined. Thus, when we think of *alternatives* we are not thinking purely and simply, or indeed primarily, in terms of consumer choice, even though such formulations enter the academic marketplace and are, as a consequence, in danger of being subsumed into its disabling structures. Indeed, if we are to register the full force of Mullaney's citation of Gramsci's definition of culture, 'a heterogeneous and irreducibly plural social formation', then we must also record that meaning is determined by the social formation itself as well as by the historical conditions within which participants in the process of producing meaning interact. Such productions do not simply constitute more 'readings' of what are otherwise stable texts, but rather seek to identify the complex conditions that ground reading itself.

Much of the recent criticism of Shakespeare has been preoccupied with what these texts have to say, as well as with what it is that they disclose. Here discursive configurations are shown to structure the text *and* the positions from which it may be read, in what has, effectively, been a devastating assault on essentialism. This emphasis upon 'constructivism', if we may use this shorthand description, was a necessary precondition of the larger challenge to traditional modes of Shakespeare criticism and scholarship. It is now time to take stock of these advances, to separate out the strands of argument which for polemical purposes were allowed to remain intertwined. Not all of the critical models which have come to the fore as materialist depend for their efficacy upon the processes of production and consumption. New historicism has concerned itself generally with the ways in which power produces itself whether or not the processes are dialogical; cultural materialism and certain kinds of radical feminism have concerned themselves with the mechanisms and strategies of resistance to the operations of power, without jettisoning a commitment to a collective morality. But such has been the influence of deconstruction, the revisions of Freud undertaken by Jacques Lacan, and of the anti-rationalist tradition generally, that what Scott Wilson has recently called 'Marx's restricted economy' opens up possibilities, as Philip Armstrong shows in his essay in this volume, beyond what Wilson again calls 'the culturalist play of morals and the materialism of socio-political context, the determinism of need and demand, and the contradictions in the mode of production' (1995: 44).

These are unquestionably major steps forward, as the historical moment of a retrospectively constructed modernity comes into direct collision with that of contemporary postmodernity. And yet it is important to remember that the kinds of advances which these collisions represent are always subject to checking and rechecking – the material practice of research itself which is often thought to be inimical to 'theory'. Such research focuses not just on the already constituted 'historical' facts, but also on the conditions, and the cultural pressures under whose influence these phenomena emerge as 'facts'. Thus the essays by Catherine Belsey, Margreta de Grazia and Bruce Smith in this volume rehearse those *aporia*s which reside at the hearts of texts, the material practices which usher in the moment of modernity, and the gendered 'subjects' over whose identities the modern cultural critic deliberates. Alan Sinfield's project of 'reading' a problematical Shakespearean text, *The Merchant of Venice*, from a position of a particular alternative subjectivity extends these considerations in a different, but no less stimulating, new direction, while Keir Elam's preoccupation with the Renaissance 'body' provides a valuable link between identity and physical stage presence.

The difficulty, as always with a Shakespearean text, is its dual existence as a piece of writing which has subsequently become venerated as 'Literature', and as an oral and visual work whose vibrancy and resonance is embodied in the actor's performance as part of a larger theatrical context. And yet, as a number of commentators have observed, the theatre itself was embroiled during this period in a 'struggle' to establish and sustain its own cultural identity. Keir Elam's reference to the theatre as plague is part of a larger avenue of investigation which extends into questions of cross-dressing, and the debates circulating around the dangers attendant on early modern stage performance. Elam's essay connects fruitfully with Dympna Callaghan's investigation of stage make-up in relation to the representations of gender and race as these issues emerge particularly in a text such as *Othello*.

It is, however, Ania Loomba's essay, 'Shakespeare and Cultural Difference', which focuses the richly interwoven strands of this provocative collection. Clearly, the way to displace 'Shakespeare' from his pedestal as supreme icon of English culture is to return him to a context. That may involve a historical context in which the dramatist's writings can be shown interacting fully with the writings of his contemporaries. It may involve those contexts in which the texts are disseminated, received, read and performed, through institutions such as the publishing industry, literary criticism, the school, the university, the organs of high culture, popular culture and so on. Not only does this mean rejecting the notion of 'alternatives' as a means of sustaining the myth of what Loomba calls 'an endlessly pliable bard', but it also foregrounds those details of cultural difference in and through which social practices are articulated. A decade ago, it was important to draw attention to the subaltern voice of Caliban in *The Tempest*, to show the extent to which traditional humanist criticism remained complicit in the colonialist strategies of what was identified as the text's imperialist dominant discourse. But as with all long views, the tendency has been to remain satisfied with a single historical model for the representation of colonialist discourse as it is represented in early modern texts. Ania Loomba's piece offers a timely reminder that history is neither as unitary, nor quite as convenient in its examples as that. There are, she asserts, *histories* of colonization which these texts mediate, and we should be sensitive to the differences between them. In tandem with the sophisticated destabilizing of gender difference that runs through a number of these essays, Loomba calls now for a destabilization of the category of 'race'. Such a project is, of course, fraught with difficulty. It pitches the discussion into another conflict, that between a metropolitan poststructuralism whose radical political project is to exploit the opportunities it finds in late capitalist fragmentation, and a subaltern identity which has yet to acquire a collective voice, and whose grand narratives, mediated through a series of institutions, need dismantling in the interests of the same radical egalitarianism.

This brings us finally to 'the gaze'. *Alternative Shakespeares* came originally to rest in materialist critical practice, involving a rewriting of the 'Elizabethan World Picture', and a rethinking of a Shakespearean text, *Henry V,* which had been the lynchpin of E. M. W. Tillyard's now familiar thesis. *Alternative Shakespeares 2* sustains and advances the materialism of its predecessor, but comes to rest in the specular economy of the theatre itself. Tillyard's 'world picture' was in some senses a misperception of historical reality, a fabricated lament for a lost unity. At best it sustained an ideology, an illusion and, by definition, a distortion of 'reality'. If ideology has now come to stand for the form and agency through which the competing interests of a society organize themselves, then we need to renew, and perhaps refocus, our interest in the detailed ways in which the imaginary and the symbolic registers function to shape and constrain social experience. Here seeing and doing as activities confront each other, and what better model than the theatre itself to explore this process? Histories of 'the gaze', the remapping and re-articulation of social space, the theatre as what Philip Armstrong calls an 'active mirror', all of these permit, even encourage, a radical rethinking of the early modern 'real'.

An Afterword is often a mark of repletion, the gesture that accompanies patriarchy in its acknowledgement of the legitimacy of its offspring. It is of the nature of *Alternative Shakespeares Vol. 2*, no less than its predecessor, that it must continue to disown its filial obligation, to bite the hands that feed it, to resist, and by resistance to empower. This act of patricide, projected onto the text of a play such as *Hamlet*, introjected in the practices of a critical enterprise noteworthy for its multilayered combativeness, is a metonym of those laws that would restrain the trajectory of Shakespeare criticism, prevent it from going where no one has gone before. This volume does not, like Prospero's Ariel, politely accept restraints as a precondition of its freedom. As a result, it offers a path forward to yet further alternatives.

Notes

1 Introduction

1 See Bate 1989: 174–84.
2 Published by Macmillan, London 1904, second edition 1905, it has remained more or less continuously in print. It was most recently republished by Macmillan in 1985 with a new introduction by John Russell Brown.
3 Reprinted in Knights 1946: 13–50.
4 All these matters and many similar ones are raised and discussed in the notes which Bradley appended to *Shakespearean Tragedy*.
5 I am here drawing on material more fully rehearsed in Hawkes 1992: 121–9 and Hawkes 1995: 10–16.
6 See Geertz 1973: 10. See also pp. 3–30 *passim*.
7 See Hawkes 1992: 3.
8 The idea of 'enriching' the concept of error is taken from Deleuze 1968. See especially pp. 150ff.
9 See the work of Geertz, above, and more particularly, the account of 'counter-Enlightenment discourse' discussed in Sahlins 1975 and 1995.

2 After the new historicism

1 An early version of this essay was first presented as a response to Miller in a talk given in 1987 at the Modern Language Association; fuller versions were later delivered at a conference titled 'The Historic Turn in the Human Sciences' (University of Michigan,

1990) and at the Institute for Advanced Study, School of Social Sciences (Princeton, 1993). For another response to Miller, also in the context of new historicism, see Montrose 1989, 1992.

2 For example, see the recent work of Joan Wallach Scott 1988.

3 For representative early works, see Orgel 1975; Montrose 1980a, 1980b; Mullaney 1980; Goldberg 1981; and Tennenhouse 1982, as well as Greenblatt's own seminal book, *Renaissance Self-fashioning* (1980).

4 As I suggest below, a more distinguishing characteristic of new historicism is its anthropological bent, its effort to produce an ethnography of cultural production that displaces and estranges both history and literature from their insular disciplinary niches.

5 Although there has been a tendency by some to situate new historicism and feminism as antagonistic movements, as in conference panels entitled 'Feminism vs. New Historicism', there has also been a great deal of salutary influence in both directions, and a significant amount of work by male and female critics alike that would be difficult to categorize as one or the other. In a recent conference address, Jean Howard provided an astute ideological critique of the institutional and disciplinary pressures that induce divisive and exclusionary positioning of such movements in the American academy, and stressed the need to resist those pressures and to pursue instead the mutually productive affiliations between various forms of cultural study. For a fuller discussion of feminist and new historicist literary criticism, see the later sections of this essay.

6 I have in mind in particular H. Aram Veeser's recent anthology (1994), which ostensibly gathers together examples of new historicists' work and critical advances beyond it. Veeser's introduction is cavalier in its representation of others' views, even when summarizing the essays included in the volume; of those essays, any mention of history seems to qualify for inclusion. To give one example, Jane Gallop's critique of certain strains of identity politics in feminist history and literary criticism is presented as being engaged in a critical (but entirely imaginary) dialogue with new historicism.

7 Although Williams is not often cited by Greenblatt, he is one of the central and often unrecognized influences on the latter's work. For others explicitly indebted to Williams, see Mullaney 1988 and the extensive series of essays by Louis Montrose.

8 For the phrase 'symbolic economy' in this context, see Mullaney 1988: 41–7, 96–7.

9 Geertz himself acknowledged this danger, warning that interpretive anthropology could all too easily become a kind of 'sociological aestheticism' out of touch 'with the hard surfaces of life – with the

political, economic, stratificatory realities within which men are everywhere contained' (1973: 30).

10 I think it is crucial to distinguish, as I have tried to do, between Geertz's method and the formalist aesthetic ideology which dictates the application of that method, and I think it is entirely possible and legitimate to do so. Vincent Pecora suggests such a distinction is impossible in his otherwise astute analysis of the Indonesian political realities effaced in Geertz's work. Pecora's charge is that new historicism inevitably performs analogous effacements, due to its methodologi cal borrowings from Geertz. At the same time, however, Pecora seems to regard his critique as an indictment of *all* anthropology, whether indulging in thick description or not; see Pecora 1989.

11 To explain the massive and unprecedented sickness and death that visited them along with the English, the Algonquians explained their strange fatalities by analogy to the equally strange and impressive weapons of the English, and with Harriot's encouragement attributed both the 'invisible bullets' that were decimating their tribe and the visible ones the English had at their disposal to the power of the English God.

12 Like others critics of Greenblatt's argument – that apparently subversive forces are not so much illusory as complex, sometimes serving to reinforce the dominant culture in the process of contesting it – Lentricchia seems oblivious to the extensive body of Marxist analysis that argues much the same point, and clearly without the defeatist message Lentricchia attributes – falsely, as far as I am concerned – to Greenblatt (see Bloch *et al.* 1980).

3 Cleopatra's seduction

1 For a wide-ranging account of the evaluation of homoeroticism in the period, see Smith 1991. Meanwhile, Jonathan Goldberg sees homophobia in the feminist attention to boys in drag. The object of male homoerotic desire is a man, he insists, and not a substitute for or an inprovement on a woman (Goldberg 1992). Gregory W. Bredbeck discusses the expansion of subjectivity implied by homoerotic possibilities in *The Sonnets* (Bredbeck 1992). See also Bredbeck 1991.

2 Stephen Orgel (1995) argues that gender was not an exclusive category in the Renaissance. More generally, inherited accounts of sexual difference as opposition are challenged in Butler 1990 and Garber 1992.

3 References to *Antony and Cleopatra* are to the Arden edition, ed. John Wilders, London: Routledge (1995).

4 See for example Hamer 1993.

5 I have followed convention is assuming that Cleopatra's allusion to the boy-actor is self-referential, but it is possible that the speech constitutes another jibe at the children's companies invoked by Rosencrantz (*Hamlet* II. ii. 337–62). This passage should probably be dated 1606–8 (Knutson 1995); *Antony and Cleopatra* is usually dated 1606–7.

6 The visual tradition was certainly familiar in England in the sixteenth and seventeenth centuries. Henry VIII owned a table-desk (now in the Victoria and Albert Museum) which is elaborately decorated in painted and gilded leather, with Venus and Cupid represented on the interior. The work is thought to have been Flemish, *c.* 1525. In 1569 Hans Eworth painted Queen Elizabeth confronting Juno, Minerva and Venus, and transcending them all. (The painting is now in Windsor Castle.) Venus has her arm round Cupid. Evidently the little boy served as a way of identifying the goddess of love at that time. Thomas Trevelyon's *Pictorial Commonplace Book* of 1608 includes a (not very seductive) image of Venus with a Cupid who is neither pretty nor particularly dimpled (fol. 204r). It looks as if it might be a copy of a popular woodcut. The Ashmolean Museum has a carved ivory Venus with a very engaging Cupid by George Petel. If this was the *Venus and Cupid* in the collection of George Villiers, 1st Duke of Buckingham, he probably bought it from Rubens in 1626, but this was nearly twenty years after the first performance of the play. I am grateful to Helen Clifford for information on this carving.

7 I owe this idea to William Dodd.

8 I owe this point to Humphrey Liddiard.

9 'The charm of a child lies to a great extent in his narcissism, his self-contentment and inaccessibility, just as does the charm of certain animals which seem not to concern themselves about us, such as cats and the large beasts of prey' (Freud 1984: 83).

10 For the history of Cupid see Panofsky 1967; Hyde 1986. J. J. Pollitt makes the point that images of Eros which appear engaging or 'cute' to modern eyes may well have been read as much more threatening in a cultural context which did not take for granted the innocence of children (Pollitt 1986: 138). (I owe this reference to James Whitley.)

11 'It is an instructive fact that under the influence of seduction children can become polymorphously perverse, and can be led into all possible kinds of sexual irregularities. This shows that an aptitude for them is innately present in their disposition. There is consequently little resistance towards carrying them out, since the mental dams against sexual excesses – shame, disgust and morality – have either not yet been constructed at all or are only in the

course of construction, according to the age of the child' (Freud 1977: 109).

12 Michael Shapiro points out that precocious bawdry and *doubles entendres* constituted part of the appeal of the plays written for the children's companies to perform. The exchanges between Cleopatra, Charmian and Iras in Act I are carried out, of course, by boys. See Shapiro 1982.

13 See also Pietro Fachetti, *Adam Receiving the Forbidden Fruit from Eve* (1602, Prado, Madrid).

14 Michelangelo's Cupid is also erotically involved with the goddess in *Venus and Love* (Museo di Capodimonte, Naples).

4 Imprints: Shakespeare, Gutenberg and Descartes

1 I wish to acknowledge my indebtedness to Neil Hertz's consideration of the practical, conceptual and mystical importance of wax (Hertz 1992: 173–8). I must also thank Peter Stallybrass for showing me Hertz's essay, as well as for his encouragement from start to finish.

2 On Descartes' wax and the topos of mutability, see Hollander 1988: 217–19.

3 For a demonstration of how poundage of wax correlates with volume of letters, see the conclusions drawn from the documented increase in the use of wax (from 3.63 pounds to 31.9 pounds) in Chancery over a fifty-year stretch in Henry III's reign, in Clanchy 1979: 45–6.

4 In Plato's *Phaedo*, Socrates draws on the same image of the imprint to describe knowledge as recollection. Here, however, the imprints come not from the outside through time, but reside inwardly from birth – imprints of 'absolutes' like equality, beauty, goodness and justice. See Plato 1926: 263 (7SD).

5 For a physiological description of this phenomenon, see the description and diagram of how impressions on the eye refigure themselves on the brain, in his '*The World*' and '*Treatise on Man*' (1629–33) (Descartes 1993a: 105). See also his description of the eye of a dead ox, 'Optics', in *Discourse and Essays* (*c.* 1630) (Descartes 1993a: 166–7).

6 In the same letter, Descartes compares the brain to paper as well as wax; and as wax is without signet, so paper is without pen. Folds in the paper take the place of any stamp or script (Descartes 1991: 233). He draws the same analogy in his letter of 29 January 1640: 'As for the impressions preserved in the memory, I imagine they are not unlike the folds which remain in this paper after it has once been folded; and so I think that they are received for the most part

in the whole substance of the brain' (143). On Descartes's punning on his own name, 'the Greek word for paper', see Nancy 1978: 9.

7 On the theory that the foetus at fertilization was complete in miniature (preformation) and on the countervailing theory that the parts and organs developed sequentially (epigenesis), see Bowler 1971: 221–44.

8 The signet/wax apparatus makes a comeback in this century, however, both in Freud's identification of the psyche with the modern day wax tablet – the mystic pad – and with Derrida's critique of that identification, in 'Freud and the Scene of Writing' (Derrida 1978: 196–231). Both writers are fully aware of the tradition behind their discussions, Freud announcing 'a return to the ancient method of writing upon tablets of clay or wax' (quoted by Derrida, p. 223) and Derrida noting, 'From Plato and Aristotle scriptural images have regularly been used to *illustrate* the relationship between reason and experience, perception and memory' (199).

9 On the Galenic one-sex model (in which female sexual parts were construed as the interiorized inversion of male), see Laqueur 1990, esp. 32–5.

10 For a discussion of Descartes's theories of generation in the context of seventeenth-century theories of preformation and epigenesis, see Fouke 1975. I wish to thank Karen Newman for showing me before publication her invaluable genealogy of generation, *Fetal Positions*.

11 In Book II of *Paradise Lost*, Milton solves the doctrinal crux of how original sin entered the world by drawing on both forms of Cartesian conception: innate ideas and epigenetic birth. Sin emerges not from any outside stimulus, neither Creation or Creator, but automatically – from Satan's own brain, its conception of sin simultaneously a sinful thought and a child named Sin (747–61).

12 I have benefited in this section from A. and J. O. Thompson's discussion of Shakespeare's use of printing, stamping and coining metaphors in relation to issues of gender difference, generation and legitimacy (1987: 177–206).

13 On the monarch's use of the signet, Privy Seal and Great Seal and their eventual preemption by the monarch's signature or 'sign manual', see Goldberg 1990: 260–3. On Hamlet's use of his father's signet as the subornation of royal power, see Goldberg 1988: 322.

14 On the various forms of copying prescribed by humanist pedagogy, see J. Goldberg's chapter 'Copies' in Goldberg 1990: 111–69; Halpern also discusses the importance of various mimetic practices in Tudor education (1991: 19–60).

15 On the circulation of folio and boy *pages*, especially among pederastically inclined pedants and pedagogues, see Pittinger

1991. On Nashe's punning use of *page* in *The Unfortunate Traveller*, see Crewe 1982: 69–73. On the male author's identification with the *pages* of his publications, see Wall's discussion of 'A Man in Print' (1993: esp. 1–2).

16 There is some suggestion that the blubbery Falstaff – called 'tallow' (*1 Henry IV*, II. iv. 111), 'greasy tallow-catch' (228) and likened to 'a candle, the better part burnt out', 'a wassail candle . . . all tallow' (*2 Henry IV*, I. ii. 156, 158) – has the capacity to serve as wax as well as signet; his claim to have lost his grandfather's signet ring (*1 Henry IV* III. iii. 79–80, 84) might be considered in this context. For a discussion of Falstaff's effeminacy, see Traub1992b: 50–70, 155, n. 19.

17 I wish to thank Albert Braunmuller for pointing out to me that women did not receive benefit of clergy until the end of the century.

18 The connection between sodomy and counterfeiting is the subject of William Fisher's essay, 'Queer Money', and I wish to thank him for sharing it before publication.

19 H. Peacham, *Minerva Britanna, or a Garden of Historical Devices*, London (1612). I am grateful to William Fisher for this reference.

20 On the poem's 'postal circuit', see Fineman 1991: esp. 195–200; on Lucrece and the humanist project of textual purification, see Jed 1989; and on her relation to the 'stigma of print', see Wall 1993: 214–20.

21 For the similarity between the two technologies, see Clanchy 1979: 160. It should be noted, however, that the letters of the press are in relief whereas the figure of the signet is recessed.

22 This is, quite literally, the rude mechanics of Shakespeare's 'rude mechanics' in *A Midsummer Night's Dream*. That it applies to both artisanal and sexual activity is apparent in the very names of the artisans, all of them alluding to the fitting together of inverse parts, sexual and artisanal. Snug the Joiner or Carpenter snugly joins pieces of wood together, like male-duftails and female-duftails. Snout the Tinkerer knows, like all tinkerers, how to stop up holes, his outstanding nose or snout giving him a natural advantage; Starveling the Tailor needles his way, thin starveling that he is, into women's garments. 'Peter' Quince find his way into women's corners or quoins, the metal or wooden shanks used to fill up gaps. And Francis the Bellows Mender, liberally (licentiously) stops the holes in womb-like bellies or bellows.

What all these names suggest is the basic phallocentricity of both making things with cloth, metal and wood and making children with bodies: different hardware, but the same mechanical principle of joining and fitting together inverse parts. The only exception is Bottom the Weaver: though his name suggests the right phallic shape of the spool around which the yarn is wound, it is, as his name also suggests, in the wrong erotic position: on the bottom, encircled rather than inserting, as Bottom is when Titania mounts him in the stretch of the play demonstrating the topsy-turvy consequences of female domination. On the names and trades of these artisans as well as their erotic counterparts, see Parker 1995: 54–5.

23 I wish to thank Ian Gadd for first telling me about bearded typefaces. Moxon discusses the cutting of beards, in *Mechanick Exercises* (1978: 24–5, 188).

24 According to C. Cockburn, printing in England has a long history of excluding women from the setting type (1991: esp. 154). Baron 1989 draws similar conclusions for nineteenth- and twentieth-century America, with attention to how definitions of masculinity were repeatedly unsettled by changes in type-setting technologies. For a full account of women's involvement in printing in the eighteenth century, despite these customary restrictions, see Mitchell 1995: 25–75. (My thanks to Simon Stern for showing me this essay.)

25 Although his interest is women's apprenticeship in the eighteenth and nineteenth centuries, K. D. M. Snell endorses studies establishing that 'the apprenticeship of girls was an accepted fact' in the earlier centuries (1984: 272–6).

26 On the invention of the forceps, the replacement of the traditional midwife with men-midwives and the sudden increase in male attendance at childbirth in the eighteenth century, see Marland 1993.

27 On the incompatibility of menstrual and technical processes in sixteenth-century France, see Davis 1980: 146.

5   L[o]cating the sexual subject

1 Versions of this essay were delivered as lectures at the Folger Shakespeare Library in Washington and at the universities of Colorado, Kansas, Maryland and Pittsburgh. A version was also circulated as a seminar paper at the 1995 meeting of the Shakespeare Association of America. I am grateful to the colleagues who invited me to speak on these occasions and to the people who listened, asked questions, resisted and pushed.

2 On the legal record see Smith 1991: 41–53; on 'Domingo Cassedon a negro' see Bray 1982: 40–1; on the Earl of Castlehaven see Bingham 1971.

3 That is to say, 'the "spontaneous" consent given by the great masses of the population to the general direction imposed on social life by the dominant fundamental group' (Gramsci 1971: 12).

4 On blood as the seat of both lust and violence see Hoeniger 1992 and Smith 1995.

5 The dates I have assigned to these plays are those suggested in the chronological table appended to Braunmuller and Hattaway 1990: 419–46.

6 All these places are catalogued in Abate 1991. The other Sodoms are in Ohio (three), Indiana (two), Oregon (two), Alabama (one), Florida (one), Kentucky (one), Illinois (one), Minnesota (one). Abate also notes several places where residents have voted to change the name.

7 See, for example, sonnet 7: 'Since you want my *cazzo* in your *cul*, / As fashionable minds prefer today, / Do with my sex whatever you fancy. / Seize it with your hand, put it inside. / You'll feel the same benefit from it / That sick men get from enemas. / For my part, it's so pleasurable / Already feeling my *cazzo* in your hand, / I'll die if now we consummate the act' (Romano *et al.* 1990: 72). On Aretino as a model for later pornography in England see Boose 1987a.

8 On the valences in the Victoria and Albert Museum see Nevinson 1938: 32–8 and plates 24–7; on the valence from the Metropolian Museum exhibition see Remington 1945: figure 34; for examples of curtains see Bunt 1961: figures 30 and 42.

9 See, for example, William Cartwright's commendatory verses for the Beaumont and Fletcher folio of 1647: '*Shakespeare* to thee was dull, whose best Jest lies / I'th'Ladies questions, and the Fools replies, / . . . / Whose wit our nice times would obsceaness call, / And which made Bawdry pass for Comicall' (reprinted in Cartwright 1651: 273).

6 How to read *The Merchant of Venice* without being heterosexist

1 Lister 1994; see Sinfield 1994a: 1–8, 19–20.

2 For a reply to her critics by McLuskie, see McLuskie 1989: 224–9, and for further comment see Dollimore 1990.

3 Another way is blatantly reworking the authoritative text so that it is forced to yield, against the grain, explicitly oppositional kinds of understanding; see Sinfield 1992: 16–24, 290–302.

4 See also Jonson 1995: III. iv. 277–8, V. iii. 580–1. On boys in theatre, see Jardine 1983: ch. 1.

5 See Bray 1982: 38–42, 70–80; Smith 1991: 47–52.

6 See Jardine 1992; Zimmerman 1992.

7 See Sinfield 1994b: 25–37; and Sinfield 1992: 127–42 (this is an extension of the discussion of *Henry V* published first in Drakakis 1985), and 237–8 (on *Tamburlaine*).

8 Bray 1982; Trumbach 1987, 1989; Sinfield 1994b: 33–42.
9 See the suggestive remarks in Goldberg 1992: 142, 273–4.
10 Anti-semitism and homophobia are linked by Fiedler 1974: ch. 2, and by Mayer 1982: 278–85.

7 'In what chapter of his bosom?': reading Shakespeare's bodies

1 See, for example, Erika Fischer-Lichte, 'The Theatrical Code as Speech' (1993: 171–256; the original German edition was published in 1983).
2 Kantorowicz 1957: 176. Various 'body' critics have also drawn upon the related distinction made by the cultural anthropologist Mary Douglas, between a 'social' and a 'physical' body, with the resulting 'continual exchange of meanings between the two kinds of bodily experience' (1970: 65). See, for example, Paster 1993: 3–5.
3 See, for example, Gaspare Pallavicino's condemnation of female promiscuity in Castiglione's *The Book of the Courtier*: 'believe not that men are so incontinent as women be . . . For of the incontinencie of woman arise infinite inconveniences, that doe not of mens' (trans. Sir Thomas Hoby (1561), London: Dent (1975), p. 219).
4 See especially Belsey 1985b; Rackin 1987; Howard 1988; Orgel 1989; Jardine 1992; Traub 1992b.
5 Compare David Kuchta's claim (1993: 244) that the Renaissance semiotics of masculinity was based on 'a hierarchy of analogies, a system of resemblances between clothing and social position'.
6 See Elam 1984: 117.
7 *The Oxford English Dictionary*, Oxford: Clarendon Press, 2nd edn (1989), vol. 8, p. 959.
8 See Spurgeon 1935; on the recurring plague image in Shakespeare, see in particular pp. 130–2.
9 Quoted in Paster 1993: 12–13.
10 On 'plague' as Elizabethan swearword, see Hughes 1991: 190.
11 'Gum' is Pope's emendation of the Folio text, which has the improbable 'Gowne'.
12 Karl Marx, *Capital*, ed. David Mclellan, London: Oxford University Press (1995), p. 85.
13 Leigh Hunt, quoted by H. J. Oliver, Arden edition, p. 153.

8 Shakespeare and cultural difference

1 The absence of race as a theoretical parameter in another influential anthology, *Rewriting the Renaissance: The Discourses of Sexual*

Difference in Early Modern Europe, (Ferguson *et al.* 1986) is equally conspicuous but has been less remarked upon, which may have something to do with Wayne's own admission of the issue in her introduction.

2 Don Wayne 1987 offers an extended discussion of the differences between British cultural materialism and American new historicism in terms of the former's greater engagement with contemporary culture. Some of these differences map onto questions of 'race' and 'cultural difference', but although there has been more attention paid in Britain to the way in which readings of texts are connected with questions of pedagogy, in the case of 'race' such attention has not been confined to critics who would call themselves cultural materialists (for example, see Dabydeen 1985). And Renaissance criticism in the US has paid more attention to questions of 'race'; but although much of it is directed to the appropriation of texts, there is very little discussion of how contemporary institutions might shape the study of cultural difference in Shakespeare. It is 'Third World' critics, not surprisingly, who have had to insistently raise the question of location.

3 Of course MLA searches are no definitive indication of existing scholarship – Howard 1994b discusses the *Fair Maid of the West* but not its second part where the theme of interracial sexuality develops most fully. Both parts are considered by Tokson 1982: 102–4, Barthelemy 1987: 162–71 and D'Amico 1991: 84–97.

4 See my discussion of the tensions between feminist criticism and issue of 'race' (Loomba 1994: 17–34). L. Brown 1994: 118–37 and F. Azim 1993: 34–6 also discuss the tensions between the emergent female subject and empire. Class is now becoming increasingly absent from analyses of these other two differences, despite widespread invocation of the desirability of addressing 'race, class and gender'. We need greater acknowledgement of and discussion about the *difficulty* of juggling these categories together (Ferguson 1994: 209–24).

5 P. Hulme 1985 and 1986, H. Carr 1985 and P. Brown 1985 offer the best examples of this work; of more recent studies Montrose 1993 is exemplary.

6 A particularly brilliant instance of this kind of reading is Montrose 1986c; see also Greenblatt 1988 and Tennenhouse 1986. For a critique of this approach see Hutson, 1996: 32.

7 For example, Montrose 1993: 187 reads *The Discovery of Guiana* as a 'legend of Sir Walter' (as pointed out by Hutson, 1996: 32). See also Greenblatt, *Walter Ralegh* (1973), which can be seen as a ur-text for his influential *Renaissance Self-fashioning* (1980). A concentration on courtly individuals might also partially explain the emphasis on New World voyaging as opposed to the Eastern travels,

whose proponents were not generally part of the charmed circle.

8 Some other scholars have tried to map precisely such transformations; see for example Quint 1985: 178–202 and Helgerson 1992: 155.

9 In fact the 'soft' liberal version of exoticism that Gillies attributes to Behn's time has been attributed to Montaigne, whom Shakespeare read, and who certainly complicates a binary division between the natural and the civilized man; see White 1978: 176–7.

10 See Chew 1937; Penrose 1952. This neglect is quite surprising given the enormous scholarship on Eastern trade for which, for starters, see bibliographies in Donald Lach's monumental *Asia in the Making of Europe* (1968–94).

11 Similarly, the speaker of John Donne's 'The Sunne Rising' claims that his mistress incorporates 'both the Indias of Spice and Myne' (Gardner 1972: 61).

12 See Vaughan 1988 for an account of how and when the connections between Caliban and the New World native became dominant.

13 This strategy asks us to suppose a presence which at first cannot be found; Spivak 1985 endorses it as the enabling fiction of the Subaltern school of Indian history.

14 Sixteenth-century English commentaries on the Turks are too numerous to list; the better known pieces are Knolles 1603; Sandys 1627; Mun 1620; Biddulph 1905 and Lithgow 1632. For commentaries see Chew 1937; Patrides 1963; Starr 1965 and Hampton 1993.

15 My essay has much in common with Jonathan Burton, *'Antony and Cleopatra* Turn'd Turk' (unpublished paper) who shares this view of the play.

16 Here I refer to sixteenth- and seventeenth-century imports from Asian languages and not to the shared Indo-European linguistic heritage. See Lach 1968–94: II, iii, 493, 525. See also his list of Asiatic words introduced into the European vocabulary (545–53), and, more generally, Yule and Burnell 1984. The impact of such rebabelization on the language of Renaissance plays, including those of Shakespeare, is an unexamined but promising area.

17 P. Parker has noted the sixteenth-century opposition of a concise, forceful, masculine, Attic style to a loquacious, effeminate 'Asiatic' expression. These sets of associations and oppositions derived as she says from a 'powerful mix of misogyny and orientalism conveyed from fifth-century Athens to Europe through the whole force of Roman tradition' ('Virile Style', unpublished manuscript: 1).

18 This desire to possess veiled women works in a variety of ways –

sometimes through the suggestion that wayward English women should emulate the subservience and obedience of Turkish wives, as in Sandys; at other times by directing the gaze and desire of Eastern women towards Western men as in plays such as Philip Massinger's *The Renegado* (1624) or John Fletcher's *The Island Princess* (1621); or often by simply positioning the white man as intimate observer of the royal harem as in Robert Withers's 'The Grand Signior's Seraglio' (1905).

19 This is not to suggest that Shakespeare accepted these stereotypes; rather his plays have evoked them, and provoked a debate about these associations.

20 According to Paul Kaplan, 'By 1500 the story of the Magi in art constituted the preeminent means of integrating the inhabitants of non-European world into the Western Christian universe.' Kaplan is quoted by Erikson who also discusses pictorial representations of Sheba.

21 For lack of space, I cannot even adequately hint at the enormous information boom and materials generated by the early years of Eastern travel, on which a wealth of secondary literature currently exists. Rich bibliographies and summaries are provided by Lach 1968–94.

22 The interest in the Americas was of course mercantile as well; still there are important differences resulting from the fact that the English did not speak of inhabiting Turkey or India, and the trade in these places was not conceived of as the exchange of baubles and trinkets for pearls and gold whose value the natives did not realize.

23 G. McMullen 1994: 224 totally bypasses the setting of *The Island Princess*, and reads it as a story about Pocahontas.

24 Conversion rituals are also described in *The Renegado* and *A True Relation of the Travailes and Most Miserable Captivitie of William Davies* (1616).

25 See also Draper 1953 and 1955. Wann includes Shylock and Othello as 'Oriental'; Barthelemy 1987 and D'Amico 1991 offer other estimates but are concerned about skin colour primarily, and Chew 1937 focuses on Muslim characters.

26 I am indebted to Haynes 1986: 75 for this observation.

27 The work of Lisa Jardine, Catherine Belsey and Jonathan Dollimore has been especially thought-provoking in this regard, as also that of Thomas Laquer, Patricia Parker, Stephen Orgel and Jean Howard and others too numerous to be mentioned here.

28 I am indebted to S. Iyengar, who suggests that, unlike the effect of cross-dressing upon the production of gender, blackface works to efface the politics of racial construction, 'White Faces, Black-face: The Production of "Race" in *Othello*', unpublished paper: 5.

29 I would like to thank Rukun Advani, Barbara Bowen, Walter
Cohen, Lars Engle, Lorna Hutson, Martin Orkin and especially
Suvir Kaul, who will recognize the ways in which this essay has
benefited from their careful readings or failed to do justice to their
comments.

9 'Othello was a white man': properties of race on Shakespeare's stage'

1 Hall notes 'Representations of Blacks, as well as actual Blacks, were
an integral part of Scottish court entertainment during James VI's
reign' (Hall 1991: 4).
2 Preston contended that Othello, the character, the *Moor* of Venice,
was white.
3 There are famous 'exceptions' to this rule, namely foreign performers and Moll Frith's musical performance. See Mann 1991:
246.
4 Valerie Wayne articulates the crucial recognition that whiteness
was 'the most visible complexion of European Renaissance society'
(1991: 11).
5 'Savages and men of Ind' are referred to, for example, in *The
Tempest* II. ii. 57. In his analysis of early modern understandings of
Africa, Eldred Jones points out: 'the peoples of Africa . . . were
strange, picturesque inhabitants of a strange, picturesque land.
Their color was a striking feature which was frequently mentioned.
Regardless of what the more informed writers may have said about
the different colors of Africans, only their blackness seems to have
registered firmly' (Jones 1965: 39).
6 Occasionally, where characters are disguised as Moors and need
to uncover themselves quickly, masks rather than blackface are
used to represent black skin, as for example in Robert Greene's
Orlando Furioso (1592). See Jones 1965: 121.
7 Similarly, P. H. Parry observes that Othello's references to his own
'begrimed' face take on greater resonance when 'what you have in
your mind as you write (or view) the play are the words spoken by
an actor who can wash his grimy blackness off an hour or so after
the words are spoken' (1990: 101).
8 My thinking here is directed by Copjec's chapter 'The Sartorial
Superego' (Copjec 1994).
9 For a fascinating account of the notion of race and cosmetics in an
unproduced eighteenth-century play, *The New Cosmetic or The
Triumph of Beauty, A Comedy* (1790) by Samuel Jackson Pratt, writing
under the pseudonym Courtney Melmoth, see Gwilliam 1994.
10 Barthelemy observes: 'The desire of so many women (nineteen in

three masques) to be freed of the sign of their otherness, the sign of their type, can neither be overlooked nor underestimated' (1987: 41). See also D'Amico 1991: 53.

11 Thomas Southerne's rendition of Aphra Behn's novella *Oroonoko*, for instance, substitutes a white woman for the black beauty Imoinda. Margaret Ferguson incisively observes, 'This change may perhaps be explained as Southerne's bow to a strikingly gendered and also colored convention of the Restoration stage which I'm still trying to understand, namely that male English actors could appear in blackface but actresses evidently could not' (Ferguson 1994: 219–20).

12 'Painting apparently was not only practised by women, for male courtiers at the end of the sixteenth century occasionally coloured their faces' (Webb 1912: 208). See Drew-Bear 1994: 27–31.

13 For a discussion of the blazon tradition in *Lucrece*, see Vickers 1986.

14 Annette Drew-Bear argues that 'In fact, extensive evidence exists that boy and adult players used makeup in Renaissance drama' (1994: 14).

15 My thinking here is indebted to Kaja Silverman's discussion of the formation of the subject in the mirror stage, which I think has considerable relevance to formations of racial identity, though it has never been addressed in that context (1992b: 90).

16 There is, of course, a Renaissance stereotype of the Italian woman as the dark lady. On the significance of Cyprus for the Renaissance see Neill 1984.

17 Other characters on stage, of course, probably also wore sumptuous dress, but the palate of colours used in these costumes was rather more muted than that used in the depiction of Moors. Andrew Gurr observes: 'It was an age of glorious variety, in which, as always in the world of fashion, new names had constantly to be chosen as new shades of color were invented. Pepper, tobacco, sea-water, and puke (a dark brown) were a few of the many Elizabethan inventions' (1992: 181–2). None of these is a bright colour.

F. M. Kelly argues for the predominance of black clothes in social dress: 'The importance of black in the collective colour-scheme of Elizabethan costume is apt to be underestimated . . . it is probably safe to say that black would be the dominant note in any average Elizabethan crowd . . . Brocades, cloth of gold and of silver were only worn by the greatest on occasions of state' (1938: 44–5).

18 John Salway observes, 'What the theatre reviewers of 1833 were, in effect, denying to Ira Aldridge was his capacity to represent a Black character in a white theatre' (1991: 121).

19 In Britain, *The Black and White Minstrel Show* was a highly popular television show until the 1970s. All of its minstrels were white men

in blackface. Ironically, it was one of the first musical shows to appear on television 'in colour'.

20 In medieval drama, for instance, blackface is not so much an impersonation as a symbolic depiction.

21 I do not have space to attend to Cleopatra here. I will only observe that she is constructed to occupy a place of pure exhibition. See my *Shakespeare Without Women* (forthcoming).

22 Similarly, when women use cosmetics, or when women act, not only is it denigrated but they are still being themselves – naturally vain, deceitful and so on.

23 Jordan 1968 observes that Africans had become virtually synonymous with slavery by the mid-sixteenth century.

24 See Jordan 1968 on the development of racialist ideology, especially chs 1 and 2. Philippa Berry has pointed out that there were very positive connotations to blackness in the thinking of Renaissance humanists like Ficino, Bruno and Miradolla. On the complex history of the marvel, see Stephen Greenblatt's brilliant *Marvelous Possessions* (1991).

25 See Parker 1994 for a compelling discussion of the parallels between the unfolding and discovery of 'foreign parts' and female genitals.

26 'Shakespeare shows that the union of a white Venetian maiden and a black Moorish general is from at least one perspective emphatically unnatural. The union is of course a central fact of the play, and to some commentators, the spectacle of the pale-skinned woman caught in Othello's black arms has indeed seemed monstrous. Yet that spectacle is a major source of Othello's emotional power. From Shakespeare's day to the present the sight has titillated and terrified predominantly white audiences' (Vaughan 1994: 51). See also Rosenberg 1961: 16–205.

27 I am indebted to the intellectual generosity of Pippa Berry, Juliet Fleming, Terence Hawkes, Peter Holland, Jean Howard and David Riggs, who kindly read earlier drafts of this essay, and to Michael Hattaway and the other members of Martin Orkin's Stratford seminar. I would also like to acknowledge Clare Hall, Cambridge, where most of it was written.

10 Watching *Hamlet* watching: Lacan, Shakespeare and the mirror/stage

1 See Levine 1986.

2 The comparison is attributed to Cicero by Donatus (Jenkins 1982: 288). Stephen Gosson refutes it at length in the 'Schoole of Abuse' (1974: 159–69).

3 All these meanings for the word 'strike' are given in the *OED*: senses 6, 7, 11, 12, 28a, b and c.

4 Cited in Frances Yates's *Theatre of the World* (1969: 143).

5 Just as Sigmund Freud and Ernest Jones took the play as a paradigm for the Oedipus complex (Freud 1976: 366–8; Jones 1949).

6 See Hawkes 1986: 92–119.

7 For example James Halliwell-Phillipps and John Dover Wilson (Jenkins 1982: 502–3).

8 For discussions of the ghost as 'uncanny' see Garber 1987 and Armstrong 1994.

9 For critiques of Lacanian 'phallogocentrism' see Brennan 1989 and Derrida 1987.

10 See, for example, Freud's essay 'Some Psychical Consequences of the Anatomical Distinction between the Sexes' (1986b).

11 Probably the most famous of Lacan's extended jokes on sexual difference occurs in his essay 'The Agency of the Letter in the Unconscious' (1977b: 150–2).

Bibliography

Abate, Frank R. (ed.) (1991) *Omni Gazetteer of the United States of America*, Detroit: Omni Graphics.

Adelman, Janet (1985) 'Male Bonding in Shakespeare's Comedies', in Peter Erickson and Coppélia Kahn (eds) *Shakespeare's 'Rough Magic'*, Newark: University of Delaware Press.

—— (1987) '"Born of Woman": Fantasies of Maternal Power in *Macbeth*', in Marjorie Garber (ed.) *Cannibals, Witches, and Divorce: Estranging the Renaissance*, Baltimore: Johns Hopkins University Press, 90–121.

Agnew, Jean-Christophe (1986) *Worlds Apart: The Market and the Theater in Anglo-American Thought, 1550–1750*, Cambridge and New York: Cambridge University Press.

Appleby, Joyce Oldham (1978) *Economic Thought and Ideology in Seventeenth-Century England*, Princeton: Princeton University Press.

Aristotle (1647) *The Problems of Aristotle, with Other Philosophers, and Physicians: Wherein are Contained Divers Questions with their Answers, Touching the Estate of Mans Bodie*, London.

—— (1935) 'On Memory and Recollection', in *On the Soul, Parva naturalia, On Breath*, trans. W. S. Hett, London: Heinemann.

—— (1986) *De anima*, trans H. Lawson-Tancred, Harmondsworth: Penguin.

Armstrong, Philip (1994) 'Uncanny Spectacles: Psychoanalysis and the Texts of *King Lear*', *Textual Practice* 8, 3: 414–34.

Artaud, Antonin (1970) 'Theatre and the Plague', in *The Theatre and its Double*, London: Calder and Boyars, 7–22.

Auden, W. H. (1963) 'Brothers and Others', in *The Dyer's Hand*, London: Faber.

—— (1969) *Collected Shorter Poems 1927–1957*, London: Faber.

Azim, F. (1993) *The Colonial Rise of the Novel*, London: Routledge.

Bakhtin, Mikhail (1984) *Rabelais and His World*, trans. Helene Iswolsky, Bloomington: Indiana University Press.

Banu, Georges (1991) *Peter Brook*: De Timon d'Athens à La Tempête, ou Le metteur en scène et le cercle, Paris: Flammarion.

Barish, Jonas (1981) *The Anti-theatrical Prejudice*, Berkeley: University of California Press.

Barker, F. and Hulme, P. (1985) '"Nymphs and Reapers Heavily Vanish": The Discursive Con-texts of *The Tempest*', in John Drakakis (ed.) (1985), 191–205.

Barker, Francis (1984) *The Tremulous Private Body: Essays on Subjection*, London and New York: Routledge.

Baron, A. (1989) 'Questions of Gender, Deskilling, and Demasculation in the U.S. Printing Industry, 1830–1915', *Gender and History* 1, 2: 178–99.

Barroll, Leeds (1991) *Politics, Plague, and Shakespeare's Theater: The Stuart Years*, Ithaca and London: Cornell University Press.

Barthelemy, Anthony Gerard (1987) *Black Face, Maligned Race: The Representation of Blacks in English Drama from Shakespeare to Southerne*, Baton Rouge: Louisiana State University Press.

Barthes, Roland (1975) *S/Z*, trans. Richard Miller, London: Cape.

Bate, Jonathan (1989) *Shakespearean Constitutions: Politics, Theatre, Criticism 1730–1830*, Oxford: Clarendon Press.

Baudrillard, Jean (1990) *Seduction*, trans. Brian Singer, London: Macmillan.

Belsey, Catherine (1985a) *The Subject of Tragedy: Identity and Difference in Renaissance Drama*, London and New York: Routledge.

—— (1985b) 'Disrupting Sexual Difference: Meaning and Gender in the Comedies', in John Drakakis (ed.)(1985), 166–190.

—— (1992) 'Desire's Excess and the English Renaissance Theatre: *Edward II, Troilus and Cressida, Othello*', in Susan Zimmerman (ed.) (1992), 84–102.

—— (1994) *Desire: Love Stories in Western Culture*, Oxford: Blackwell.

Bennington, Geoffrey (1994) *Legislations: The Politics of Deconstruction*, London and New York: Verso.

Berger, Harry (1981) 'Marriage and Mercifixion in *The Merchant of Venice*: The Casket Scene Revisited', *Shakespeare Quarterly* 32: 155–62.

Bergeron, D. (1971) *English Civic Pageantry 1558–1642*, London: Edward Arnold.

Biddulph, W. (1905) 'Part of a Letter of Master William Biddulph from Aleppo', in S. Purchas (1905), vol. 8.

Biersack, Aletta (1989) 'Local Knowledge, Local History: Geertz and Beyond', in Lynn Hunt (ed.) *The New Cultural History*, Berkeley and Los Angeles: University of California Press, 72–96.

Bingham, Caroline (1971) 'Seventeenth-Century Attitudes Toward Deviant Sex', *Journal of Interdisciplinary History* 1: 447–72.

Birdwood, G. and Foster, W. (1893) *The Register of Letters etc. of the Governour and Company of Merchants of London Trading into the East Indies, 1600–1619*, London: Bernard Quartich.

Blagden, C. (1960) *The Stationers' Company: A History, 1403–1959*, London: Allen and Unwin.

Bloch, Ernst *et al.* (1980) *Aesthetics and Politics*, trans. R. Taylor (ed.), London: Verso.

Bloom, Harold (1994) *The Western Canon*, New York and London: Harcourt Brace.

Booker, Christopher (1992) 'A Modern Tragedy of Errors', in *The Daily Telegraph*, April 23.

Boose, Lynda E. (1987a) '"Let It Be Hid": Renaissance Pornography, Iago, and Audience Response', in Richard Marienstras and Dominique Goy-Blanquet (eds) *Autour d'Othello*, Amiens: Presses de l'UFR CLERC, Université Picardie.

—— (1987b) 'The Family in Shakespeare Studies; or – Studies in the Family of Shakespeareans; or – The Politics of Politics', *Renaissance Quarterly* 40: 707–42.

—— (1994) '"Getting a Lawful Race": Racial Discourse in Early Modern England and the Unrepresentable Black Woman', in M. Hendricks and P. Parker (eds) (1994).

Bourdieu, Pierre (1977) *Outline of a Theory of Practice*, trans. Richard Nice, Cambridge: Cambridge University Press.

Bowler, P. (1971) 'Preformation and Pre-existence in the Seventeenth Century: A Brief Analysis', *Journal of the History of Biology* 4: 223–44.

Bradley, A. C. (1904) *Shakespearean Tragedy: Lectures on Hamlet, Othello, King Lear and Macbeth*, London: Macmillan.

Braunmuller, A. R. and Hattaway, Michael (1990) *The Cambridge Companion to English Renaissance Drama*, Cambridge: Cambridge University Press.

Bray, Alan (1982) *Homosexuality in Renaissance England*, London: Gay Men's Press.

—— (1990) 'Homosexuality and the Signs of Male Friendship in Elizabethan England', *History Workshop* 29: 1–19.

Bredbeck, Gregory W. (1991) *Sodomy and Interpretation*, Ithaca: Cornell University Press.

—— (1992) 'Tradition and the Individual Sodomite: Barnfield, Shakespeare and Subjective Desire', in Claude J. Summers (ed.) *Homosexuality in Renaissance and Enlightenment England: Literary Representations in Historical Context*, New York: Haworth Press, 41–68.

Brennan, Teresa (ed.) (1989) *Between Feminism and Psychoanalysis*, London and New York: Routledge.

Brinsley, J. (1612) *Ludus literarius: or, the Grammar Schoole*, facs. rpt. 1964, Menston: Scolar Press.

Bristol, Michael D. (1985) *Carnival and Theater: Plebeian Culture and the Structure of Authority in Renaissance England*, New York and London: Routledge.

—— (1990) 'Charivari and the Comedy of Abjection in Othello', *Renaissance Drama* 21 (new series): 3–21.

Brown, L. (1994) 'Amazons and Africans: Gender, Race, and Empire', in M. Hendricks and P. Parker (eds) (1994).

Brown, P. (1985) '"This Thing of Darkness I Acknowledge Mine": *The Tempest* and the Discourse of Colonialism', in J. Dollimore and A. Sinfield (eds) (1985).

Bunt, Cyril G. E. (1961) *Tudor and Stuart Fabrics*, Leigh-on-Sea: F. Lewes.

Butler, Judith (1990) *Gender Trouble: Feminism and the Subversion of Identity*, London and New York: Routledge.

—— (1994) 'Against Proper Objects', *differences* 6, 2 and 3: 1–26.

Calderwood, James L. (1989) *The Properties of Othello*, Amherst: University of Massachusetts Press.

Callaghan, Dympna (1989) *Woman and Gender in Renaissance Tragedy*, Brighton: Harvester; Atlantic Highlands, NJ: Humanities Press International.

—— (1993) '"And All is Semblative a Woman's Part": Body Politics and *Twelfth Night*', *Textual Practice* 7: 428–52.

Campbell, Mary B. (1992) 'The Illustrated Travel Book and the Birth of Ethnography: Part I of de Bry's *America*', in D. G. Allen and R. A. White (eds) *The Work of Dissimilitude*, Newark: University of Delaware Press.

Carr, H. (1985) 'Woman/Indian: "The American" and his Others', in Francis Barker *et al.* (eds) *Europe and its Others*, vol. 2, Colchester: University of Essex.

Cartwright, William (1651) *Comedies, Tragi-comedies, with Other Poems*, London: Humphrey Moseley.

Case, S. (1991) 'The Eurocolonial Reception of Sanskrit Poetics', in Sue-Ellen Case and Janelle Reinelt (eds) *The Performance of Power*, Iowa: Iowa University Press.

Certeau, Michel de (1984) *The Practice of Everyday Life*, trans. Steven F. Rendall, Berkeley and Los Angeles: University of California Press.

Chartier, Roger (1990) *Cultural History: Between Practices and Representations*, trans. Lydia G. Cochrane, Ithaca: Cornell University Press.

Chatterji, P. (1986) *Nationalist Thought and the Colonial World*, London: Zed Books, for the United Nations University.

Chew, S. (1937) *The Crescent and the Rose: Islam and England During the Renaissance*, New York: Oxford University Press.

Clanchy, M. T. (1979) *From Memory to Written Record: England, 1066–1307*, London: Edward Arnold.

Cockburn, C. (1991) *Brothers: Male Dominance and Technological Change*, London and Concord, Mass.: Pluto Press.

Cohen. W. (1987) 'Political Criticism of Shakespeare', in J. Howard and M. F. O'Connor (eds)(1987), 18–46.

Coke, Edward (1660) *The Third Part of the Institutes of the Laws of England*, 3rd edn, London: J. Fleshner.

Coleridge, Samuel Taylor (1969) Terence Hawkes (ed.) *Coleridge on Shakespeare*, Harmondsworth: Penguin Books.

Comaroff, Jean and John L. (1991) *Of Revelation and Revolution: Christianity, Colonialism, and Consciousness in South Africa*, vol. 1, Chicago and London: University of Chicago Press.

Conway, J. F. (1986) 'Syphilis and Bronzino's London Allegory', *Journal of the Warburg and Courtauld Institutes* 49: 250–5.

Copjec, Joan (1994) *Read My Desire: Lacan Against the Historicists*, Cambridge, Mass.: MIT Press.

Corbeiller, le C. (1961) 'Miss America and her Sisters, Personifications of the Four Parts of the World', *The Metropolitan Museum of Art Bulletin*, 19, 8 (new series): 209–23.

Cornwallis, William (1600) *Essayes*, London: Edmund Mattes.

Cowhig, Ruth, (1985) 'Blacks in English Renaissance Drama and the Role of Shakespeare's Othello', in David Dabydeen (ed.) (1985).

Crewe, J. V. (1982) *Unredeemed Rhetoric: Thomas Nashe and the Scandal of Authorship*, Baltimore and London: Johns Hopkins University Press.

Dabydeen, David (ed.) (1985) *The Black Presence in English Literature*, Manchester: Manchester University Press.

D'Amico, J. (1991) *The Moor in English Renaissance Drama*, Tampa: University of South Florida Press.

Darnton, Robert (1984) *The Great Cat Massacre and Other Episodes in French Cultural History*, New York: Basic Books.

Davis, N. Z. (1980) 'Women in the *Arts Mécaniques*', in *Lyon et l'Europe, hommes et sociétés: Mélanges d'histoire offerts à Richard Gascon*, vol. 1, Lyon: Presses Universitaires de Lyon.

—— (1994) 'Iroquois Women, European Women', in M. Hendricks and P. Parker (eds) (1994).

de Grazia, M. (1991) *Shakespeare Verbatim: The Reproduction of Authenticity and the 1790 Apparatus*, Oxford: Clarendon Press.

—— (1994) 'The Scandal of Shakespeare's Sonnets', *Shakespeare Survey* 46: 35–49.

—— (1995) 'The Question of the One and the Many', *Shakespeare Quarterly*, 46, 2: 1–7.

Dekker, Thomas (1884–6) *The Seven Deadly Sinnes of London* (1606), in A. B. Grosart (ed.) *The Non-dramatic Works of Thomas Dekker*, vol. 2, London: The Huth Library.

Deleuze, Gilles (1968) *Difference and Repetition*, trans. Paul Patton, London: Athlone Press, 1994.

Derrida, J. (1978) *Writing and Difference*, trans. Alan Bass, Chicago: University of Chicago Press.

—— (1979) *Spurs: Nietzsche's Styles*, trans. Barbara Harlow, Chicago: University of Chicago Press.

—— (1987) 'Le Facteur de la vérité', in *The Post Card: From Socrates to Freud and Beyond*, trans. Alan Bass, Chicago: University of Chicago Press, 413–96.

—— (1992) *Acts of Literature*, ed. Derek Attridge, New York and London: Routledge.

Descartes, R. (1953), *Descartes: Oeuvres et Lettres*, ed. André Bridoux, Paris: Bibliothèque de la Pléiade.

—— (1993a) *The Philosophical Writings of Descartes*, vol. 1, ed. J. Cottingham, R. Stoothoff, D. Murdoch, Cambridge: Cambridge University Press.

—— (1993b) *The Philosophical Writings of Descartes*, vol. 2.

—— (1991) *The Philosophical Writings of Descartes*, vol. 3.

Doanne, Mary Ann (1991) *Femmes Fatales: Feminism, Film Theory, Psychoanalysis*, New York: Routledge.

Dolan, Frances E. (1993) 'Taking the Pencil Out of God's Hand: Art, Nature and the Face Painting Debate in Early Modern England', *PMLA* 108: 224–39.

Dollimore, Jonathan (1984) *Radical Tragedy: Religion, Ideology, and Power in the Drama of Shakespeare and his Contemporaries*, Brighton: Harvester; Chicago: University of Chicago Press.

—— (1990) 'Shakespeare, Cultural Materialism, Feminism and Marxist Humanism', *New Literary History* 21: 471–93.

—— (1992) *Sexual Dissidence: Augustine to Wilde, Freud to Foucault*, Oxford: Clarendon Press.

Dollimore, Jonathan and Sinfield, Alan (eds) (1985) *Political Shakespeare: New Essays in Cultural Materialism*, Ithaca: Cornell University Press; Manchester, Manchester University Press, 2nd edn 1994.

Donne, John (1965) *The Elegies and The Songs and Sonnets*, ed. Helen Gardner, Oxford: Clarendon Press.

Douglas, Mary (1970) *Natural Symbols: Explorations in Cosmology*, New York: Pantheon.

Drakakis, John (ed.) (1985) *Alternative Shakespeares*, London: Routledge.

—— (ed.) (1994) *Antony and Cleopatra* (New Casebooks), London: Macmillan.

Drake, St. Clair (1990) *Black Folk Here and There*, 2 vols, Los Angeles: University of California Press.

Draper, J. (1953) 'Shakespeare and India', *Annales publiées par la Faculté des Lettres de Toulouse*, Nov: 2–12.

—— (1955) 'Indian and Indies in Shakespeare', *Neuephilologische Mitterlungen* 56: 103–22.

Drew-Bear, Annette (1981) 'Face-painting in Renaissance Tragedy', *Renaissance Drama* 12 (new series): 71–93.

—— (1994) *Painted Faces on the Renaissance Stage: The Moral Significance of Face-painting Conventions*, Lewisburg, PA: Bucknell University Press.

Earle, John (1629) *Micro-cosmographie: or, a Peece of the World Discovered; in Essayes and Characters*, enlarged edition, London: Robert Allot.

Eccles, A. (1982) *Obstetrics and Gynaecology in Tudor and Stuart England*, London: Croom Helm.

Eco, Umberto (1976) *A Theory of Semiotics*, Bloomington: Indiana University Press.

Eden, R. (1577) *The History of Travayle East and West*, London.

Elam, Keir (1980) *The Semiotics of Theatre and Drama*, London: Routledge.

—— (1984) *Shakespeare's Universe of Discourse: Language-games in the Comedies*, Cambridge: Cambridge University Press.

—— (1996) 'The Fertile Eunuch: *Twelfth Night*, Early Modern Intercourse and the Fruits of Castration', *Shakespeare Quarterly* 47, 1: 1–36.

Erickson, Peter (1985) review of *The (M)other Tongue: Essays in Feminist Psychoanalytic Interpretation*, in *Hurricane Alice: A Feminist Review* 3: 6–7.

—— (1987)'Rewriting the Renaissance, Rewriting Ourselves', *Shakespeare Quarterly* 38: 327–37.

—— (1993) 'Representations of Blacks and Blackness in the Renaissance', *Criticism* 35, 4: 499–527.

Everden, D. (1993) 'Mothers and Midwives in Seventeenth-Century London', in Hilary Marland (ed.) (1993).

Fabricius, Johannes (1994) *Syphilis in Shakespeare's England*, London: Jessica Kingsley.

Ferguson, Margaret W. (1994) 'Juggling the Categories of Race, Class and Gender: Aphra Behn's *Oroonoko*', in M. Hendricks and P. Parker (eds) (1994).

Ferguson, Margaret, Quilligan, Maureen and Vickers, Nancy J. (eds) (1986) *Rewriting the Renaissance: The Discourses of Sexual Difference in Early Modern Europe*, Chicago: University of Chicago Press.

Ferris, Leslie (1990) *Acting Women: Images of Women in Theatre*, New York: New York University Press.

Fiedler, Leslie (1974) *The Stranger in Shakespeare*, St Albans: Paladin.

Fineman, J. (1991) *The Subjectivity Effect in Western Literary Tradition: Essays Toward the Release of Shakespeare's Will*, Cambridge, Mass. and London: MIT Press.

Finkelpearl, Philip J. (1969) *John Marston of the Middle Temple: An Elizabethan Dramatist in his Social Setting*, Cambridge: Harvard University Press.

Fischer, S. K. (1985) *Econolingua: A Glossary of Coins and Economic Language in Renaissance Drama*, Newark, N.J.: University of Delaware Press.

Fischer-Lichte, Erika (1993) *The Semiotics of Theatre*, trans. Jeremy Gaines and Doris L. Jones, Bloomington: Indiana University Press.

Fish, Stanley (1980) *Is There a Text in This Class? The Authority of Interpretive Communities*, Cambridge, Mass.: Harvard University Press.

Fisher, W. (1994) 'Queer Money', unpublished manuscript.

Foucault, Michel (1971) *The Order of Things: An Archaeology of the Human Sciences*, trans. Alan Sheridan, London: Tavistock.

—— (1977) *Discipline and Punish: The Birth of the Prison*, trans. Alan Sheridan, New York: Pantheon; Harmondsworth: Penguin Books.

—— (1979) *The History of Sexuality, Volume 1:, An Introduction*, trans. Robert Hurley, New York: Pantheon; Harmondsworth: Penguin Books.

Fouke, D. (1975) 'Mechanical and Organical Models in Seventeenth-Century Explanations of Biological Reproduction', *Science in Context* 3, 2: 366–88.

Freud, Sigmund (1976) Angela Richards and Albert Dickson (eds) *The Penguin Freud Library, Volume 4:, The Interpretation of Dreams*, trans. James Strachey, London and New York: Penguin.

—— (1977) 'On Sexuality', in *The Penguin Freud Library Volume 7:, On Sexuality*, 31–169.

—— (1979) 'The Pathogenesis of a Case of Homosexuality in a Woman', in *The Penguin Freud Library Volume 9, Case Histories II*, 369–400.

—— (1984) 'On Metapsychology: The Theory of Psychoanalysis', in *The Penguin Freud Library*, vol. 11.

—— (1985) 'The Uncanny', in *The Penguin Freud Library*, vol. 14: Art and Literature, 339–76.

—— (1986a) 'Beyond the Pleasure Principle', in Anna Freud (ed.) *The Essentials of Psycho-analysis*, trans. James Strachey, London and New York: Penguin, 218–68.

—— (1986b), 'Some Psychical Consequences of the Anatomical Distinction between the Sexes', in Anna Freud (ed.) *The Essentials of Psycho-analysis*, trans. James Strachey, London and New York: Penguin, 402–11.

Gainsford, Thomas (1616) *The Rich Cabinet Furnished with Varietie of Excellent Discriptions, Exquisite Charracters, Witty Discourses, and Delightful Histories, Devine and Morrall*, London.

Gallagher, Catherine (1989) 'Marxism and the New Historicism', in Aram H. Veeser (1989), 37–48 .

Garber, Marjorie (1987) *Shakespeare's Ghost Writers: Literature as Uncanny Causality*, London and New York: Routledge.

—— (1992) *Vested Interests: Cross Dressing and Cultural Anxiety*, London and New York: Routledge.

Gardner, H. (ed.) (1972) *The Metaphysical Poets*, Harmondsworth: Penguin.

Garner, Shirley Nelson (1989) 'Let her Paint an Inch Thick', *Renaissance Drama* 20: 123–39.

Gay, Penny (1994) *As She Likes It: Shakespeare's Unruly Women*, New York and London: Routledge.

Geary, Keith (1984) 'The Nature of Portia's Victory: Turning to Men in *The Merchant of Venice*', *Shakespeare Survey* 37: 55–68.

Geertz, Clifford (1973) *The Interpretation of Cultures: Selected Essays*, New York: Basic Books.

—— (1980) *Negara: The Theatre State in Nineteenth Century Bali*, Princeton: Princeton University Press.

—— (1983) *Local Knowledge: Further Essays in Interpretive Anthropology*, New York: Basic Books.

Gesta Grayorum (1968) ed. Desmond Bland, Liverpool: Liverpool University Press.

Giddens, Anthony (1979) *Central Problems in Social Theory: Action, Structure, and Contradiction in Social Analysis*, Berkeley: University of California Press.

Gillies, J. (1994) *Shakespeare and the Geography of Difference*, Cambridge: Cambridge University Press.

Ginzburg, Carlo (1980) *The Cheese and the Worms: The Cosmos of a Sixteenth-Century Miller*, trans. John and Anne Tedeschi, Baltimore: Johns Hopkins University Press.

Goldberg, Jonathan (1981) *Endlesse Worke: Spenser and the Structures of Discourse*, Baltimore: Johns Hopkins University Press.

—— (1982) 'The Politics of Renaissance Literature: A Review Essay', *English Literary History* 49: 514–42.

—— (1983) *James I and the Politics of Literature*, Baltimore: Johns Hopkins University Press.

—— (1986) 'Textual Properties', *Shakespeare Quarterly* 37, 1: 213–17.

—— (1988) 'Hamlet's Hand', *Shakespeare Quarterly* 39, 3: 307–27.

—— (1990) *Writing Matter: From the Hands of the English Renaissance*, Stanford: Stanford University Press.

—— (1992) *Sodometries: Renaissance Texts, Modern Sexualities*, Stanford: Stanford University Press.

—— (1995) 'Hal's Desire, Shakespeare's Idaho', in Nigel Wood (ed.) *Henry IV Part One and Two*, Buckingham: Open University Press.

Gosson, Stephen (1974) *Markets of Bawdrie: The Dramatic Criticism of*

Stephen Gosson, ed. Arthur F. Kinney, Salzburg: Institut für Englische Sprache und Literatur.

Gramsci, Antonio (1971) *Selections from the Prison Notebooks*, ed. and trans. Quintin Hoare and Geoffrey Nowell Smith, London: Lawrence & Wishart.

Greenblatt, Stephen J. (1973) *Walter Ralegh: The Renaissance Man and his Roles*, New Haven: Yale University Press.

—— (1980) *Renaissance Self-fashioning. From More to Shakespeare*, Chicago: University of Chicago Press.

—— (ed.) (1982) *The Power of Forms in the English Renaissance*, Norman, Okla.: Pilgrim Books.

—— (1985) 'Invisible Bullets: Renaissance Authority and its Subversion', in Jonathan Dollimore and Alan Sinfield (eds) (1985), 18–47 .

—— (1988) *Shakespearean Negotiations: The Circulation of Social Energy*, Berkeley: University of California Press.

—— (1989) 'Towards a Poetics of Culture', in Aram H. Veeser (1989), 1–14.

—— (1990a) 'Resonance and Wonder', in Peter Collier and Helga Geyer-Ryan (eds) *Literary Theory Today*, Ithaca: Cornell University Press, 74–90 .

—— (1990b) 'Filthy Rites', in *Learning to Curse: Essays in Early Modern Culture*, New York: Routledge.

—— (1991) *Marvelous Possessions: The Wonder of the New World*, Chicago: University of Chicago Press.

Greg, W. W. and Boswell, E. (1930) *Records of the Court of the Stationers' Company, 1576 1602*, London: The Bibliographic Society.

Greville, F. (1987) *The Life of the Renowned Sir Philip Sidney*, in Mark Caldwell (ed.) *The Prose of Fulke Greville, Lord Brooke*, New York: Garland.

Gurr, Andrew (1992) *The Shakespearean Stage 1574–1642*, 3rd edn, Cambridge: Cambridge University Press.

Gwilliam, Tassie (1994) 'Cosmetic Poetics: Coloring Faces in the Eighteenth Century', in Veronica Kelly and Dorothea Von Mücke (eds) *Body and Text in the Eighteenth Century*, Stanford: Stanford University Press, 144–59.

Hahn, T. (1978) 'Indians East and West: Primitivism and Savagery in English Discovery Narratives of the Sixteenth Century', *The Journal of Medieval and Renaissance Studies* 8: 77–114.

Hakluyt, R. (1904) *The Principall Navigations, Voyages and Discoveries of the English Nation*, Glasgow: James MacLehose and Sons.

Hall, Kim F. (1991) 'Sexual Politics and Cultural Identity in The Masque of Blackness', in Sue Ellen Case (ed.) *The Performance of Power*, Iowa City: University of Iowa Press.

—— (1993) 'Reading What Isn't There: "Black" Studies in Early Modern England', *Stanford Humanities Review* 3, 1: 23–33.

—— (1994) '"I Rather Would Wish to be a Black-moor": Beauty, Race and Rank in Lady Mary Wroth's Urania', in Margo Hendricks and Patricia Parker (eds) (1994).

—— (1995) *Things of Darkness: Economies of Race and Gender in Early Modern England*, Ithaca: Cornell University Press.

Halperin, David M. (1992) 'Historicizing the Sexual Body: Sexual Preferences and Erotic Identities in the Pseudo-Lucianic *Ertes*', in Domna C. Stanton (ed.) *Discourses of Sexuality from Aristotle to AIDS*, Ann Arbor: University of Michigan Press.

Halpern, R. (1991) *The Poetics of Primitive Accumulation: English Renaissance Culture and the Genealogy of Capital*, Ithaca and London: Cornell University Press.

Hamer, Mary (1993) *Signs of Cleopatra: History, Politics, Representation*, London and New York: Routledge.

Hampton, T. (1993) '"Turkish Dogs": Rabelais, Erasmus, and the Rhetoric of Alterity', *Representations* 41, Winter: 58–82.

Hawkes, Terence (1986) *That Shakespeherian Rag: Essays on a Critical Process*, London and New York: Routledge.

—— (1992) *Meaning by Shakespeare*, London and New York: Routledge.

—— (1995) *William Shakespeare: King Lear*, Plymouth: Northcote House/British Council.

Hawking, Stephen W. (1990) *A Brief History of Time*, New York: Bantam.

Haynes, J. (1986) *The Humanist as Traveler*, London and Toronto: Associated University Presses.

Heath, B. (1869) *Some Account of the Worshipful Company of Grocers of the City of London*, London: Chiswick Press.

Helgerson, R. (1992) *Forms of Nationhood: The Elizabethan Writing of England*, Chicago and London: University of Chicago Press.

Hendricks, Margo and Patricia Parker (eds) (1994) *Women, 'Race,' and Writing in the Early Modern Period*, New York and London: Routledge.

Herford, C. H. and Simpson, Percy and Evelyn (1941) *Ben Jonson: Complete Works*, Oxford: Clarendon Press.

Hertz, N. (1992) 'Dr. Johnson's Forgetfulness, Descartes' Piece of Wax', *Eighteenth Century Life* 16, 3: 167–81.

Heywood, Thomas (1978) Richard H. Perkinson (ed.) *'An Apology for Actors' (1612); 'A Refutation of The Apology for Actors' (1615) by I. G.*, New York: Scholars' Facsimiles and Reprints.

Hill, Errol (1984) *Shakespeare in Sable: A History of Black Shakespearean Actors*, Amherst: University of Massachusetts Press.

Hill, R. F. (1975) '*The Merchant of Venice* and the Pattern of Romantic Comedy', *Shakespeare Survey* 28: 75–87.

Hobbs, Mary (1992) *Early Seventeenth-Century Verse Miscellany Manuscripts*, Aldershot: Scolar Press.

Hoeniger, F. David (1992) *Medicine and Shakespeare in the English Renaissance*, Newark: University of Delaware Press.

Hollander, J. (1988) *Melodious Guile: Fictive Patterns in Poetic Language*, New Haven and London: Yale University Press.

Holstun, James (1989) 'Ranting at the New Historicism', *English Literary Renaissance* 19: 189–225.

Howard, Jean E. (1986) 'The New Historicism in Renaissance Studies', *English Literary Renaissance* 16: 13–43.

—— (1987) 'Renaissance Anti-theatricality and the Politics of Gender and Rank in *Much Ado About Nothing*', in Jean E. Howard and Marion F. O'Connor (eds) (1987), 163–187.

—— (1988) 'Crossdressing, the Theatre, and Gender Struggle in Early Modern England', *Shakespeare Quarterly*, 39, 4: 418–40.

—— (1994a) *The Stage and Social Struggle in Early Modern England*, London: Routledge.

—— (1994b) 'An English Lass Among the Moors: Gender, Race, Sexuality and National Identity in Heywood's *Fair Maid of the West*' in M. Hendricks and P. Parker (eds) (1994).

Howard, Jean E. and O'Connor, Marion F. (eds) (1987) *Shakespeare Reproduced: The Text in History and Ideology*, New York and London: Routledge.

Howe, Elizabeth (1992) *Enter the Actress: Women and Drama 1660–1700*, Cambridge: Cambridge University Press.

Hughes, Geoffrey (1991) *Swearing: A Social History of Foul Language, Oaths and Profanity in English*, Oxford: Blackwell.

Hulme, Peter (1986) *Colonial Encounters: Europe and the Native Caribbean, 1492–1797*, New York and London: Routledge.

—— (1985) 'Polytropic Man: Tropes of Sexuality and Mobility in Early Colonial Discourse', in Francis Barker *et al.* (eds) *Europe and its Others*, vol. 2, Colchester: University of Essex.

Hunter, G. K. (1978) *Dramatic Identities and Cultural Tradition*, Liverpool: Liverpool University Press.

Hutson, L. (1996) 'Chivalry for Merchants, or Knights of Temperance in the Realms of Gold', unpublished manuscript.

Hyde, Thomas (1986) *The Poetic Theology of Love: Cupid in Renaissance Literature*, London and Toronto: Associated University Presses.

Hyman, Lawrence W. (1970) 'The Rival Loves in *The Merchant of Venice*', *Shakespeare Quarterly* 21: 109–16.

Irigaray, Luce (1985) *Speculum of the Other Woman*, trans. Gillian C. Gill, Ithaca: Cornell University Press.

James I (1643) *Wittie Observations Gathered from our late Soveraign King James in his Ordinarie Discourse*, London.

James, Mervyn (1988) *Society, Politics and Culture: Studies in Early Modern England*, Cambridge: Cambridge University Press.

Jardine, Lisa (1983) *Still Harping on Daughters: Women and Drama in the Age of Shakespeare*, Brighton: Harvester.

—— (1992) 'Twins and Travesties: Gender, Dependency and Sexual Availability in *Twelfth Night*', in Susan Zimmerman (ed.) (1992), 27–38.

Jed, S. (1989), *Chaste Thinking: The Rape of Lucretia and the Birth of Humanism*, Bloomington: Indiana University Press.

Jenkins, Harold (ed.) (1982) *Hamlet* (The Arden Shakespeare), London and New York: Routledge.

Johnson, Samuel (1969) *Dr. Johnson on Shakespeare*, ed. W. K. Wimsatt, New York: Hill and Wang; Harmondsworth: Penguin Books.

Jones, A. R. (1991) 'Italians and Others', in D. Kastan and P. Stallybrass (eds) *Staging the Renaissance*, New York and London: Routledge.

Jones, E. D. (1962) 'The Physical Representation of African Characters on the English Stage During the 16th and 17th Centuries', *Theatre Notebook* 17, 1: 17–21.

—— (1965) *Othello's Countrymen: The African in English Renaissance Drama*, London: Oxford University Press.

—— (1971) *The Elizabethan Image of Africa*, Charlottesville: University of Virginia Press.

Jones, Ernest (1949) *Hamlet and Oedipus*, London: Gollancz.

Jonson, Ben (1995) *Poetaster*, ed. Tom Cain, Manchester: Manchester University Press.

Jordan, Winthrop (1968) *White Over Black: American Attitudes Toward the Negro, 1550–1812*, Chapel Hill: University of North Carolina Press,

Kahn, Coppélia (1981) *Man's Estate: Masculine Identity in Shakespeare*, Berkeley: University of California Press.

—— (1985) 'The Cuckoo's Note: Male Friendship and Cuckoldry in *The Merchant of Venice*', in Peter Erickson and Coppélia Kahn (eds) *Shakespeare's 'Rough Magic'*, Newark: University of Delaware Press.

Kantorowicz, Ernst (1957) *The King's Two Bodies: A Study in Medieval Political Theology*, Princeton: Princeton University Press.

Kastan, David Scott (1986) 'Proud Majesty Made a Subject: Shakespeare and the Spectacle of Rule', *Shakespeare Quarterly* 37: 459–75.

Kastan, David Scott and Stallybrass, Peter (eds) (1991) *Staging the Renaissance: Reinterpretations of Elizabethan and Jacobean Drama*, New York and London: Routledge.

Kaul, S. (1994) 'Reading Literary Symptoms: Colonial Pathologies and the *Oroonoko* Fictions of Behn, Southerne, and Hawkesworth', *Eighteenth-century Life* 18, 3 (new series): 80–96.

Keesing, Roger M. (1987) 'Anthropology as Interpretive Quest', *Current Anthropology* 28: 161–76.

Kelly, F. M. (1938) *Shakespearean Costume for Stage and Screen*, London: Adam and Charles Black.

Kermode, Frank (1988) 'The New Historicism', *The New Republic* February 29: 31–4.

Kleinberg, Seymour (1985) '*The Merchant of Venice*: The Homosexual as Anti-Semite in Nascent Capitalism', in Stuart Kellog (ed.) *Literary Visions of Homosexuality*, New York: Haworth Press.

Knights, L. C. (1946) *Explorations*, London: Chatto.

Knolles, Richard (1603) *A Generall Historie of the Turkes*, London.

Knopp, Lawrence (1995) 'Sexuality and Urban Space: A Framework for Analysis', in David Bell and Gill Valentine (eds) *Mapping Desire: Geographies of Sexualities*, London: Routledge.

Knutson, Roslyn L. (1995) 'Falconer to the Little Eyases. A New Date and Commercial Agenda for the "Little Eyases" Passage in *Hamlet*', *Shakespeare Quarterly* 46: 1–31.

Kristeva, Julia (1974) *La Révolution du langage politique*, The Hague: Mouton (partial English translation in Toril Moi [ed.] *The Kristeva Reader*, Oxford: Basil Blackwell, 1990, 89–135).

Kuchta, David (1993) 'The Semiotics of Masculinity in Renaissance England', in James Grantham Turner (ed.) *Sexuality and Gender in Early Modern Europe: Institutions, Texts, Images*, Cambridge: Cambridge University Press, 233–46.

Lacan, Jacques (1972) 'Seminar on "The Purloined Letter"', trans. Jeffrey Mehlman, *Yale French Studies* 48: 38–72.

—— (1977a) 'Desire and the Interpretation of Desire in *Hamlet*', trans. James Hulbert, *Yale French Studies* 55/56: 11–52.

—— (1977b) *Ecrits: A Selection*, trans. Alan Sheridan, London: Tavistock.

—— (1979) *The Four Fundamental Concepts of Psychoanalysis*, trans. Alan Sheridan, Harmondsworth: Penguin.

—— (1982) *Feminine Sexuality: Jacques Lacan and the Ecole Freudienne*, ed. and trans. Juliet Mitchell and Jacqueline Rose, London: Macmillan.

—— (1988a) *The Seminar of Jacques Lacan*, vol. 1: *Freud's Papers on Technique 1953–1954*, trans. John Forrester, Cambridge: Cambridge University Press.

—— (1988b) *The Seminar of Jacques Lacan*, vol. 2: *The Ego in Freud's Theory and in the Technique of Psychoanalysis 1954–1955*, trans. Sylvana Thomaselli, Cambridge: Cambridge University Press.

Lach, Donald (1968–94) *Asia in the Making of Europe*, 3 vols, Chicago and London: Chicago University Press.

Laqueur, Thomas (1990) *Making Sex: Body and Gender from the Greeks to Freud*, Cambridge, Mass.: Harvard University Press.

Lentricchia, Frank (1989) 'Foucault's Legacy: A New Historicism?', in Aram H. Veeser (1989), 231–42.

Lenz, Carolyn, Swift, Ruth, Green, Gayle and Neely, Carol Thomas (eds) (1980) *The Woman's Part: Feminist Criticism of Shakespeare,* Urbana: University of Illinois Press.

Levine, Laura (1986) 'Men in Women's Clothing: Anti-theatricality and Effeminization from 1579 to 1642', *Criticism* 28: 121–43.

—— (1994) *Men in Women's Clothing: Anti-theatricality and Effeminization 1579–1642,* Cambridge: Cambridge University Press.

Lingis, Alphonso (1994) *Foreign Bodies,* New York and London: Routledge.

Lister, David (1994) 'Shylock: Unacceptable Face of Shakespeare', *Independent on Sunday,* April 17, 3.

Lithgow, William (1632) *Rare Adventures and Painfull Peregrinations,* London.

Little, Arthur L., Jr (1993) '"An Essence That's Not Seen": The Primal Scene of Racism in *Othello*', *Shakespeare Quarterly* 44, 3: 304–24.

Liu, Alan (1989) 'The Power of Pluralism: The New Historicism', *English Literary History* 56: 721–71.

Loomba, A. (1989) *Gender, Race, Renaissance Drama,* Manchester: Manchester University Press.

—— (1994) 'The Colour of Patriarchy: Critical Difference, Cultural Difference and Renaissance Drama', in M. Hendricks and P. Parker (eds) (1994).

—— (1996) *Of Queens and Spices: Renaissance Drama and the East Indies,* unpublished manuscript.

Lotman, Yuri M. (1981) 'Semiotica della scena', *Strumenti critici* 15,1: 1–29.

Lott, Eric (1993) *Love and Theft: Blackface, Minstrelsy, and the American Working Class,* Oxford: Oxford University Press.

Lyotard, Jean-François (1984) *The Postmodern Condition: A Report on Knowledge,* trans. Geoff Bennington and Brian Massumi, Manchester: Manchester University Press.

McLuskie, Kathleen (1985) 'The Patriarchal Bard: Feminist Criticism and Shakespeare', in Jonathan Dollimore and Alan Sinfield (eds) (1985), 2nd edn 1994.

—— (1989) *Renaissance Dramatists,* Atlantic Highlands, NJ: Humanities Press International; Hemel Hempstead: Harvester Wheatsheaf.

McMullen, G. (1994) *The Politics of Unease in the Plays of John Fletcher,* Amherst: University of Massachusetts Press.

Mann, David (1991) *The Elizabethan Player: Contemporary Stage Representation,* New York and London: Routledge.

Marland, Hilary (ed.) (1993) *The Art of Midwifery,* London and New York: Routledge.

Marotti, Arthur F. (1995) *Manuscript, Print, and the English Renaissance Lyric,* Ithaca: Cornell University Press.

Mayer, Hans (1982) *Outsiders*, trans. Denis M. Sweet, Cambridge, Mass.: MIT Press.

Merleau-Ponty, Maurice (1962) *Phenomenology of Perception*, trans. Colin Smith, London: Routledge.

Midgley, Graham (1960) '*The Merchant of Venice*: A Reconsideration', *Essays in Criticism*, 10: 119–33.

Miller, J. Hillis (1987) 'Presidential Address 1986: The Triumph of Theory, the Resistance to Reading, and the Question of the Material Base', *PMLA* 102: 281–91.

Mitchell, C. J. (1991) 'Women in the Eighteenth-Century Book Trades', in O. M. Brack, Jr (ed.) *Writers, Books, and Trade*, New York: AMS Press, 25–75.

Montrose, Louis Adrian (1980a) '"Eliza, Queene of Shepheardes" and the Pastoral of Power', *English Literary Renaissance* 10: 153–82.

—— (1980b) 'The Purpose of Playing: Reflections on a Shakespearean Anthropology', *Helios* 7 (new series): 51–74.

—— (1983a) 'Shaping Fantasies: Figurations of Gender and Power in Elizabethan Culture', *Representations* 2: 61–94.

—— (1983b) 'Of Gentlemen and Shepherds: The Politics of Elizabethan Pastoral Form', *English Literary History* 50: 415–59.

—— (1986a) 'Renaissance Literary Studies and the Subject of History', *English Literary Renaissance* 16: 5–12.

—— (1986b) 'The Elizabethan Subject and the Spenserian Text', in Patricia Parker and David Quint (eds) *Literary Theory/Renaissance Texts*, Baltimore: Johns Hopkins University Press, 303–40.

—— (1986c) '*A Midsummer Night's Dream* and the Shaping Fantasies of Elizabethan Culture: Gender, Power, Form', in M. Ferguson *et al.* (eds) (1986).

—— (1988) '"Shaping Fantasies": Figurations of Gender and Power in Elizabethan Culture', in Stephen Greenblatt (ed.) *Representing the English Renaissance*, Berkeley: University of California Press.

—— (1989) 'Professing the Renaissance: The Poetics and Politics of Culture', in Aram H. Veeser (ed.) (1989), 15–36.

—— (1992) 'New Historicisms', in Giles Gunn and Stephen Greenblatt (eds) *Redrawing the Boundaries of Literary Study*, New York: Modern Language Association.

—— (1993) 'The Work of Gender in the Discourse of Discovery', in Stephen Greenblatt (ed.) *New World Encounters*, Berkeley: University of California Press.

Moretti, Franco (1982) '"A Huge Eclipse": Tragic Form and the Deconsecration of Sovereignty', in S. Greenblatt (ed.) (1982), 7–40.

Moxon, J. (1978) *Mechanick Exercises on the Whole Art of Printing* (1683–4), ed. Herbert Davis and Harry Carter, London: Oxford University Press.

Mullaney, Steven (1980) 'Lying Like Truth: Riddle, Representation and Treason in Renaissance England', *English Literary History* 47: 32–48.

—— (1983) 'Strange Things, Gross Terms, Curious Customs: The Rehearsal of Cultures in the Late Renaissance', *Representations* 3: 40–67.

—— (1988) *The Place of the Stage: License, Play, and Power in Renaissance England*, Chicago: University of Chicago Press.

—— (1989) Review of Greenblatt (1988), *Shakespeare Quarterly* 40: 495–500.

Mun, S. T. (1620) *A Discourse of Trade from England unto the East Indies*, London.

Nancy, J. (1978) 'Dum Scribo', *Oxford Literary Review* 3: 6–20.

Nashe, Thomas (1972) *The Unfortunate Traveller and Other Works*, ed. J. B. Steane, Harmondsworth: Penguin.

Neely, Carol Thomas (1988) 'Constructing the Subject: Feminist Practice and New Renaissance Discourses', *English Literary Renaissance* 18: 5–18.

Neill, Michael (1984) 'Changing Places in Othello', *Shakespeare Survey* 37: 115–31.

—— (1989) 'Unproper Beds: Race, Adultery, and the Hideous in *Othello*', *Shakespeare Quarterly* 40, 4: 383–412.

Neill, S. (1966) *Colonialism and Christian Missions*, New York: McGraw Hill.

Nevinson, John L. (1938) *Catalogue of English Domestic Embroidery of the Sixteenth and Seventeenth Centuries*, London: Victoria and Albert Museum.

Newman, Karen (1991) *Fashioning Femininity*, Chicago: University of Chicago Press.

—— (1986) 'Renaissance Family Politics and Shakespeare's *The Taming of the Shrew*', *English Literary Renaissance* 16: 86–100.

—— (1987) '"And Wash the Ethiop White": Femininity and the Monstrous in *Othello*', in J. Howard and M. O'Connor (eds) (1987), 143–62.

—— (forthcoming) *Fetal Positions: An Essay on Individualism, Science and Visuality*, Stanford: Stanford University Press.

Newton, Judith Lowder (1989) 'History as Usual?: Feminism and the "New Historicism"', in Aram H. Veeser (ed.) (1989), 152–67.

Orgel, Stephen (ed.) (1969) *Ben Jonson: the Complete Masques*, New Haven: Yale University Press.

—— (1975) *The Illusion of Power: Political Theater in the English Renaissance*, Berkeley and Los Angeles: University of California Press.

—— (1989) 'Nobody's Perfect: Or Why Did the English Stage Take Boys for Women?', *South Atlantic Quarterly* 88: 7–29.

—— (1995) 'Insolent Women and Manlike Apparel', *Textual Practice* 9: 5–25.

Orkin, Martin (1987) 'Othello and the "Plain Face" of Racism', *Shakespeare Quarterly* 38: 166–88.

Orlin, Lena Cowen (1994a) 'The Elizabethan Long Gallery and the Progress of Privacy', unpublished manuscript.

—— (1994b) *Private Matters and Public Culture in Post-Reformation England*, Ithaca: Cornell University Press.

Ortner, Sherry B. (1984) 'Theory in Anthropology Since the Sixties', *Comparative Studies in Society and History* 26: 126–66.

Panofsky, Erwin (1967) 'Blind Cupid', in *Studies in Iconology: Humanistic Themes in the Art of the Renaissance*, New York: Harper and Row, 95–128.

Parker, J. (1965) *Books to Build an Empire: A Bibliographic History of English Overseas Interests to 1620*, Amsterdam: N. Israel.

Parker, Patricia (1987) *Literary Fat Ladies: Rhetoric, Gender, Property*, London and New York: Routledge.

—— (1994) 'Fantasies of "Race" and "Gender": Africa, Othello and Bringing to Light', in M. Hendricks and P. Parker (eds) (1994).

—— (1995) 'Rude Mechanicals', in M. de Grazia, P. Stallybrass, and M. Quilligan (eds) *Subject and Object in Renaissance Culture*, Cambridge: Cambridge University Press.

Parry, P. H. (1990) 'The Boyhood of Shakespeare's Heroines', *Shakespeare Survey* 42: 99–109.

Partridge, Eric (1955) *Shakespeare's Bawdy*, London: Routledge.

Paster, Gail Kern (1993) *The Body Embarrassed: Drama and the Disciplines of Shame in Early Modern England*, Ithaca: Cornell University Press.

Patrides, C. A. (1963) '"The Bloody and Cruell Turke": The Background of a Renaissance Commonplace', *Studies in the Renaissance* 10: 126–35.

Pechter, Edward (1987) 'The New Historicism and its Discontents: Politicizing Renaissance Drama', *PMLA* 102: 292–303.

Pecora, Vincent P. (1989) 'The Limits of Local Knowledge', in Aram H. Veeser (ed.) (1989), 243–76.

Penrose, B. (1952) *Travel and Discovery in the Renaissance 1420–1620*, Cambridge, Mass.: Harvard University Press.

Pittinger, E. (1991) 'Dispatch Quickly: The Mechanical Reproduction of Pages', *Shakespeare Quarterly* 42: 389–409.

Plantin, Christophle (1567) *La Première, et La Second partie des dialogues francois pour les jeunes enfans*, Anvers.

Plato (1926) *Euthyphro, Apology, Crito, Phaedo, Phaedrus*, trans. H. N. Fowler, London: Heinemann; New York: G. Putnam.

—— (1988) *Theaetetus*, trans. R. Waterfield, Harmondsworth: Penguin.

—— (1989) *Symposium*, trans. A. Nehamas and P. Woodruff, Indianapolis, Indiana: Hackett Publishing Company.

Pollitt, J. J. (1986) *Art in the Hellenistic Age*, Cambridge: Cambridge University Press.

Porter, Carolyn (1988) 'Are We Being Historical Yet?', *South Atlantic Quarterly* 87: 743–86.

Pratt, M. L. (1994) 'Transculturation and Autoethnography: Peru 1615/1980', in F. Barker, P. Hulme and M. Iverson (eds) *Colonial Discourse/Postcolonial Theory*, Manchester: Manchester University Press.

Prynne, William (1633) *Histrio-Mastix: The Players Scourge, or, Actors Tragaedie*, London.

Purchas, S. (1614) *Purchas: His Pilgrimage*, 2nd edn, London.

—— (1905) *Hakluytus Posthumous, or Purchas His Pilgrimes*, 20 vols, Glasgow: James MacLehose and Sons.

Quint, D. (1985) 'The Boat of Romance and Renaissance Epic,' in Kevin and Marina Brownlee (eds) *Romance: Generic Transformation from Chrétien de Troyes to Cervantes*, Hanover, N.H.: University Press of New England.

Rackin, Phyllis (1972) 'Shakespeare's Boy Cleopatra, the Decorum of Nature, and the Golden World of Poetry', *PMLA* 87: 201–12 (reprinted in John Drakakis [ed.] [1994], 78–100).

—— (1987) 'Androgyny, Mimesis and the Marriage of the Boy Heroine on the English Renaissance Stage', *PMLA* 102: 29–41.

—— (1994) 'Foreign Country: The Place of Women and Sexuality in Shakespeare's Historical World', in R. Burt and J. M. Archer (eds) *Enclosure Acts: Sexuality, Property, and Culture in Early Modern England*, Ithaca and London: Cornell University Press.

Rainolds, John (1599) *Th'overthrow of Stage-playes*, Middleburg.

Raman, S. (1994) *Looking East: 'India' and the Renaissance*, unpublished Ph.D. thesis, Stanford University.

Ramussio (1550) *Naviggationi e viaggi*, Venice.

Reade, Simon (1991) *Cheek By Jowl: Ten Years of Celebration*, London: Absolute Press.

Remington, Preston (1945) *English Domestic Needlework of the XVI, XVII, and XVIII Centuries*, New York: Metropolitan Museum of Art.

Riviere, Joan (1986) 'Womanliness as a Masquerade', in Victor Burgin, James Donald and Cora Kaplan (eds) *Formations of Fantasy*, London and New York: Methuen, 35–44.

Roberts, Jeanne (1991) *The Shakespearean Wild: Geography, Genus, and Gender*, Lincoln: University of Nebraska Press.

Robinson, Amy (1994) 'It Takes One to Know One: Passing and Communities of Common Interest', *Critical Inquiry* 20, 4: 715–36.

Rogin, Michael (1987) *Ronald Reagan, the Movie and Other Episodes in Political Demonology*, Berkeley: University of California Press.

Romano, Giulio, Raimondi, Marcantonio, Aretino, Pietro and Count Jean-Frederic-Maximilien de Waldeck (1990) *I modi: The Sixteen*

Pleasures, ed. Lynne Lawner, Evanston: Northwestern University Press.

Rorty, Richard (1980) *Philosophy and the Mirror of Nature*, Oxford: Basil Blackwell.

Rosenberg, Marvin (1961) *The Masks of Othello: The Search for the Identity of Othello, Iago, and Desdemona by Three Centuries of Actors and Critics*, Berkeley: University of California Press.

Rouse, R. H. and Rouse, M. A. (1990) 'The Vocabulary of Wax Tablets', *Harvard Library Bulletin* 1 (new series): 1–13.

Rowse, A. L. (1974) *Simon Foreman: Sex and Society in Shakespeare's Age*, London: Weidenfeld and Nicholson.

Sahlins, Marshall (1975) *Culture and Practical Reason*, Chicago: University of Chicago Press.

—— (1985) *Islands of History*, Chicago: University of Chicago Press.

—— (1995) *How 'Natives' Think: About Captain Cook, For Example*, Chicago, University of Chicago Press.

Said, Edward (1978) *Orientalism*, London: Routledge and Kegan Paul.

Salway, John (1991) 'Veritable Negroes and Circumcised Dogs: Racial Disturbances in Shakespeare,' in Lesley Aers and Nigel Wheale (eds) *Shakespeare in a Changing Curriculum*, New York and London: Routledge, 108–24.

Sandys, George (1627) *Relation of a Journey begun An. Dom. 1610*, 3rd edn, London.

Sawday, Jonathan (1995) *The Body Emblazoned: Dissection and the Human Body in Renaissance Culture*, London: Routledge.

Schoenbaum, S. (1991) *Shakespeare's Lives*, 2nd edn, Oxford: Clarendon Press.

Scobie, E. (1985) 'The Black in Western Europe', in Ivan Van Sertima (ed.) *African Presence in Early Europe*, New Brunswick and Oxford: Transaction Books.

Scott, Joan Wallach (1988) *Gender and the Politics of History*, New York: Columbia University Press.

Sedgwick, Eve Kosofsky (1985) *Between Men*, New York: Columbia University Press.

Serpieri, Alessandro (1985) 'Reading the Signs: Towards a Semiotics of Shakespearean Drama', in John Drakakis (ed.) (1985), 119–43.

Sewall, William (1989) 'Toward a Theory of Structure: Duality, Agency, and Transformation', CSST Working Paper 29.

Shakespeare, William (1599) *The Most Excellent and Lamentable Tragedie, or Romeo and Juliet*, facsimile reprint in Michael J. B. Allen and Kenneth Muir (eds) *Shakespeare's Plays in Quarto*, Berkeley: University of California Press.

—— (1623) *The First Folio of Shakespeare*, facsimile reprint, ed. Charlton Hinman, New York: Norton, 1968.

—— (1986) *The Sonnets and A Lover's Complaint*, ed. J. Kerrigan, Harmondsworth: Penguin Books.

Shapiro, Michael (1982) 'Boying her Greatness: Shakespeare's Use of Coterie Drama in *Antony and Cleopatra*', *Modern Language Review* 77: 1–15.

Shorter, Edward (1984) *A History of Women's Bodies*, Harmondsworth: Penguin Books.

Shyllon, Folarin (1977) *Black People in Britain 1555–1833*, Oxford: Oxford University Press.

Sidney, Philip (1962) *The Poems of Sir Philip Sidney*, ed. William A Ringler, Oxford: Clarendon Press.

—— (1966) *A Defence of Poetry*, ed. J. A. Van Dorsten, Oxford: Oxford University Press.

Silverblatt, I. (1994) 'Andean Witches and Virgins: Seventeenth-Century Nativism and Subversive Gender Ideologies', in M. Hendricks and P. Parker (eds) (1994).

Silverman, Kaja (1992a) *Male Subjectivity at the Margins*, New York and London: Routledge.

—— (1992b) 'The Lacanian Phallus', *Differences* 4, 1: 84–115.

Sinfield, Alan (1992) *Faultlines*, Berkeley: University of California Press; Oxford: Oxford University Press.

—— (1994a) *Cultural Politics – Queer Reading*, Philadelphia: University of Pennsylvania Press; London: Routledge.

—— (1994b) *The Wilde Century*, London: Cassell; New York: Columbia University Press.

Singh, Jyotsna (1994) 'Othello's Identity, Postcolonial Theory, and Contemporary African Rewritings of *Othello*', in M. Hendricks and P. Parker (eds) (1994).

Skulsky, Harold (1964) 'Pain, Law, and Conscience in *Measure for Measure*', *Journal of the History of Ideas* 51: 157.

Smith, Bruce R. (1991) *Homosexual Desire in Shakespeare's England: A Cultural Poetics*, Chicago: University of Chicago Press.

—— (1992) 'Making a Difference: Male/Male "Desire" in Tragedy, Comedy and Tragi-comedy', in S. Zimmerman (ed.) (1992).

—— (1995) 'Rape, Rap, Rupture, Rapture: R-rated Futures on the Global Market', *Textual Practice* 9, 3: 421–43.

Snell, K. D. M. (1984) *Annals of the Labouring Poor: Social Change and Agrarian England, 1660–1900*, Cambridge: Cambridge University Press.

Spenser, Edmund (1980) *The Faerie Queene*, ed. A. C. Hamilton, London: Longman.

Spiegel, Gabrielle M. (1990) 'History, Historicism, and the Social Logic of the Text in the Middle Ages', *Speculum* 65: 59–86.

Spivak, G. (1985) 'Subaltern Studies: Deconstructing Historiography', in R. Guha (ed.) *Subaltern Studies IV: Writings on South Asian History and Society*, Delhi: Oxford University Press.

Spurgeon, Caroline F. (1935) *Shakespeare's Imagery and What it Tells Us*, Cambridge: Cambridge University Press.

Stallybrass, Peter (1986) 'Patriarchal Territories: The Body Enclosed', in M. Ferguson *et al.* (eds.) (1986), 123–42.

—— (1987) 'Reading the Body and the Jacobean Theater of Consumption', *Renaissance Drama* 18: 121–48 (reprinted in D. Kastan and P. Stallybrass [eds] [1991], 210–20).

Stallybrass, Peter and White, Allon (1986) *The Politics and Poetics of Transgression*, Ithaca: Cornell University Press.

Starr, G. A (1965) 'Escape from Barbary: A Seventeenth-Century Genre', *Huntington Library Quarterly* 29: 35–52.

Stewart, Susan (1993) *On Longing: Narratives of the Miniature, the Gigantic, the Souvenir, the Collection*, Durham: Duke University Press.

Stubbes, Phillip (1877) *The Anatomie of Abuses*, ed. Frederick J. Furnivall, London: New Shakespeare Society.

Tennenhouse, Leonard (1982) 'Representing Power: *Measure for Measure* in its Time', in S. Greenblatt (ed.) (1982), 139–56.

—— (1986) *Power on Display*, London: Routledge.

Thomas, D. (1936) *Type for Print*, London: Joseph Whitaker & Sons.

Thompson, A. and Thompson, J. O. (1987) *Shakespeare: Meaning and Metaphor*, Brighton: Harvester.

Todorov, T. (1984) *The Conquest of America: The Question of the Other*, trans. Richard Howard, New York: Harper and Row.

Tokson, Elliot H. (1982) *The Popular Image of the Black Man in Elizabethan Drama 1550–1688*, Boston, Mass.: G. K. Hall.

Tory, G. (1529) *Champ Fleury*, Paris.

Traub, Valerie (1992a) 'The (In)Significance of "Lesbian" Desire in Early Modern England', in S. Zimmerman (ed.) (1992), 150–69.

—— (1992b) *Desire and Anxiety: Circulations of Sexuality in Shakespearean Drama*, London and New York: Routledge.

—— (1995) 'The Psychomorphology of the Clitoris', *GLQ* 2: 81–113.

Trumbach, Ralph (1987) 'Sodomitical Subcultures, Sodomitical Roles, and the Gender Revolution of the Eighteenth Century: The Recent Historiography', in Maccubin, Robert Purks (ed.) *'Tis Nature's Fault*, Cambridge: Cambridge University Press.

—— (1989) 'Gender and the Homosexual Role in Modern Western Culture: The 18th and 19th Centuries Compared', in Altman, Dennis, Vance, Carole, Vicinus, Martha, Weeks, Jeffrey (eds) *Homosexuality, Which Homosexuality?* London: Gay Men's Press.

Ure, Peter (ed.) (1956) *Richard II* (The Arden Shakespeare), London and New York: Routledge.

Vaughan, A. T. (1988) 'Shakespeare's Indian: The Americanization of Caliban', *Shakespeare Quarterly* 39, 2: 137–53.

Vaughan, Virginia Mason (1994) *Othello: A Contextual History*, Cambridge: Cambridge University Press.

Vecellio, Cesare (1598) *Habiti antichi et moderni di tutte il mondo*, 2nd edn, Venice.

Veeser, Aram H. (ed.) (1989) *The New Historicism*, New York and London: Routledge.

—— (1994) *The New Historicism Reader*, New York and London: Routledge.

Vickers, Nancy J. (1986) 'This Heraldry in Lucrece' Face', in Susan Rubin Suleiman (ed.) *The Female Body in Western Culture: Contemporary Perspectives*, Cambridge, Mass.: Harvard University Press.

Wall, W. (1993) *The Imprint of Gender: Authorship and Publication in the English Renaissance*, Ithaca and London: Cornell University Press.

Wallerstein, Immanuel (1991) 'The Ideological Tensions of Capitalism: Universalism Versus Racism and Sexism', in Immanuel Wallerstein and Etienne Balibar, *Race, Nation and Class: Ambiguous Identities*, London: Verso, 29–36.

Walvin, James (1971) *The Black Presence: A Documentary History of the Negro in England, 1555–1860*, London: Orbach and Chambers.

Wann, L. (1914) 'The Oriental in Renaissance Drama', *Modern Philology* 12, 6: 423–47.

Warmistry, T. (1658) *The Baptized Turk, or a Narrative of the Happy Conversion of the Signior Rigep Dandulo*, London.

Warner, Michael (1994) 'New English Sodom', in Jonathan Goldberg (ed.) *Queering the Renaissance*, Durham, NC: Duke University Press.

Warren, F. M. (1914) 'The Enamoured Moslem Princess in Orderic Vital and the French Epic', *PMLA* 29: 341–58.

Wayne, Don E. (1984) *Penshurst: The Semiotics of Place and the Poetics of History*, London: Methuen.

—— (1987) 'Power, Politics, and the Shakespearean Text: Recent Criticism in England and the United States', in J. Howard and M. O'Connor (eds) (1987), 47–67.

Wayne, Valerie (ed.) (1991) *The Matter of Difference: Materialist-Feminist Criticism of Shakespeare*, Ithaca and London: Cornell University Press.

Webb, Wilfred Mark (1912) *The Heritage of Dress: Being Notes on the History and Evolution of Clothes*, London: Times Book Club.

Welsford, E. (1926) *The Court Masque*, New York: Russell and Russell.

Whigham, Frank (1988) 'Encoding the Alimentary Tract: More on the Body in Renaissance Drama', *English Literary History* 55: 333–50.

White, H. (1978) *Tropics of Discourse: Essays in Cultural Criticism*, Baltimore and London: Johns Hopkins University Press.

White, H. O. (1935) *Plagiarism and Imitation During the English Renaissance: A Study of Critical Distinctions*, Cambridge, Mass.: Harvard University Press.

Whitelaw, Billie (1995) 'Billie Whitelaw . . . Who He?', *Sunday Times*, 27 August, 10: 13.

Whythorne, T. (1962) *The Autobiography*, ed. J. Osborne, Oxford: Oxford University Press.

Williams, David (1988) '*Timon of Athens*: An Account', in David Williams (ed.) *Peter Brook: A Theatrical Casebook*, London: Methuen, 245–51.

Williams, E. C. (1970) *Anne of Denmark*, London: W. & J. Mackay.

Williams, Raymond (1978) *Marxism and Literature*, Oxford: Oxford University Press.

Wilson, Richard and Dutton, Richard (eds) (1992) *New Historicism and Renaissance Drama*, London: Longman.

Wilson, Scott (1995) *Cultural Materialism: Theory and Practice*, Oxford: Blackwell.

Withers, R. (1905) 'The Grand Signior's Seraglio', in S. Purchas (ed.) (1905), vol. 9, 322–406.

Withington, R. (1918) *English Pageantry: An Historical Outline*, vol. 1, Cambridge, Mass.: Harvard University Press.

Woodbridge, Linda (1984) *Women and the English Renaissance*, Urbana: University of Illinois Press.

Yates, Frances (1969) *Theatre of the World*, London: Routledge.

—— (1994) *The Art of Memory*, London: Pimlico.

Yule, H. and Burnell, A. C. (1984) *Hobson-Jobson*, Delhi: Munshiram Manoharlal.

Zimmerman, Susan (1992) 'Disruptive Desire: Artifice and Indeterminacy in Jacobean Comedy', in S. Zimmerman (ed.) (1992).

—— (ed.) (1992) *Erotic Politics: Desire on the Renaissance Stage*, New York and London: Routledge.

Index